Praise for **Born to Bark**

"It's the story of an underdog—the one who should have failed. A heartwarming read proving that there is no such thing as impossible."

—*Toronto Star*

"Internationally recognized dog expert . . . writes about one of his own extraordinary dogs. Charming . . . blends Coren's personal history into the story of his much loved Cairn terrier, with lots of insightful information."

—*The Vancouver Sun*

"If you like animal stories that give you a chuckle or make your eyes well up, pick up psychologist Stanley Coren's new book about the dogs he has known who have brought warmth, love, and humor to his life. . . . His relationship with Flint became the stuff of legend. Delightful."

—*The Free Lance–Star* (Fredericksburg, Va.)

"Coren's sharp insight into the species and man's relationship to it is magnified in this first-person story of true grit that ranges from perceptive narrative to tough realism. In the process, Coren serves up plenty of doggy escapades, accented with spot-on behavioral tips and why they work. Through the journey, Coren delivers humor, angst, perception, and correction."

—SeattleKennelClub.com

"Stanley Coren's funny and touching memoir, *Born to Bark*, reveals how the mentor we've come to know and love became so expert at reading the minds and hearts of dogs."

—Ted Kerasote, author of the *New York Times* bestseller *Merle's Door: Lessons from a Freethinking Dog*

"A deeply thoughtful yet lighthearted, fun read, this book had me alternately laughing and crying, and reflecting on my relationship with my own dog. I recommend this book to anyone who has ever loved a dog or tried to train one."
—Stacey O'Brien, author of *Wesley the Owl*

"Just as Stanley Coren's important books on dogs deserve prime spots in every animal lover's library, so will his Cairn terrier, Flint, win a special place in each dog lover's heart. This little dog with a big soul will utterly captivate you. Even when he's misbehaving (which is rather often) you can't help but love Flint's fierce terrier courage, his boundless energy, and his mischievous sense of humor. In this personal and personable memoir, Dr. Coren offers respectful and penetrating insights into the lively mind of a special dog—and revealing glimpses into his own soul as well."
—Sy Montgomery, author of *Birdology*

"Dr. Stanley Coren writes about the dogs he has owned, in particular his soul mate, Flint. . . . At every stage, Dr. Coren's profound knowledge of dogs shines through as he relates inspiring and heartwarming stories of his precious time with Flint. This book will inform and educate, amuse and entertain any and all dog owners as well as those thinking of getting a dog. Yet another great contribution from Dr. Coren."
—Professor Nicholas H. Dodman, author of *The Dog Who Loved Too Much*

"I've learned more from Stanley Coren about dogs and people than from just about any other writer and thinker on the subject. He . . . teaches us so much about ourselves and the intense way we connect with our dogs. Coren understands better than anyone how dogs think. Now he teaches us about how we think about them. A wonderful read for anyone who has ever loved a dog."
—Jon Katz, author of *Soul of a Dog*

ALSO AVAILABLE BY COREN

Why Does My Dog Act That Way?

How Dogs Think

How to Speak Dog

The Pawprints of History

The Intelligence of Dogs

Sleep Thieves

The Left-Hander Syndrome

What Do Dogs Know? (with Janet Walker)

Why We Love the Dogs We Do

The Modern Dog

Born to Bark

My Adventures with an Irrepressible and Unforgettable Dog

STANLEY COREN

ATRIA PAPERBACK

New York London Toronto Sydney New Delhi

ATRIA PAPERBACK
A Division of Simon & Schuster, Inc.
1230 Avenue of the Americas
New York, NY 10020

This Atria Paperback edition January 2015

ATRIA PAPERBACK and colophon are trademarks of Simon &
Schuster, Inc.

For information about special discounts for bulk purchases, please
contact Simon & Schuster Special Sales at 1-866-506-1949 or
business@simonandschuster.com.

The Simon & Schuster Speakers Bureau can bring authors to your
live event. For more information or to book an event, contact the
Simon & Schuster Speakers Bureau at 1-866-248-3049 or
visit our website at www.simonspeakers.com.

Book design by Oh Snap! Design

Manufactured in the United States of America

10 9 8 7 6 5 4 3 2

The Library of Congress has catalogued the Free Press hardcover
edition as follows:

Coren, Stanley.
    Born to bark: my adventures with an irrepressible and
unforgettable dog / Stanley Coren.
        p. cm.
    Includes index.
    1. Cairn terrier—Biography.   2. Coren, Stanley.   I. Title.
    SF429.C3C67 2010
    636.755092'9—dc22   2010013608

ISBN 978-1-4391-8920-7
ISBN 978-1-4391-8921-4 (pbk)
ISBN 978-1-4391-8922-1 (ebook)

This book is dedicated to my wife Joan, and to Flint and Wiz,

who I hope are waiting for me somewhere.

CONTENTS

❖ ❖ ❖

Born to Bark

CHAPTER 1

FIRST MEMORIES

For Christmas the woman who would become my wife bought me a dog—a little terrier. The next year her Christmas gift to me was a shotgun. Most of the people in my family believe that those two gifts were not unrelated.

The dog's name was Flint. He was an oversized Cairn terrier, mostly gray with black pricked ears and a black mask. Weighing about 23 pounds and standing something over 13 inches at the shoulder, he looked for all the world like a jumbo version of Toto in the original film version of *The Wizard of Oz*. For thirteen years he was my dearly beloved companion, and for thirteen years he and my wife were at war with each other.

I was trained as a researcher and a psychologist; however, Flint was a key that unlocked for me a way of looking at canine behavior and human relationships with dogs. Some people consider me to be an expert on dog behavior and the bond that humans have with their dogs. If the opinion of those people is correct, then I must admit that my primary education came from growing up around dogs and watching and interacting with them. My university-level education came from my research and study of the scientific literature on how dogs think, but my postgraduate training was the result of living with Flint. It was Flint who taught me how to watch dogs and the reactions that they cause in the human world that they live in. He also introduced me to the world of "Dog People," some of whom may be fanatical, loony, and misguided, but most of whom are empathetic, caring, and dedicated to their canine companions. Many of these Dog People became my friends and the source of much of the pleasure that I have experienced over the years.

My life's activities are divided between two different environments. The first is the ordered and structured world of the university, scientific research, data, and research publications. It is a world populated with many staid, serious, and predictable people and equally predictable and structured situations. My other living space is the chaotic world of dogs, dog training, and dog competitions. This world is populated by dog owners, trainers, handlers, judges, and competitors, many with strange or unique ideas. It is also filled with dogs of every variety and temperament, some well trained, steady, and friendly, and others that have been allowed basically to run wild in their human habitat. The canine universe seems to be driven more by emotions than logic, so apparently random things may happen. As Flint soon taught me, often the best response to such unpredictable events is a sense of humor. Going back and forth between these two worlds is much like looking at a Hollywood feature film where the director is trying to give you a glimpse of the workings of the mind of a schizophrenic, alternating between ordered reality and delusional fantasy.

Flint became a part of both of those lives. He soon showed me that I had a lot more to learn about dogs and that there were some clear holes in my knowledge of how dogs think. However, there were even more holes in my understanding of the nature of the bond that humans have with dogs—or, as in my wife's case, the bond we may *not* have with a particular dog.

🐾 🐾 🐾

Let me start by giving you a bit of history about myself before that canine whirlwind arrived on the scene. Dogs have been the signposts that have marked the various stages in my life's journey. For as long as I can remember there was always a dog in my home. The first dog of my memory is a beagle named Skipper, but there was at least one dog earlier than that. I have seen photos of me rolling around on the ground with Rex, who was a husky-type dog, either a Malamute or a Siberian husky. If we can read anything from the few photos we had, I dearly loved that dog and, according to my mother, he adored me. One photograph provides some evidence of why our bond was so strong. In it I am sitting next to Rex and I am happily chewing on a dog biscuit. My mother claimed that in that photo Rex was looking at me with great love and affection, but it appears to me that he was looking at the dog treat and hoping that something edible was about to happen for him.

One day, when I was around eight or nine years of age, my mother and her sister, my Aunt Sylvia, were having coffee together and looking at some old family snapshots. As they sat chatting and laughing at the black-and-white images, the page turned to reveal that particular picture of Rex and me. Sylvia was appalled.

"Chesna, that is disgusting!" my aunt said, and immediately went into the lecturing mode that she used when she felt that she needed to instruct someone and bring them to her own moral and intellectual high ground, "Stanley is chewing on a dog biscuit. It's unsanitary. It's unhealthy! It's nearly child abuse!"

"Sylvia, it's just a dog biscuit," my mother gently replied. "The first time I gave Stan a biscuit to give to Rex, he started to chew on it himself. I don't think that he much liked the taste, but he liked the fact that Rex would hang around him until he finally gave him what remained of the treat. After that, Stan wouldn't go anyplace without a dog treat in his pocket, and Rex would never be more than an arm's length away from him. That's what saved Stanley's life."

During the early years of World War II, just after my father, Ben, had earned his officer's commission, he had been assigned to Fort Knox, Kentucky, where we lived in a mostly military community just outside the gates of the camp. It was sort of rural, and the place we rented was pretty bare and run-down, but it did have a little fenced yard where Rex and I could play. My mother was inside doing the wash one day when she heard me give a frightened shout, followed by angry sounds from Rex. When she ran out of the house she found me hiding behind Rex who was barking and growling at a "nasty-looking snake, pink and black and orange, making hissing and buzzing sounds." Rex had defensively put himself between me and the snake. My mother shouted for us to get back and as soon as she could, she pulled me away. Meanwhile, Rex dived at the snake and caught it in the middle of its body, but it swung around and bit him on the face. Rex yelped and dropped it and then grabbed its neck and snapped it up and down. When it stopped moving, Rex looked a bit dazed and blood was oozing from puncture wounds on his face.

My mother's shouts and Rex's barking attracted the attention of our next-door neighbor, who came running out to help. She was from Georgia and recognized the snake as a copperhead rattlesnake, which is poisonous but not as bad as a cottonmouth or some others, although such snakes can certainly kill a young child or dog. Fortunately, she knew what to do about Rex's wounds. She made a little X-shaped cut over each of the bite holes and squeezed them until there was a good flow of blood that helped drain the poison. Afterward, Rex was pretty sick and his face swelled up, but he pulled through.

As my mother looked at the photo, she recalled that Rex and I had acted as if we were glued together, and that I had used

Rex had put himself right in front of me for my protection.

those dog treats that I always had with me as rewards, managing to teach Rex dozens of different words and several tricks.

When my father left with the troops to go to Europe, my mother began to pack our belongings to go back to her family in Philadelphia. Shortly before we left, a driver lost control of his Jeep and hit Rex, who died on our front lawn. My mother looked across the room to where I was sitting and told me, "You took it pretty hard. You kept kissing Rex's face and telling him to wake up. For the next few weeks you insisted on taking a dog biscuit to bed with you because you said that Rex would expect it to be there when he came home."

My mother told me the story of Rex only that one time, but it hurt me a great deal. Here was a dog who had loved me so much that he had nearly given his life for me, and I had no memory of him, no matter how hard I tried to recall the events. In fact, the only evidence that I had that he had ever lived was in a couple of small, faded black-and-white photos. It is difficult to imagine that I might never have survived to live the rest of my life if it had not been for an unremembered dog who had stayed close to me in the hopes of getting an occasional bit of dog treat, and whom I had clearly cherished.

❧ ❧ ❧

My first personal memories of a dog are all about Skipper, a beagle. He arrived in my life after we were back in Philadelphia, the war was over, and my father was home. I don't remember Skippy as a puppy. In my mind he was always a full-sized beagle who loved to snuggle and run. Mostly he loved to sniff things, and he had enough strength and traction so that when he was on leash he could drag my light young body over to any target he needed to explore. I always carried around bits of food with me that I could use to reward Skipper to get him to do the things that I wanted him to. A typical beagle, Skipper was not particularly trainable, but he was sweet and social and willing to curl up next to me while I read, worked, or slept. I loved him dearly, in spite of my having been bitten by a rabid dog not too long before Skipper joined our family.

When I was growing up, dogs were not commonly being vaccinated, rabies was a greatly feared disease, and dog bites were the most usual means of transmission. Rabies symptoms include partial paralysis, an inability to speak or swallow, and psychological deterioration with confusion, anxiety, agitation, paranoia, hallucinations, bouts of hostility, and delirium. Without treatment, and once the symptoms show themselves, rabies is one hundred percent fatal within 2 to 10 days. Death by rabies is quite ugly and excruciatingly painful. Before 1885, the year when Louis Pasteur and Émile Roux first successfully cured a victim bitten by a rabid dog, the most common treatment for human rabies was euthanasia—doctors or close family members actually smothered the patient with a pillow, which was considered to be much kinder than allowing him to suffer an agonizing death from the disease.

Thankfully, when I was bitten, a treatment was available for the disease, but that treatment was itself painful and traumatic. I had gone to visit my Aunt Sylvia and Uncle Alex and my cousins who had rented a house for the summer in Atlantic City. Only one day into my holiday, I was approaching a dog with my hand out to pet it when it bit me. Although it hurt, my principal emotion at the time was surprise, since dogs had always responded well to me and I'd never been bitten before. Someone grabbed me and lifted me off the ground and away from the dog while someone else grabbed the dog by the collar, dragged it away, and locked it into another yard behind a gate.

The dog was believed to be rabid, and treatment—a series of horribly painful shots—was started immediately. The shots were given with a wide-bore needle (which looked like a lance to my young eyes) and injected directly into the abdominal muscles with no anesthetic. I came to dread the sight of the doctor and his needle, and left his office shaking and sobbing, pleading with my mother and aunt not to take me back for the next injection. Everybody in the family was in a state of panic, but after the fifth and last shot, since I wasn't showing any symptoms, they knew that I would survive.

A colleague who is a clinical psychologist has told me that, given the pain involved in that treatment process, I should have been left with persistent posttraumatic stress–related symptoms that should appear whenever I am around dogs. It would be reasonable to expect that I would have a lifelong fear of dogs, but I have no fear or negative residual feelings for dogs because the dog hurt me a little bit and just once, while the doctors hurt me a lot, and many times. As a result I have been left with a lifelong discomfort associated with doctors and hospitals.

At the time that I had Skippy, we were living in West Philadelphia, in a duplex, where my family lived upstairs and my mother's parents, Jake and Lena, lived downstairs. My grandmother was a significant influence when I was growing up. Since both of my parents were working, that meant that except for weekends I got to see my parents for only a few hours at night and in the morning, so my grandmother was my primary caretaker. In the early evenings I would curl up in my grandparents' living room next to the large radio, which was our principal form of entertainment. This radio was a big piece of furniture, a floor model that stood about 4 feet high. Skipper would curl up beside me as I listened to the three radio programs that I loved: *Superman*, *The Lone Ranger*, and *Lassie*. Of the three, *Lassie* was my favorite.

The *Lassie* radio adventures were true to the spirit of the original Eric Knight story, in which Lassie was clearly a dog, not a human in a fur coat. Lassie never spoke human language, but simply barked. Pal, the dog who played Lassie in the original movies, also did the barking on the radio show, but listeners were never told that the whining, panting, snarling, and growling were all convincingly done by a human actor named Earl Keen.

Each episode involved Lassie playing a different dog in a different setting and situation. The show had a certain magical charm about it because of the dog's intelligence, emotion, and dedication. Virtually every episode also demonstrated that somehow we humans could understand and communicate with dogs. Lassie did not speak English, Spanish, German, French, or any other human tongue, but her family and everybody who heard her understood her completely, nonetheless. In one episode Lassie's barking could mean that a child was hurt and in need of rescue, in another that the house was on fire, or even "Your mother still loves you and wants you to come home."

I would listen carefully, trying to work out the nuances of the barks, without great success. I was jealous of Lassie's family and neighbors, who could all understand the language of dogs and knew how to make their dog understand exactly what they were saying as well. While I sat next to the big radio fondling Skippy's long, flannel-textured ears and feeling linguistically inept, I began to form a resolve. I would learn how to talk to dogs and understand what they were saying in return.

❀ ❀ ❀

I got a head start in my attempts to learn all I could about dogs because my mother believed that it was possible to teach children how to read at a very young age and that such early literacy would give me an educational advantage. So she spent several hours each Saturday and Sunday morning teaching me how to read. I loved it and began to read everything I could lay my hands on. Well before my sixth birthday I could read at a third-grade level. This turned out to be fortunate, since my mother was now pregnant with my brother Dennis and our weekend mornings spent improving my reading ability were becoming shorter and less frequent.

In a sort of enlightened self-interest, my mother next arranged for me to get my own library card at the Cobbs Creek Parkway branch of the Philadelphia Public Library. Anticipating that her time with me would be radically more limited with the arrival of the new baby, she knew that, if I had an interesting book to read, I would tend to hide in a corner and pore over it, my dog beside me, rather than hanging around getting underfoot. I used that library card quite a bit, and by the time I was 7 or 8 years old I had read every book on dogs, wild animals, biology, and science that was in its tiny children's collection. I also often read them aloud to Skipper, trying to imitate the instructional tones that my mother and first-grade teacher used when teaching. Sometimes, if it was a good story, I would try to read it dramatically, changing my voice according to what I thought the people in the book might sound like. My grandparents or my parents would occasionally walk into the room while I was doing one of my melodramatic readings for the dog and smile or stop for a few minutes to watch and listen, but they never interrupted me or commented.

I not only read those books for myself, but often read them aloud to Skipper.

It was a good time in my life, until Skipper disappeared. I now know that Skippy had contracted *canine distemper,* a viral disease that is almost always fatal. There is no treatment for it, although now there are effective vaccines to prevent it. Even if there had been a treatment for distemper, however, my family had so little money then that sometimes adequate food for the humans could not be assured. My parents would rather have died than to have sought financial help if that meant that people would look upon us as being poor and unable to make it on our own. So if our dog became sick, home remedies were all that we could afford to offer, and if they didn't work, the dog was simply lost.

Distemper is a virulent disease and the symptoms are ugly, with vomiting, diarrhea, discharge from the nose, red eyes, shivering, convulsions, and breathing difficulties. When a dog contracts it, the disease escalates rapidly and death often comes quickly. My parents had decided that this would be too gruesome and traumatic for me to see, since they remembered how hard it had been for me to deal with the loss of Rex. They thought that they were doing something kind when they secretly moved Skipper to the basement, next to the coal furnace where he would be warm but out of sight. They then told me that someone had accidentally left the door open and Skipper had run out and was now lost.

Today, I know that my parents were trying to ease my pain, but at the psychological level it was the worst thing that they could have said to a child. Death, especially by disease, is not something that carries with it feelings of shame, failure, or desertion. Individuals do not choose to die, and their passing away does not make a statement about those who they leave behind. Abandonment is something else. The idea that my dog had run away when I thought that he loved me and I cared for him so dearly meant that I had personally failed that dog. It meant that I had not communicated to him how important he was—that I was to blame for his deciding that he did not want to live with me any longer.

When my parents put me to bed that night, I was crying. As soon as they put out the light I dressed myself again and left the house. I was going to find Skipper and let him know that I loved him. I was going to bring him home where we could be together again, and I would never do anything to make my dearest friend unhappy. The police found me wandering the streets calling for

Skippy at around 3 A.M. When I was finally brought back home my parents were nearly hysterical with worry.

By the next night my parents had spoken to someone who apparently explained to them what might be going on in my head. So my father and my mother tried to tell me that Skippy had gotten very sick and died. They tried to reassure me that it was not my fault and he had not run away. They told me that the only reason they had lied to me was that they didn't want me to see my dog looking so awfully sick. I didn't believe them but thought that they were now lying to try to make me feel better, rather than letting me face the horrible truth that I had inadequately understood and loved my dog, and he had left me for those reasons. Truth is a powerful weapon, but only if it is the first shot fired. I had built armor against it by then, and my pain and doubt about Skipper would not be washed away by later explanations.

My mother seemed to know that something further had to be done to lift me out of my grief. So she took the day off from work and had me help her clean the house with some especially nasty-smelling cleaner that was dissolved in water. She explained to me that it was a disinfectant and that we had to disinfect the house so that we could bring another dog into the house and the germs from Skipper's disease would not hurt our new dog.

I still didn't believe her. "We can't have a new dog," I protested. "When Skippy comes back and finds a new dog he'll think that I don't love him and don't want him."

My mother knelt down beside me and quietly said, "Skippy is not coming back because he can't. He died. He is with God now, and he will wait for you. Because he loves you and knows that you loved him, he also knows that you need another dog as a friend. He wouldn't want his germs to hurt that new dog. So we are going to make our home clean and safe for dogs. First, we will kill all of the germs with this disinfectant, and then we will air the house out for a couple of days. After that, we will see if there is another dog in the world that God wants you to have, since he has Skipper as his own pet for now."

It sounded like the truth and only cleaning up after a disease could justify using such awful smelly stuff to wash the floors and walls. It was then that I finally began to believe that Skipper was really dead. I turned to the bucket with its malodorous disinfectant solution and began to damp mop every surface of the house that I could reach—no other dog was going to die in that house if I could help it. I cleaned everything so vigorously that I could barely lift my arms at the end of the day. That night I fell asleep dreaming of God sitting on a white throne, with Skippy curled up next to his foot. Skipper was still my dog; he hadn't run away from me because I wasn't kind to him. I was sad, but God was a good person whom I could trust to take care of my dog until I got to be with him again.

🐾 🐾 🐾

My mother clearly had a plan for me, because on Saturday morning she took me to the library, pushing the baby stroller that contained my brother Dennis. On the way she explained to me that if and when we got a new dog, it would be a puppy and I would have to learn how to take care of it and to train it. I would have to learn what I needed to know by reading books about dogs.

We bumped the stroller up the library steps and entered through the big double set of doors. The high-ceilinged familiar space was filled with dark wooden bookshelves, and I took in that subtle smell of books that I had come to love. Near the doors was the circulation counter and next to it a few desks for the librarians. There were three alcoves off of the main area. The small one to the right was the children's section, which I was very well acquainted with since it was the only one that I was allowed to go into with the green library card that was issued to kids. My mother didn't even glance in that direction but went to the counter and placed my library card down on it.

"I'd like to upgrade my son's library card to a regular one," she said.

The librarian was a thin older lady with glasses and gray hair pulled back into a bun. She recognized me from my twice weekly visits to the library and gave me a slight smile, and then turned to my mother.

"How old is he?" she asked.

"Eight."

"A child must be twelve years old before we can let them use the adult section."

"He can read well enough to use the adult books," my mother said quietly, "and he needs material that is not in the children's collection. For example, there are no books in the children's section on dog care or training."

"Well, why don't you just take those books out on your card and let him read them?"

My mother sighed slightly. "I work and can't make it here very often. He needs to be able to select the books that have the information that he is looking for and take them out on his own."

"Some of that material in the main section is very difficult to read for a child, and some books on the open shelves contain inappropriate material for someone his age."

"You can test his reading skills right now if you like, and I will give you or anyone else on the library staff the right to prevent him from taking out books with unsuitable material in them."

The librarian hesitated, then leaned down and asked me, "So, you like dogs?"

I nodded. She pulled over her desk chair, motioned for me to sit down, and walked away. A few moments later she reappeared carrying a book with the title *Bruce* and a picture of a collie on the cover. It was a novel by Albert Payson Terhune, a writer who had died a few years before and was best known for his fictional adventures of collies, the breed that he truly loved. She opened the book to the first chapter and randomly pointed at a paragraph and said, "Start reading here. Out loud, please."

It was like reading to Skipper, which I had done so many times before. I adopted my best oratorical voice and began.

"Her 'pedigree name' was Rothsay Lass. She was a collie— daintily fragile of build, sensitive of nostril, furrily tawny of coat. Her ancestry was as flawless as any in Burke's Peerage.

"If God had sent her into the world with a pair of tulip ears and with a shade less width of brain-space she might have been cherished and coddled as a potential bench-show winner, and in time might even have won immortality by the title of 'CHAM-PION Rothsay Lass.'

"But her ears pricked rebelliously upward, like those of her earliest ancestors, the wolves . . ."

I was caught up in the story virtually from the moment that I began and went on reading with my attention glued to the page in front of me. I had no idea what my mother and the librarian were doing until the librarian tapped me on the shoulder and said, "That's okay for now. We need you to sign your name right here on your library card."

That tan-colored card was my key to rest of the library collection. The library did not have a big collection of books on dogs even in the main area, but there was a book on puppies and another on general dog care, which I checked out along with the Albert Payson Terhune novel that had served as my reading test. Over the next year or so I would ultimately read every dog book that Terhune had ever written. Like the dogs in the books by Eric Knight, who wrote about Lassie, Terhune's dogs were intelligent, empathetic, and courageous, but they were not "cartoon" dogs that could talk. Like real dogs they reasoned and acted in response to circumstances. Because of those books my dreams were often filled with beautiful collies, and my ambitions included not only understanding more about dogs, but perhaps someday writing about dogs.

I read the book on puppies and the book on dog care several times. Meanwhile, I checked each morning and on my return from school each day to see if there was another dog in the world that "God wanted me to have" who might have arrived when I was asleep or away from home.

CHAPTER 2

TIPPY

A round a month after Skipper died, my father arrived
home carrying something wrapped in a blue terrycloth bath towel. I followed him the length of the
short hallway and into the kitchen where he sat down. Puzzled,
curious, and hopeful, I tried to see what he had brought me. He
placed the bundle in my arms and leaned over to say, "Give him
a name. Give him a life."

My father smiled in a way that made his gray eyes twinkle.
I collapsed into a cross-legged heap on the floor and was staring
into the dark eyes of a puppy in the bundle that I held. He would
grow up to be a classic smooth fox terrier; his face was dark,
long, and tapered almost to a point. His ears were typical of his
breed and would grow to be erect, with only the top hanging
down to make the V-shaped flap that dog breeders call "button
ears." As an adult he would weigh around 17 pounds and would
stand around 15 inches at the shoulder on thin, elegant legs that
were designed for running.

He was mostly white but had a chestnut-brown saddle-
shaped patch that reached over his back and down his sides
almost to his belly. The brown started again near the base of

his carrot-shaped tail and moved upward about three quarters of its length, leaving a prominent white tip. The color and the patterning (except for his face) were almost identical to that of my beagle, Skipper. Most important was that he had a white tail tip, which Skippy had also had and I had always thought was a unique aspect of Skippy's coloring. When I looked at this new dog with the same special color markings as my beloved beagle, I knew that God had sent him to me and that this dog was supposed to keep me company in the same way that Skipper had. That white tail tip marking gave him his name, which would be "Tippy."

Many years later I would learn that this color pattern is not at all unique among dogs. Dogs use their tails to signal their emotional state, including threats, assertions of dominance, and expressions of submission. A white tip helps to make the position and movement of the tail more visible to other dogs. But at my age, then just shy of nine years, I simply viewed that white tail tip as a divine message that this dog was destined to take the place of my beagle.

🐾 🐾 🐾

Having read the puppy-training books I had taken from the library, I knew how to begin civilizing my dog. First, I had to housebreak him. At that time, the use of kennel crates for housebreaking (to my mind the most efficient method) was not widely known. So housebreaking became an extended process, and the occasional "accident" continued to occur at intervals until Tippy was about a year of age.

Coincidentally, my brother Dennis was just over 3 years old and going through the late stages of his own toilet training at the time. My mother tried to make the process for Dennis as nonconfrontational as possible, but other people were involved in my brother's toilet training as well. Since my mother had gone back to work, my brother was often left with my grandmother, Lena, who felt that Dennis was being coddled and pampered. She would frequently point out that, when she grew up in Eastern Europe, a child of my brother's age would be punished if he did not make it to the toilet in time. She was not one to use physical punishment, but when he had an occasional "accident," she would wave a finger sternly in Dennis's face and say, "You're a bad boy!"

Because Dennis was bright, he quickly learned what the words meant and immediately put them to use whenever he found a wet spot, or worse, left by Tippy. He would track down my dog and wave his finger in his face and say, "Bad dog!" with as much seriousness as his squeaky little voice could manage. This occurred pretty often, and I suspect that Tippy came to believe that "Bad Dog" was another one of his names, like "Little Foxy," which my father sometimes called him, and "Needle Nose," which my mother sometimes used. As little Dennis stood there waving a finger at him, Tippy would lick his hand and wag his tail—apparently quite happy with the extra attention that he was getting, regardless of the motivation behind it.

🐾 🐾 🐾

One day when Tippy was about 9 or 10 months old, he had an episode of "terrier frenzy" that had some important consequences for me. Tippy would go crazy trying to catch a spot of light moving jerkily across the floor, so his frenzy was really my fault, because I had borrowed my mother's hand mirror to reflect sunlight. Our living room served as a playroom for my brother and me and, of course, Tippy. It had a frayed sofa next to a round pedestal-style table with a red glass-based lamp, and one worn but comfortable chair. A sort of chest of drawers stood in the far corner and served as another table, on top of which was an old-fashioned 78 rpm record player and a table radio.

The only other thing in the room was a big, round, virtually indestructible rug made of a fat braid of rags that my mother had coiled in a big spiral and stitched together.

As Tippy chased the spot of light, he became more and more energized, charging this way and that, and then circling the room at high speed to return to chasing the quickly moving spot of light. Tippy ultimately became so excited that he forgot the game and was taken over by a manic or berserk state of mind, circling the room again and shooting out the door, down the short hall, and into the kitchen, where he started racing around the kitchen table. When he had done this before, he dashed up and down the hall a few times, until his frenzy had subsided, then he would return to me. This particular form of play was safe only when no one was working in the kitchen, but this was a Sunday and my mother was home baking. She was somewhere between the oven and table when my four-footed tornado hit.

When I heard my mother's yelp I was already halfway down the hall, yelling, "Tippy, come!" over and over. The little dog dashed back to me, circled me two or three times, and then headed back to do some more circuits of the kitchen. My commands to sit or lie down had no effect.

Suddenly I heard a thud and the clatter of something hitting the floor. Then there was a sudden cessation of the sound of scrabbling feet coming from my dog. When I got to the kitchen I saw that Tippy had entangled himself in my mother's legs as he raced around the room. She had lost her balance, and although she did not actually fall, she had fumbled the muffin tin that she had just taken out of the oven so that it had hit the table at an odd angle and spilled several muffins onto the floor. For Tippy, as for most dogs, food focuses the mind. At the sight of edible things falling to the ground from above, his mania stopped and he tried to gulp down pieces of the still-hot pastries. My mother grabbed a couple of muffins that were still intact and looked at me as I stood in the doorway fearing for my dog's future.

*Tippy would frantically chase any spot of light moving
erratically on the floor.*

"Come sit," she said directed me, pointing at a chair. As
Tippy continued his search for crumbs and bits on the floor, my
mother went to the pantry to gather the ingredients to make a
replacement batch of muffins. She did not look at Tippy at all
and did not look at me again until she was ready to mix the batter. Then she stopped and waved a wooden spoon at me.

"Tippy is your dog, so you have responsibility for not only
what happens to him, but also for what he does."

I glanced down to see my dog still patrolling the kitchen floor for any food fragments he might have missed. I was dreading what my penalty for his misbehavior was going to be.

My mother continued, "You called him and he didn't come. You told him to sit and he didn't sit. You told him to lie down and he didn't even slow up. Your dog is disobedient and he is not under control. It is your fault!" she said pointing the spoon at me for emphasis.

She said nothing for several minutes while she stirred the batter and poured it into the muffin tin. As she placed the tin in the oven and closed the door, she said to me, "It's your fault because you didn't train him. I will give you exactly eight weeks from today. After that I will give you a test. I want that dog to know how to come, sit, lie down, stay in place, and walk on a loose leash at the end of that time. If he fails that test . . ."

My mother just left that sentence uncompleted, leaving me to imagine terrible fates for both Tippy and me.

I did not know how to train a dog. I had taught my beagle Skipper a few things by waving food at him and he had listened and responded, at least most of the time, but even his best performance would not be enough to pass a test. Tippy was going to have to learn an awful lot and I didn't really know where to start. Even worse—it was Sunday and the library was closed, so I had nowhere to go to get the help that I needed.

🐾 🐾 🐾

The next day when school finished, I went directly to the library and pawed through the drawers full of cards that cataloged the books until I hit the subject topic "Dogs." The library had only one book in its collection that was indexed under "Dogs— training of." I scribbled down the number and nearly ran to the appropriate shelf, worried that someone may have already checked it out. However, there it was, *Training You to Train*

Your Dog by Blanche Saunders. I could not have known that of the few books available on the topic at the time I had accidentally hit upon the best of the lot. Through the 1950s, the dog training methods used throughout most of Europe and North America were still strongly influenced by the German military and their service dog training practices. The techniques used to train dogs reflected the attitudes of the military at the time and were based upon strict discipline supported by force if necessary, so a military dog trainer's tools included a leash that was braided and made rigid at the loop end so that it could be turned around and used as a whip if the dog failed to obey. These forceful methods worked and became the standard the rest of the world followed for most of the next century. Only later did people learn that more than one-third of the dogs subjected to such training regimens would break under the pressure and eventually fail.

Probably the most significant person during these early years was Colonel Konrad Most, arguably the father of modern "traditional" dog training. Konrad Most understood the importance of rewards and punishments, but believed that the best motivator for dogs was their desire to avoid punishment. Although a word of praise or occasional petting might be useful, choke collars, leash jerks, and even an occasional whipping were the mainstays of his training methods.

Hollywood would add a certain glamour to such compulsive dog training methods because of the success of dog trainers such as the American colonel Lee Duncan, who became known for his exceptional dog Rin Tin Tin. In 1918, Duncan found a bombed-out German war-dog kennel in Lorraine, France, that contained a German shepherd and her litter of pups. Duncan took one pup and named him Rin Tin Tin after the one-inch-tall wool puppets that French civilians gave to the liberating American soldiers for good luck. One of the captured German kennel masters taught him the techniques employed by Konrad Most, and Duncan used these to train his dog. Rin Tin Tin would go on to star in 26 Hollywood films and was credited for saving the fledgling Warner Brothers Studio from financial ruin during the silent film era.

The second Hollywood influence on dog training came from Carl Spitz, a German immigrant who was another student of Most. In 1927 he opened the Hollywood Dog Training School and became famous for being the trainer of many canine film stars, such as Terry, who played Toto in *The Wizard of Oz*.

One more direct import from Germany rounded out this early dog training world. Josef Weber learned to train dogs from Konrad Most's training manual when he was an instructor in the Berlin Police Force dog training unit. Ultimately he set up a "residential" dog training school in Princeton, New Jersey, for the dogs of people who were too busy (or uninterested) in training their own pets. His clients were an international Who's Who of the wealthy and famous. One person who came to him for instruction, not for her dog, but for herself as a dog trainer, was Blanche Saunders.

Destined to change the way dogs would be trained, Saunders never would have started on that career path had it not been for a breeder of standard poodles, Helene Whitehouse Walker. At that time (and even today), many people thought that poodles were wimpy, stupid, and useless dogs—fit only to be primped and coifed and shown in beauty pageants. Walker's experience with the breed had shown her that they were actually intelligent and hardworking.

While visiting Europe, Mrs. Walker saw some dog obedience competitions and wanted her dogs trained to perform these tasks in order to demonstrate to the world how clever poodles really were. Josef Weber recommended that Saunders do the actual training and also handle the demonstrations, noting, "She is very good with dogs, although she inclines toward being somewhat too gentle with them. However, for a breed like a poodle, that might be a virtue."

Blanche Saunders would later say that she was sitting on a tractor when Mrs. Walker approached her and said, "I'm told that you are good with dogs. How would you like a real job training them?" Saunders did not ask for any details but simply jumped off the tractor and asked, "When do I start?"

While Saunders trained the poodles, Walker used her persuasive skills and approached dog clubs and breeders with the idea of holding competitive obedience tests at dog shows. To further popularize the new sport of dog obedience, Saunders organized public demonstrations, some held in highly visible settings, such as Rockefeller Center, Madison Square Garden, and at sporting events at Yankee Stadium during intermissions.

In 1936 the American Kennel Club (AKC) agreed to award titles to dogs who reached a high enough standard of performance at dog obedience trials. Once the rules were in place Walker and Saunders engaged in a nationwide trek to popularize dog obedience as a sport. Together they loaded three poodles and all of their jumps and other gear into a trailer and started a 10,000-mile tour around the country. Going from one dog show to another, they stopped to give many public performances under a "Train Your Dog" banner. These made Blanche Saunders one of the most respected dog trainers of the time and, when her book appeared in 1946, it was virtually guaranteed to be a success.

Even though her mentor Josef Weber thought that she was "too gentle" with dogs, Saunders had not completely broken away from the force-based, military-style training inherited from Germany. She did, however, bring a broader understanding of the principles of learning to the field of dog training. Specifically, she observed, "Dogs learn by associating their acts with a pleasing or displeasing result. They must be disciplined when they do wrong, but they must also be rewarded when they do right."

Force and compulsion were still acceptable means of training for Saunders. Thus, the main tools that she used were the leash and the choke collar, usually a length of light metal chain with a ring at either end. When the chain is slipped through one of the rings and the leash is attached to the other ring it creates a nooselike device. When the leash is pulled or jerked, the noose tightens, causing discomfort as it cuts off the dog's air supply. Releasing pressure on the leash removes the pressure on the dog's neck. With choke-collar training, the dog is basically working to avoid the punishing effects of the tight collar. Saunders's innovation was that, along with the forceful guidance, she tried to add some positive rewards, noting, "There is magic charm in pieces of cooked liver and chicken." She anticipated what modern dog trainers call *positive dog training* methods when she said, "It is important that you know that kindness will accomplish much more than harshness and cruelty. A dog has a wonderful memory and he won't forget your attitude toward him."

When I was only 9 years of age, none of the specifics of the history of dog training methods mattered to me, but it did matter to me that Saunders wrote, "The reason that dogs and children get along so well must be that they are so much alike. They think alike, act alike, and they even train alike." I read this passage as meaning that it was reasonable to think that I could train my dog even if I had not yet grown up. As far as necessary equipment went, I already had a leash, so all that I needed was the choke collar.

🐾 🐾 🐾

My family was hard-pressed for money, so I dared not ask for funds to buy a second collar for Tippy that would be used just for training. But I remembered that one of our neighbors had had an old dog that had died a few months earlier and that she had worn what looked like the choke collar shown in Blanche Saunders's book. I gathered up my courage and crossed the street to their home. I knocked on the door and Mrs. Friedman answered. My voice quavered a bit as I started speaking, since I knew that my parents would not have been pleased to find out that I was asking the neighbors for any sort of "handout."

"Hello, Mrs. Friedman," I said. "I'm really sorry that Rosy died. I have my own dog now and his name is Tippy. My mother says that I have to train him, and I got this book that shows me how to do it, but it says that I have to use a choke collar and I don't have one. I was wondering if you kept Rosy's collar and if I could borrow it until I trained my dog or until you get another dog. I'll give it back afterward."

Mrs. Friedman smiled sympathetically and said, "Well, Rosy was a lot bigger than the little dog that I've seen you walking. But if you think that it will help, I'll give you her collar."

She disappeared for a few minutes and then returned with what seemed like an enormous piece of chain. Rosy had been a very large Labrador retriever. Her collar was two or three times longer than what was required to circle the slim neck of a fox terrier, but it was a choke collar and it was not costing me anything, so it would just have to do.

I thanked Mrs. Friedman and ran home. I sat in front of Tippy and looked at the picture in the book that showed Blanche Saunders shaping a chain like the one that I now had into a loop collar while a black poodle watched her with a happy expression. It looked easy. Next I slipped the collar over Tippy's head and when I released it I heard a clunking sound. The collar was so large that if Tippy nodded his head just a few inches the ring that hung down would bang against the floor. My trim little dog wearing the long, wide-linked heavy metal collar looked like a prisoner chained in a dungeon that I'd read about in books about knights and castles.

"It's okay, Tippy," I reassured him. "You only have to wear this when you are being trained. The rest of the time you can wear your own leather collar."

Tippy gave a little wave of his tail suggesting that he understood, or at least forgave me for the indignity of it all.

Carefully following the instructions in the book, I began training Tippy to sit and lie down on command. Physically positioning and guiding the dog was an important part of Saunders's training procedure, so I would tug up on the choke collar and push Tippy's hind quarters down to get him to sit. Getting him to lie down involved a bit of a wrestling match, with me grabbing his paws to pull him down and if necessary even lying down on top of him to keep him in position. As Blanche Saunders hinted, sneaking him a bit of food when he cooperated really helped.

Every day after school, I would put that enormous chain collar on my dog and work with him for an hour. On weekends I would train him for an hour or so early in the morning before the rest of the house was awake. The sounds of "Come!" "Sit!" "Down!" "Heel!" and "Stay!" uttered with all of the power that my high-pitched young voice could manage became the background music to my family's life.

Looking back, it is a great wonder to me that Tippy learned anything. My timing was awful, and all of those jerks, pulls, pushes, and tugs should have ruined my relationship with him. Perhaps the treats helped offset the buildup of any negative emotions, plus I gave him a lot of patting and praise. Unfortunately, a significant obstacle to my success was the "Dennis Factor."

My brother Dennis, 6 years younger than I, thought my dog training efforts were hilarious and invented a game in which he would try to distract Tippy or get him to disobey me whenever possible. When I would tell Tippy to "Stay!" in a sitting position, Dennis would run around or make catlike meowing sounds to try to get him to move or lie down. When I would give Tippy a "Come!" command he would stand on the side and call the dog while waving a bit of food to entice him away from me. When I would tell Tippy to lie down and stay, while I moved across the room to stand for a minute or so, Dennis would bounce a ball in front of Tippy, and, if that didn't cause him to move, would run behind him and tug on his tail. Whenever Tippy responded to him instead of obeying my instructions, Dennis would wag his finger at him and yell, "Bad dog!" and then roll on the floor laughing hysterically. When I tried to get my mother to intervene, she would smile and tell me that I was doing a good job training Tippy and that Dennis would learn by watching me so that he would be able to train his own dog when he got older. Dennis was standing beside me when I had this conversation and he responded by waving his finger at me and squeaking, "Bad dog!" He then fell to the floor laughing again while I tried to imagine some form of unpleasant retribution.

🐾 🐾 🐾

The 8 weeks flew by, but Tippy did seem to be under a reasonable degree of control now. His test was scheduled for a Sunday morning. We all went into the living room and my father, mother, and Dennis sat down on the sofa. My mother then said, "So show us!"

Tippy seemed to understand that something important was happening and was calmer and more observant than usual. He even seemed to give a little nod of encouragement to me, punctuated by the end of his long choke collar chain thumping against the floor.

I began by walking Tippy around the room, keeping him beside me in what trainers call the "heel position." Left turn, right turn, fast, slow, halt, and sit—all seemed perfect and he moved as if he were glued to my left leg. Then I placed him in a sit, stood in front of him, and told him to lie down, then to sit, both of which he did precisely. Next I told him to stay and I marched across the room.

"Tippy, come!" I called. The handsome little terrier bounded to me dragging his overlong chain collar along the floor and sat directly in front. Then I showed off his crowning achievement. Standing tall, I told him "Tippy, go around!" He stood up, circled behind me in a clockwise direction and sat down by my left side. My mother actually applauded and my father gave a smile that made his pale eyes sparkle. Tippy had passed the test and all was well.

Dennis gave his usual comment, "Bad dog!" but this time I didn't mind.

Later that week I returned the choke chain to Mrs. Friedman. I would still occasionally practice obedience commands with Tippy, but I had promised him that he would only have to wear that chain collar while I was training him, and I now considered him to be a perfectly well-trained dog.

🐾 🐾 🐾

Three or four weeks had passed since Tippy's obedience test, and on a weekend day my mother was in the kitchen making a big pot of split pea soup. I had a library book in my hand and was thinking about going outside, where the sun was shining and I could read for a bit. My plan was to find Tippy and take him out with me for company, so I had his leash in my other hand. It was then that I heard Tippy barking in the living room. It was his frantic bark and it was superimposed on the sounds of my brother Dennis laughing. I dashed down the hall and into our little living room to see what was happening.

Dennis was using a flashlight to cast a bright spot on the floor, moving it erratically and laughing and shouting "Bad dog!" as Tippy dashed this way and that trying to catch it.

Even though Tippy was trained, if he became overexcited and entered that state of terrier frenzy, I could not be sure that he would still respond to my commands, and the consequences of him dashing into the kitchen and another collision with my mother were too dreadful to contemplate.

I shouted, "Dennis, stop that!" but he only laughed and jumped up on the sofa while moving the light spot on the floor faster and faster. Tippy was becoming more and more excited, so I quickly closed the living room door to prevent him from charging down the hall. I called "Tippy, come!" No response.

"Tippy, down!" No response.

Accelerating, the little terrier made his dash for the door. Finding the door unexpectedly closed, he made a quick turn to avoid a collision, but lost his footing and slid a short distance on the bare wood floor only to bang against the rickety wooden pedestal table beside the sofa. Time slowed as I watched the table tilt and the red glass lamp tip over and crash to floor, breaking into several large pieces. The noise and the near miss from a large falling object brought Tippy to a halt long enough for me to grab him and clip the leash onto his collar.

Dennis was still jumping up and down on the sofa, laughing and shouting, "Bad dog!" when I opened the living room door and raced down the hall dragging my dog. I had to get him away from this newest disaster. Suddenly I had a flash of inspiration. I shouted, "Mom! Dennis was jumping on the sofa and knocked over the lamp and it broke. I'm gonna take Tippy outside so that he doesn't cut his feet on the glass. Dennis is still in there."

I felt no remorse. Dennis was ultimately responsible for this mess, and I doubted that he could shift the blame to Tippy, but I wanted my dog out of sight just in case. Perhaps my dog—my wonderfully trained dog—could avoid suffering the consequences of this latest lapse in control.

I sat on the front steps of the house, my arms around my dog. The warm sunshine helped calm me and I stopped shaking. Tippy turned and gave my face a lick. I faintly heard my mother's angry voice drift through the window and my brother's insistent explanation of "Bad dog!" which did not seem to be carrying much weight today. I chuckled to myself and whispered in Tippy's ear, "Good dog!"

CHAPTER 3

PENNY

Many dogs would come to live under my parents' roof, although not all at the same time. The array would ultimately include two schnauzers, an Irish setter, and two Cavalier King Charles spaniels. There would also be a cavalcade of cats including a sweet gray cat, a nasty purple Persian, and eventually four Siamese cats of differing shades and temperaments. The dogs belonged to us kids: me, Dennis, and eventually my youngest brother Arthur. When we boys no longer lived in the house, the dogs belonged to my father. The cats belonged to my mother.

Every dog that touched our existence had its own character, with a variety of strengths and foibles. Each had a life story, and each added its experiences to our lives. During the years that I lived in my parents' home, one special dog would set the stage for how I would think about dogs for the rest of my life. She was a boxer named Penny.

Penny was there at times of great change and transition in my life—when I finished high school, when I began and later returned from my active military service, and through my undergraduate college years. Like all of my dogs, her job was to be my companion, but occasionally she was a therapist and teacher.

❧ ❧ ❧

I never understood how, or from where, my father got our dogs. Even though we had very little money, my father wanted a traditional household and didn't want my mother to have to work, but circumstances were such that she always had at least a part-time job. By the middle of my high school years, however, our financial condition was better. My parents had their own house and enough income to meet the mortgage payments. Money was still a concern (so I worked part-time jobs to pay for textbooks, school fees, and personal things), and there was really not enough left over to allow us to afford luxuries. Certainly an expensive purebred dog would have fit in the category of luxury—yet we always had them.

One of my uncles later told me that my father bought most of our dogs with straight labor, rather than money. Dad was a wonderful craftsman and could build or repair just about anything. Our dogs were usually purchased in exchange for his doing some kind of construction or repair job for people. This involved working weekends and some evenings with the only payment being a puppy when the job was completed. He never explained the circumstances to us, and if we asked he would just say, "The dog is here with us now and that is all that matters."

Penny may have been different, since when my father placed the towel-wrapped puppy in my arms, he announced, "Her name is Penny because that is what I paid for her. She is a boxer. Give her a life." Since he usually left the naming of the dog to the son who would care for her, this was a clear difference, and although he never offered any further explanation, it seemed to matter to my father.

My brother Dennis looked at the puppy and observed, "Her face is so flat she looks like she walked into a wall. That's one ugly dog!"

My mother also peered over my shoulder and laughed, "She is so ugly that she is actually cute!"

Penny would never grow up to have the classic look of the breed. She was somewhat smaller and lighter than the norm, and her legs would not be quite as long and elegant as her body mass required. She was the classic fawn color of a boxer, though, with a white chest and white "socks," or paws. Her face was a dark mask that shadowed the area around her eyes and muzzle, although it was not quite as square and jowly as those of show dogs. But her dark eyes were set in a perpetually friendly, attentive look.

I thought she was beautiful. I got down on my knees, unwrapped the towel, and put her on the floor. She immediately began to sniff around, checking each person in turn, and then began inspecting the room.

I called to her in as happy a voice as I could produce, "Penny, come!" and she immediately trotted over to me and shoved her dark face in my hand. She then sat and looked at me with those dark eyes, and if people could melt because of the warmth of a look of love, I would have turned into a puddle at that moment.

Disaster struck a month later. Our house was on a residential street in West Philadelphia, but it got more traffic than most such streets because it was used by many people as a shortcut to bypass two busy intersections. The people who used it that way were obviously impatient and tended to travel at higher than normal speeds for such a narrow lane. This made the street too hazardous for the neighborhood children to play in.

One day my mother was outside talking to the woman who lived next door. Somehow, Penny got out of the house, and wandered between two parked cars and into the street where she was hit by a speeding car. Fortunately, she was clipped by it and not actually run over, but she flew several yards and landed in an unconscious heap. The car did not stop, and the driver may not have even seen her emerge and might not have known that he had nearly killed my small, young dog.

My mother rushed Penny to a veterinarian, who treated her immediately and later said that if the puppy had been older and had received an impact like that she probably would have been crippled for life. As it was, he was able to patch her up so that all that was left physically was a slight wobble in her hips that gave her a gait that looked much like someone who has had too much alcohol to drink but is trying to hide the fact by walking as gracefully as possible.

Penny's greatest injury, however, was psychological, for the accident left her with an intense fear of streets and oncoming cars. Taking Penny on walks was nearly impossible. She would not step off a curb to cross a street. If you tried to force the issue she would actively resist, all the while whimpering pitifully. This meant that Penny's life became confined to our home and our small backyard. Her exercise would be a few circuits around the block, or occasionally I would drive her to a park for a bit of a romp. In all other ways she was as courageous as any other boxer. Ultimately my education as a psychologist would teach me some techniques that might have been able to rid her of her fears, but that was years away and sadly too late for Penny.

When I got Penny, I was in my last year of high school and doing quite well academically. My personal life was orderly if not exciting, since, as the oldest child, my extended family had basically planned my future. My parents and maternal grandfather had even decided who I would marry. My father had planned my entry into the army as soon as I graduated. My mother had arranged to make sure that my scholarship for college would be held until I left active military service. My parents had also decided which university I would attend, namely, the University of Pennsylvania "because it is an Ivy League school."

My future career was also planned for me. My reading and interests mostly leaned toward the behavioral and biological sciences, since I had retained my childhood dream of being something like Dr. Doolittle, learning to communicate with animals and to understand what they were thinking. It was the 1960s, however, when the race between the United States and Russia for the domination of space filled the news. Physicists, engineers, and computer scientists were the heroes of the time, and psychologists and biologists did not get anywhere near the same attention or respect. My parents assumed that I'd select a profession that would involve research in the physical sciences or perhaps an engineering or technological specialization, and they exerted every pressure they could to make sure that their expectations came to pass, including continually talking about how I would become a great astrophysicist, nuclear scientist, or aviation engineer. Although I had my own dreams and desires, I was not particularly rebellious and had respect for my parents, believing that they had my best interests in mind. Furthermore, I simply assumed that this kind of control was what everyone my age experienced.

In later years, my parents would ease their attempts at controlling their children's lives, which would benefit my brothers, but I was their firstborn and they did not tolerate much questioning about their plans for me. I occasionally balked, but in most instances, their constant pressure made me conform. Nonetheless, my parents were not tyrants, so if I was insistent enough for long enough, they would let me take my own course of action, although they did not make it easy and would not let me forget that I had deviated from the path expected of "a good son."

Under this benevolent dictatorship, I felt socially isolated. I had no confidants to whom I could talk and work out my options. My small circle of friends tended to talk about "things" and "events," not feelings, personal goals, and futures—and never about relationships with our parents. Ultimately Penny would become the companion with whom I shared my secrets.

I had a part-time job on Thursday and Friday evenings and all day Saturday. When I was home, I spent a lot of time in my small room studying. I had a little desk there with a goose-necked lamp on it. There was also an old rocking chair near the window. Next to the bed was a floor pillow on which Penny slept. When I would go upstairs to work, Penny would follow me, lie down on the pillow, and watch me at the desk. When I sat in the rocking chair reading she would hop up on my narrow single bed and nap. The reverberation of her gentle snoring became the comforting background music for my life, and ever since I have always found it easier to write or work when I can hear the noise of a dog breathing nearby.

Often, when there were issues that I had to work through, decisions that I had to make, or parental decisions that I was supposed to abide by, I would close the door to my room and "discuss" them with Penny. Nowadays, psychologists have shown that it is not unusual for people to talk to their dogs in much the same way that they might talk to another human—conversationally. A lot of evidence has accumulated that such interactions between people and their dogs can be important for psychological health. For most people the bulk of their social interactions come from other humans. However, elderly people, those who live alone, or someone who was having difficulty speaking to his family about important matters (as I did) can get some of the same benefits from talking to a dog. Certainly my conversations with Penny helped me over some rough spots in my life and ultimately allowed me to make some important decisions—including some that would not please my parents.

One scientific survey, published in the 1990s, found that 96 percent of all people talk to their dogs in this way. Nearly everybody admitted that they usually greet their dogs when they come home and also usually bid them farewell when they leave.

Sometimes they will explain to the dog that some recent behavior was "stupid," "naughty," "helpful," or "funny." Sometimes they will extend the comment into a short narrative such as "It's a good thing that I found this mess before Mom did. You would catch a lot of grief if she knew what you did." Virtually everyone admits to asking questions of their dogs about matters they feel the dogs care about, such as "Do you want to go for a walk?" or "Do you want a snack?"

Conversations with canine companions also include questions that the dog really can't be expected to answer (or even care much about), such as "Do you think that there is any chance that it might rain today?" or "Do you think that Alan will forgive me for forgetting about our scheduled meeting for lunch yesterday?" Of course, this talking usually is a monologue, since the dog provides a friendly presence but no real input.

Some "dialogues" with dogs are more complex interactions, where there appears to be some give and take between the dog and the person, even though only the human is speaking. Overhearing this kind of conversation is similar to listening to one side of a phone conversation. A snippet of it might go, "I've asked Sally out to dinner with me on Saturday. Where do you think we should go?" [Pause for a few seconds.] "No, I took her out for Chinese food last time. How about an Italian restaurant this time?" [Another brief pause.] "You know, you're right, there is that new Argentinean restaurant with all the meat served from skewers." [Pause.] "Of course! I had forgotten that on Saturdays they have that Latin band there. This could be a lot of fun. That's a really good suggestion, Lassie."

In another variety of human-and-dog conversations that is familiar to many dog owners but might appear to be strange to an outsider, the person not only talks to the dog, but also provides audible answers, essentially speaking the words that he believes the dog would say in response. Parents often engage in this kind of conversation when talking to young babies: when a mother gives her child a toy, she might say something such as, "Would you like this teddy bear?" When the baby smiles or reaches, she adds (often in a higher-pitched, more childlike voice), *"Oh yes, Mommy. I like that bear."* When a person provides both his own dialogue and that of his dog, however, the conversation sounds much like the often used Hollywood movie sequence where a mentally deranged individual carries on an argument among his various multiple personalities—each with a distinctive voice and character.

Perhaps the best-known such conversations with a dog were recorded by John Steinbeck, the Nobel Prize–winning author who wrote about a trip across the United States with his black standard poodle in *Travels with Charley*. In truth, the book could just as well have been titled *Conversations with Charley*. A sample of one such conversation occurred when he found Charley simply staring blankly off into space. Steinbeck began the following bit of dialogue and provided both parts of the conversation, presumably out loud:

"What's the matter, Charley, aren't you well?"
His tail slowly waved with his replies. *"Oh, yes. Quite well, I guess."*
"Why didn't you come when I whistled?"
"I didn't hear you whistle."
"What are you staring at?"
"I don't know. Nothing, I guess."
"Well, don't you want your dinner?"
"I'm really not hungry. But I'll go through the motions."

And some quite hilarious conversations are featured in A. R. Gurney's popular play, *Sylvia*, in which the dog Sylvia speaks clearly to her owner about many big and small matters, although only her owner (and the audience) understands her. Many of my discussions with Penny were like those in *Trav-*

els with Charley. I would say something to her and then give her answer in a voice that mimicked that of the Disney cartoon character Goofy. I have given every dog that I have spoken to its own unique voice. I have no idea why I chose that particular voice for Penny, especially since many of our conversations were fairly deep and personal, and many of the comments that I filled in for her in that silly voice were emotion-laden and the suggested actions often had important personal consequences. Perhaps I chose Penny's voice because at one level I still considered the idea of intense personal conversations with a dog to be "goofy," or perhaps to keep matters light and to remind me that "the dog's comments" were not to be interpreted as commands or requirements for action. To an eavesdropper, such conversations would probably sound as if I had lost my mind, so I always closed the door before Penny and I "talked."

🐾 🐾 🐾

Immediately following my graduation from high school, I entered the army, which took me to Fort Knox, Kentucky, for basic training, and then to Fort Monmouth, New Jersey, for training as a still photographer. My coursework scores and my evaluations as a photographer were very good, and I soon found myself being sent out on various interesting photographic assignments for the army's Public Information Office. This took me around the country and allowed me to meet a large number of interesting people and their dogs.

According to my mother, Penny had been quite upset at my leaving. She would spend long hours upstairs guarding my room and barring entry to anyone except my mother. She refused to sleep anywhere else but on her pillow by my bed, and if her way into my room was blocked, she would set up a howl until she was allowed inside. However, matters did change a bit with a new arrival in our family.

By the time that I returned home to restart my civilian life, my youngest brother Arthur had been born and was now an unsteady toddler wandering around the house. In my absence Penny had adopted Arthur, and her maternal instincts caused her to act as a protective shield around him. One day Arthur grabbed the electrical cord attached to a ceramic table lamp, and when he tugged, it toppled to the floor, breaking into several large chunks.

My brother Dennis, who was in the room, shouted, "Arthur, get away from there!" as he leapt from his seat and dashed across the room to try to keep his brother from cutting himself on the broken pottery. To Penny, however, his loud vocalization and sudden movement toward "her child" looked like an attack, so she vaulted from her position to interpose her body between Dennis and Arthur. When Dennis reached for my brother, she produced a low grumbling growl and then used her head and blunt muzzle to move Arthur toward the door, away from his larger brother. At that moment my mother entered the room, lifted Arthur from the floor, and then carried him into the next room. Only then did Penny seem to relax, as she followed my mother to monitor what was happening to "her child."

Penny's relationship with Arthur was special, and she would tolerate many misdemeanors and abuses from him that would have brought out hostility toward anyone else. For example, one day when Penny was peacefully resting in the living room. Arthur waddled into the room carrying two large metal spoons. He looked across the room at the peacefully resting boxer and clanged the spoons together to produce a sharp sound while he announced "Glock!"

Arthur then proceeded in an unsteady waddle across the room toward the dog, clanging the spoons together and with each impact he repeated "Glock!"

"Glock! Glock! Glock! Glock! Glock!" Now he was in front of Penny, who lifted her head and looked up at him. Arthur then slipped one spoon under her chin, and took the other one and banged down across the top of her muzzle. His shout of "Glock!" was partly cut off by the fact that Penny leapt to her feet and in the process knocked the unsteady toddler off of his feet. She looked at him, shook her head as if trying to clear some fogginess from her eyes, and then walked over to the other end of the living room and lay down again.

Arthur rolled over and pulled himself upright. With spoons banging he marched back across the room toward Penny: "Glock! Glock! Glock! Glock!"

When he was a foot or two in front of her, she rose to her feet, bumped her square muzzle against his chest, and watched him topple backward. She then walked over to him, licked his face, and went to the far end of the room.

The whole process then repeated itself, Arthur wobbling across the room with his "Glock! Glock! Glock! Glock!" Penny knocking him over, licking his face, and retreating to the far side of the room.

Back and forth they went in their little dance of "Glock and tumble." Arthur apparently enjoying the game, Penny showing incredible degrees of forgiveness.

My mother ended the show by announcing, "Come on, now, we can't just sit and let him abuse the dog." She removed the spoons from his hands and picked Arthur up. Arthur reached his tiny hand out in the direction of the dog, opening and closing it and repeating "Glock!"

The next time Arthur saw Penny, she was resting and he was not carrying spoons. However, he ran over and flopped on top of her and announced "Glock!" Suddenly and spontaneously, my family concluded that they may have been observing more than a game, and to Arthur at least, this was a naming ritual and thereafter Penny had a new nickname, although it was used differently by different family members. My mother used it as a noun and as a synonym for the word "dog" as in the query

"Have you fed the glock yet?" Arthur, Dennis, and I tended to use it as just another name for our dog, as in "I'm going to take Glock for a walk." Penny accepted the name as just another strange label that was being applied to her and responded to commands like "Glock, come!" with the same reliability that she responded to "Penny, come!"

🐾 🐾 🐾

In spite of her protectiveness toward Arthur, Penny still spent her nights sleeping on a pillow next to my bed. Because I was a sound sleeper, I needed a loud alarm clock to wake me, so I had bought a spring-wound clock with two large bells on top. The noise that this clock made when the alarm went off virtually shattered the furniture around it—certainly no one could easily sleep through it. Penny hated it. Because the clock made some sort of sound as it approached the time set for the alarm, Penny quickly learned that if she could awaken me just before the time set for the alarm, I would glance at the clock, and, since it was near the time when I intended to wake up I would turn off the alarm and get out of bed. So each morning I was awakened by 50 pounds of boxer landing on my chest. Because of this very effective biological alarm clock, the entire time that I was at university I never missed a class because of oversleeping.

🐾 🐾 🐾

I was following the path of a major in physics, in order to prepare myself for one of the professions my parents had decided upon for me, although it brought me little joy. One evening when my parents were out and my brothers asleep, I made myself some tea and sat down to talk with Penny. Lying halfway on her favorite fringed floor pillow, she had the courtesy to keep her eyes open and to look at me.

Penny was lying halfway on her favorite fringed floor pillow but had the courtesy to keep her eyes open and to look at me.

"I really don't like this physics and math stuff all that much," I admitted to my dog.

"*Well, you are doing okay in those courses,*" Goofy's voice replied.

"I really want to do something that holds my interest, especially if I am going to be doing it for the rest of my life."

"*So, what catches your interest?*"

"Understanding what you and other dogs say and think is part of it. But I've also been reading some things about how people and animals see and hear, and that is fascinating stuff that I would like to do some research on."

"*Is there something in the university that will let you study both?*"

"Psychology, I guess, but Mom and Dad don't have a very high opinion of psychologists. They would explode if I told them I was leaving physics to major in psychology."

"*It's not their life, you know.*"

"Yeah, but they can make it very uncomfortable if I go against their wishes."

There was a long pause, during which Penny walked over to me and nuzzled my hand. Then the Goofy voice announced, "*Well, you still have your job working in a physics laboratory. You could tell your parents that you want to explore psychology because it has caught your interest, but you can emphasize the fact that you are keeping your job in the physics lab so that you can always go back to that as a major.*"

I looked into the dog's dark eyes and said, "But that's not the way it really works in the university, you know."

Penny lay herself down at my feet and the Goofy voice said, "*Well, then, you may never get to really understand what I am thinking, and you may end up in a well-paying job that you don't really like. But if you volunteer to live in a dungeon that your parents have designed for you, don't complain to me later that you don't like wearing chains. Besides, you can just take the courses and not tell them that you are thinking about becoming a psychologist.*"

That was the longest oration I had ever put into Penny's voice up to that time, but it reflected exactly the degree of emotion and turmoil that was going through my head.

The next evening I told my parents that I was going to take a few psychology courses, but they shouldn't worry because I was keeping my job in the physics lab. They were concerned, and my mother complained that with all that Freud business, and that total concern with sex, it was not a very reputable profession.

Keeping my job in the physics lab calmed things a bit as my conversation with Penny had suggested it might. As a survival strategy I also eliminated the words *psychology* and *psychologist* from my vocabulary when I was at home. Instead, I would tell my parents that I was studying "animal behavior" and "human and animal sensory processes." The fact that my academic major had changed to psychology would not be mentioned until late in my senior year when I had already been accepted for graduate studies at Stanford University.

🐾 🐾 🐾

Regardless of their feelings about psychologists, my parents did like the friends that I made while working in psychology. It was during a visit from a couple of these friends that Penny showed another of her behavioral quirks. Most of my dogs have demonstrated a liking for beer—at least flat beer, since most dogs don't like to inhale the bubbles into their noses. Penny was unique in developing an appetite for bourbon. Rye or sometimes scotch would occasionally suffice, but bourbon was her passion, and she was exactly the right height to be able to shove her face into a glass of whisky when it was placed on a coffee table or an end table next to the sofa. Often the unfortunate owner of the drink did not discover that my dog had emptied his glass until he heard her crunching on the ice cubes (which she used as sort of chaser). With a body weight of only around 50 pounds, Penny was quickly affected by even a little alcohol, and so, after drinking some whisky on the sly, she would become slightly inebriated, stagger to the middle of the room, lie down, and start to snore. This prompted my father to observe, "Your dog is a noisy drunk."

🐾 🐾 🐾

Penny was extremely important to me as a companion and confidante, and she also taught me something very important about courage by personal example. Some individuals are fearless, but it is not the fearless hero who demonstrates courage; real courage is shown only by people who have strong fears. Courage is defined as the willingness to act even when you are wracked by fear for your own life or safety.

One Sunday afternoon I was standing outside our house and chatting with Barry, a neighbor who also attended the University of Pennsylvania. He had joined the hockey team and was telling me about some of the team's exploits (and embarrassing gaffes). I had let Penny out on the small front lawn to sniff about a bit. She would not wander very far and certainly would not go out into the street because of her paralyzing fear of stepping off a curb even when she was on leash.

My mother appeared briefly and asked me to keep an eye on Arthur while she was in the basement doing the laundry. A moment later my 3-year-old brother emerged from the front door pushing a big yellow ball. It bounced down the steps and stopped at the line of rocks that edged our little front lawn. As Arthur carefully made his way down the steps, Penny came over and sat down a few feet from him. I knew that she would not let "her little boy" out of her sight when he was out of the house. Arthur had now reached the bottom of the steps, where he picked up the ball and tossed it over the low row of stones and continued to play.

I became engrossed in Barry's entertaining tale and let my attention drift from my baby-minding duties. Suddenly I heard what sounded for all the world like a woman's shriek of pain or fear. I looked up and saw that the sound had actually come from Penny who was darting across the pavement and, much to my astonishment, off the curb and between two parked cars, just as a bright red automobile raced past the very place where my dog had vanished. I ran faster than I ever remember running before or after—crossing the few yards between the front steps and the street in seconds. When I arrived at the gap between the vehicles, I found Arthur struggling to get across the street, where I could see his yellow ball resting on the other side. Another car flashed rapidly past, missing my brother by inches. The only thing keeping Arthur from being hit by the passing traffic was Penny, who had gripped the crossed rear straps that held up his corduroy pants and braced herself to keep him from making any further movements forward. All the while she was whimpering plaintively.

I grabbed my brother and lifted him back to the safety of the pavement, with a loud, "Stay there! I'll get your ball." My heart was beating strongly enough that I could actually hear my pulse in my ears. My heroic dog, who had saved my brother's life, still stood there, in the street that she feared so intensely. She was between two parked cars in virtually the same situation that she had been just before her own painful, life-threatening accident. There was a small puddle of urine in the place where she stood, visible evidence of the extreme fear she had felt.

I called her to me, and she moved in a slow, dazed manner as she stepped back onto the pavement. I bent down to pet her and felt her trembling and panting in rapid, shallow, fearful breaths. My dog had fought her greatest fear and protected "her child." She took another step or two toward Arthur, then licked his face before sinking slowly to the ground, where she lay trembling and panting for several more minutes before she finally regained enough strength to move back toward the house.

In the movies, when a person faces his ultimate fear and survives, that individual is always cured and never has to suffer that fear again. My dog Penny had showed incredible courage in facing her utmost fear in order to save my brother's life. However, she was not cured. I never saw her spontaneously step into the street again, and she seemed, if anything, to be even more fearful of traffic. She also became even more strongly protective of Arthur and would interpose her body between him and the street when he appeared to be approaching too close to the curb.

That night I sat down in front of my courageous dog, poured two glasses of bourbon, held them up in front of me, and announced, "I'd like to honor my brave dog with a toast. Remember that courage is just being equal to the tasks that life puts in front of us. By that standard, you are indeed a courageous dog. I would be honored if the most heroic boxer that I ever met would join me in a drink. Here's to you, Glock!"

As I set one of the glasses on the floor in front of her, the Goofy voice announced, *"The street still scares me. You know, if you had given me this drink before Arthur tried to run out onto the road, I probably would have been a lot more courageous!"*

All else was lost in the sounds of lapping and ice cubes and liquid splashing around in a wide glass tumbler.

CHAPTER 4

THE DOG-LESS YEARS

From the moment that I decided to switch my major to psychology at the University of Pennsylvania, I felt that I was really home. I loved studying both human and animal behaviors and how we form our conscious picture of the world in our minds.

So much was happening in psychology at that time. B. F. Skinner was formalizing his discoveries about the process of learning, David Hubel and Torston Wiesel, who would later win the Nobel Prize, were uncovering the neurological basis for how the brain puts together visual images, while another Nobel Prize winner, George von Békésy, was uncovering the mechanisms by which we interpret the sounds that we hear. The structure of DNA had recently been discovered, and new tools for looking at how behaviors could be determined genetically were being developed. There were also new discoveries and data about the behavior of dogs and other canines. Another Nobel Prize winner, Konrad Lorenz, had written two exciting books, *Man Meets Dog*, about the domestication of dogs and the human-animal bond, and *King Solomon's Ring*, which gave an overview of his research on dog behavior, social structure, and the way dogs communicate. L. David Mech had started his wolf studies, which would expand our knowledge of canine behavior even further. J. Paul Scott and John Fuller were applying the newly developed methods for studying behavior genetics to dogs at the Jackson Laboratory in Bar Harbor, Maine, while Michael W. Fox was exploring the effects of early developmental experiences on the later adult behavior of dogs.

Caught up in all of these advances, I began doing research in two areas: how animals perceive the world and the nature of curiosity in animals. Much of this work had to be done at odd hours, since I still was working at two part-time jobs that I needed to provide me with enough money to pay for my books, laboratory fees, and other necessities. However, several faculty members gave me keys and access to the labs and I would often be found testing animals at 6 A.M., well before my classes started for the day. I had already sent in my applications to several of the top graduate programs in psychology and was awaiting their responses.

The future of my personal life was also becoming clearer. In their usual manner, my parents and grandfather had already decided who I was to marry and had been applying pressure for a number of years. I had had dates and pleasant evenings with a number of girls over the years, but nothing that seemed destined to turn into a lasting relationship.

Then there was Marcia—the chosen one—whom I always called Mossy, although I have no memory of why. Her family lived only about three city blocks from one of my childhood homes in West Philadelphia. Her mother and father (Goldie and Denny) were very pleasant, and my maternal grandfather, Jake, knew Denny quite well. Mossy's family was pretty much at the same financial and social level as my own, and coming from the same neighborhood we shared a number of common views and attitudes.

A year younger than I was, Mossy and I began to spend

more time together during our years at West Philadelphia High School, which both our families encouraged. After my stint in the army, and Mossy's completion of her training as an X-ray technologist, I continued to see her, and we dated while I was doing my undergraduate work at Penn.

Although this seems as close to an arranged marriage as one gets in the modern Western world, it was not a matter of compulsion. It involved a lot of subtle pressures, such as conversations that began "When you and Marcia get married . . ." or suggestions like "If you will be working for your doctoral degree in a university that is outside of the city, you and Marcia should probably get married in June at the end of your senior year," or questions like "Have you and Marcia decided how long you will wait before making us grandparents?"

I did like Mossy. Everyone liked her. She was verbal, intelligent, had a good sense of humor, and was a great and enthusiastic dancer. She was also a wicked card player, a good observer of people, and she told interesting stories. Her behaviors and moods were predictable and never much cause for stress. We were comfortable with each other and had both accepted our parents' presumption that we would get married. The problem, for me, was that there was simply no passion in our relationship. To me, it was more like a longtime friendship.

I talked this over with Penny, who was lying on her pillow in my bedroom, and explained my doubts.

"I don't know if I should go through with this marriage thing with Mossy," I said to my brown-eyed dog. "Everyone says that you should get married because of love—that there should be lots of fire and excitement and all of that."

The Goofy voice answered, *"So who do you know who kindles that kind of fire in you?"*

"No one, right now."

"Do you want to start looking for some 'passion pet' now?"

"Come on, I've got too much going on, what with the two

jobs, the research, my studies, and all of that. Where would I find the time or the energy?"

"Do you like her?"

"Of course I do."

"If you've got to go away, say to California, for graduate work, would you rather go alone or with her?"

That was really the crucial question. "I suppose that I would like her company. We do get along together, and I don't like the thought of starting a new life in a different place alone."

I sat on the floor stroking my dog and thinking my life was not a random stroll through some garden, where I could change my path any time I wanted to look at interesting flowers or plants. Rather, my life was a railroad train, and it was taking me in the only direction that the tracks led. At the time, I probably did not require much passion in my personal life, since I was pouring virtually all my emotional reserves into research and studies. Although I had abandoned physics as my major I was still working for the physics department, liquefying helium for use by the cryogenics group. Cryogenics is the study of things that happen at very cold temperatures, and many research projects use liquid helium as a refrigerant, since it remains liquid at temperatures less than 1 degree above absolute zero (theoretically the lowest temperature obtainable is -459°F).

The cryogenics research group met once each week to discuss its ongoing work. Kenneth Atkins, the director of the group, invited me to attend, since I was treated as one of the regular departmental staff. Listening to these brilliant scientists wrestling with complex problems gave me an insight as to how research was conducted and how creative thinking could be applied to problems. I could not have gotten this kind of education any other way. It taught me how to turn questions into concrete tests, how to simplify complicated descriptions in a way that left only the vital elements. During these think-tank sessions I even began to learn how to present complex theories and ideas in a basic manner that any layperson can understand. Watching these scientists wrestle with concepts at the far limits of our knowledge made me want to test my own creative abilities by applying these same mental skills to psychological and behavioral problems.

With the benefit of hindsight, I can see that research had clearly become my passion. It was addictive, and I was spending the majority of what free time I had gathering data, writing, analyzing—lost in my own intellectual world. I had become that clichéd Hollywood version of a scientist, immersed in his work while forgetting or neglecting his family and other relationships. I finished my undergraduate studies with four published research articles, including a study in one of the most important research journals in the world, *Science*. That publication, as much as my grades and other qualifications, led to my being accepted by Stanford University for doctoral studies in psychology.

🐾 🐾 🐾

I graduated from Penn in the beginning of June 1964, and less than two weeks later Mossy and I were married, making two sets of parents and my grandfather very happy, and convincing them that all was right with the world. Later that summer, Mossy and I loaded everything that we owned (which wasn't all that much) into the almost-new blue station wagon that my grandfather had given me for our cross-country trek to California.

The last thing I did before climbing into the car to begin the journey was to bend down to say good-bye to Penny. I held her big square head in my hands, looked into her deep brown eyes, and quietly told her, "I love you, girl."

Normally the Goofy voice would have answered me with some snarky comment, but there were people around and I didn't want them to think that I had gone mad. So the Goofy voice was silent this time.

"Wait for me, Glock. I'll be back for you."

It would be two years before I could return to my parents' home in Philadelphia, and Penny could not wait. I never saw those brown eyes again and never again heard that Goofy voice.

🐾 🐾 🐾

Because I had served in the military, when Mossy and I arrived at Stanford University we were eligible for subsidized married student housing. These accommodations were in a place called Stanford Village, which made it sound like some idyllic, tree-lined setting. It actually was a set of narrow, one-story wooden army barracks located behind Stanford Research Institute. These buildings had been used as a military hospital during World War II, but now had been converted to apartment units by building thin walls to subdivide the area into apartments. Each housing unit was composed of a small bedroom, a living room, a tiny kitchen, and a walk-in-closet-sized bathroom with no bathtub and only a metal shower stall. The walls had been hastily and cheaply put up with no sound insulation between units, and in some places there were gaps of around a half inch between the top of the wall and the ceiling. This gave us little privacy but lots of information about our neighbors' private lives, since even whispers freely drifted through the walls and gaps into our apartment. Nonetheless, it was a place to live and it was very inexpensive.

At that time, Stanford had one of the most respected psychology departments in the world. It could boast more winners of the American Psychological Association's Distinguished Psychologist Award (psychology's equivalent of the Nobel Prize) than any other department in existence. I was going to work with one of their superstars, Leon Festinger, who is best known for his *theory of cognitive dissonance*, which explains the ways that people form and change their attitudes, but who also made significant contributions to social psychology, learning, perception, statistics, and even paleopsychology (which is the attempt to reconstruct social and other everyday behaviors from the kinds of things that archeologists and paleontologists turn up when exploring the caves and primitive settlements where primitive humans lived tens of thousands of years ago).

One of the most brilliant people that I have ever met, Leon could shed new insights on any problem to which he turned his attention. His analytic abilities were astonishing. In his weekly research meetings with his students and a few colleagues, he was a delight to watch as his mind worked behind the ever-present cloud of cigarette smoke. He would tease apart theoretical notions and then reassemble them in new forms. He had a talent for extracting the essence of a theory and then creating a very simple experimental procedure to test it.

In spite of my admiration of him, Leon and I clashed several times during my first year at Stanford because I did not want to be a technician simply carrying out a principal researcher's instructions, no matter how much of a genius he was. I had my own research ideas and my own interests, and Leon admitted that some were very interesting. Ultimately, he offered me a compromise. He gave me a large room as a laboratory and told me that as long as I completed the various research projects that we were doing collaboratively, I could do any other research that I wanted to do on my own and he would support it financially. This worked for both of us, and I always had three or four experiments going at the same time, each set up in a different corner of my big lab space.

🐾 🐾 🐾

I was yearning for a dog, but pets were not permitted in our housing complex. So although cats are really not my cup of fur, I allowed myself to get involved in a research project that involved a cat. Socializing with a cat is certainly better than having no animal companion. She was a purebred Siamese with the registered name of Shen Wa's Just Fu Too, but I just called her Fu. She had been selected because she was extremely cross-eyed and because of the odd way that the visual system of Siamese cats is wired to their brains. If we could, in essence, get her to tell us what she was actually seeing by teaching her to respond to some special types of visual displays, it might shed light on a newly developed theory about how humans see their world.

I designed the apparatus that Fu was to be tested in. She had only a very simple task to perform. All that she had to do was to look at a display that controlled the information that came into each eye separately, and then push a lever on the right if she saw one line and a lever on the left if she saw two. Pigeons can do this sort of task, so there was no reason to expect that a cat would have any difficulty. The actual testing was being done by a more junior graduate student named Charlie. Leon had asked me to keep an eye on Charlie's progress, which I gladly did since it gave me the excuse to drop by the lab at various times and, if testing was not in progress, I got to play a bit with Fu. She was incredibly beautiful, with deep blue eyes, and was, at least for a cat, very loving.

Unfortunately, Fu turned out to be too dumb to even learn the preliminary tasks needed for her to be tested. Charlie became rather despondent about how the experiment was going, and Leon was annoyed at the lack of progress. Since Charlie was following the procedures exactly as specified, Leon's displeasure focused on the cat, and he decided to end the testing and have her put down.

I felt sorry for Fu, since she had at least partly filled the need that I had for a pet over the past 8 or 9 months. So when I heard his plans to terminate her life, I offered to take her. Leon was sufficiently frustrated and angry that he openly expressed a strong desire to see the animal dead and had already arranged to have her euthanized later that afternoon. With the limited time left I made the best pitch that I could think of.

"Look, Leon, you have some affection for your own cat, Max, don't you?" Max was a tailless Manx cat.

"What difference does that make?" he grumbled as he reached into his pocket to take out a cigarette. This was a good sign, since it meant that he was not so upset that he had forgotten to smoke.

"Well, maybe you can understand how I feel about Fu. I know what we paid for her, and I am willing to buy her from you."

"Buy her? Where the hell are you going to get the money to buy her given your bountiful salary?" I was earning $235 a month and we would have starved if it was not for the fact that Mossy was working as an X-ray technician. Fu would cost nearly half a month's wages if I paid her full price, an amount we really couldn't afford. "Furthermore, I don't give a damn about the money," Leon grumbled. "I just want her destroyed today so I can put her out of my misery."

He took a deep puff on his cigarette, looked at the ceiling, and exhaled. After a moment, he looked back at me and asked, "Is she really that important to you?"

I nodded.

"All right, simply on behalf of my feelings for Max, you can have her, and it won't cost you anything. However, there are two conditions. First, you get that cat out of the lab immediately. I never want to see it again. Second, I want you to promise me that you will never tell me that the cat is happy in its new home. I don't want to even know where its new home is, and I don't want you to say another word about her in my presence. Her name should have been Phooey! Now get that cat out of my lab before I change my mind."

I dashed over to Charlie's office and told him to cancel the euthanasia request, then raced down to the workshop and with the help of the shop technician, cobbled together an ugly but usable kennel crate, using a wooden packing box from some recently received equipment. With this in hand I went to Charlie's lab and removed Fu.

Since there was no place else to leave her, I smuggled the cat into our apartment. In two days Mossy and I would be driving back to Philadelphia for a visit, since classes had ended for the Christmas holiday. This meant that the likelihood that the cat would be discovered was low.

As I sat with Fu in my lap later that evening, I found that I wanted to talk to her as I had talked to Penny. So I said, "You know that you are very lucky. If Leon had delayed his decision to kill you by just a day or two, I would have been on my way to Philadelphia and would have missed the opportunity to save your life. Instead, you are going to become our Christmas gift to my parents."

Fu did not answer, and I did not expect her to. Although I felt comfortable talking to her, I had no desire to give her a voice or engage in any real interactive conversation with her—after all, she was only a cat.

🐾 🐾 🐾

By the time I had finished my doctoral research, a number of changes had occurred in my life. Surrounded by many brilliant minds in Stanford's psychology department, and its intense focus on scientific investigation, I had become virtually addicted to my research and writing. Mossy was supportive in her quiet way, but she did not understand either the issues that I was dealing with in my research or my passion for doing it. Because I was so occupied with my research, our relationship had weakened and we became more distant and uninvolved. We both noticed that this was happening and both of us wanted the marriage to prosper and continue, but I did not want to stop my work to make things better and Mossy did not have the skills or inclination to be involved with my studies.

I did not know how to remedy our personal situation or even how to begin to work my way through the various alternative options that I might have. Because pets were not allowed in these apartments, I had no dog to serve as a confidant and sounding board to allow me to have the kind of therapeutic and exploratory "conversations" that I had had with Penny. Apparently I had become more dependent on those "dialogues" than I realized. Thus the idea that a lot of my own behaviors and choices were weakening my bond with my wife never truly entered my consciousness. Like so many other married couples confronted with a cooling relationship, Mossy and I decided that the solution was to have a baby.

Although this method of trying to heal our marriage was, as is usually the case, a failure, I never regretted bringing our daughter Rebecca into the world. A pretty child, she had her mother's dark hair and my mother's sparkling blue eyes. While my relationship with Mossy did not permanently improve, it did get a little better for a while, and perhaps the downhill slide slowed a bit. I gave up some of my time in the lab to spend more time at home with Rebecca.

Ultimately, as my addiction to my research took over again, I spent less time at home and more time working. When I finally finished my thesis and got my doctorate, I had published an additional half dozen articles in scientific journals. This was considered to be a remarkable level of productivity at that time, and so several well-respected universities offered me jobs. At the same time Leon Festinger had decided to leave Stanford to take an endowed professorial chair at the Graduate Faculty of the New School for Social Research in New York City. Originally from New York, Leon adored that city and, in addition, he had fallen in love with a woman who was on the faculty of New York University. He was offered the opportunity to start his own research program with a suite of laboratories in a new building. Leon asked me if I would accept a faculty position at the New School and become the director of the new Perception Laboratory that he was founding. He also guaranteed research funding for the first two years. My loyalty to Leon inclined me to accept, the availability of research funding was a great incentive, and furthermore, New York was easy driving distance from Philadelphia where my family still lived, now with their new dog, a schnauzer named Baron, and their well-loved, blue-eyed Siamese cat named Fu. So it was off to New York with my wife and daughter.

CHAPTER 5

THE DOG THAT WASN'T MINE

I t was time to complete my family with a dog, but once we reached New York, we had a lot of trouble finding a dog-friendly apartment building. I believed that a puppy would make us a true family unit.

Besides longing for a dog, I may have been trying to model myself after my father and the loving home he had created for us with the dogs he had brought home. I had convinced myself that this dog would be for my daughter—it would not be my dog; it would have to bond with Rebecca more strongly than to me. Even though I wanted another canine companion, I nonetheless believed that this was the right thing to do. So we got a little gray prick-eared Cairn terrier and named him Feldspar. Almost from the beginning my daughter called him Felfy, so Mossy and I did too.

Virtually from the first day that I arrived at the New School for Social Research, I began to organize my lab and start a series of research projects. In a replay of what had happened at Stanford, my hours got longer and longer and I was seldom at home, which meant that I was not there to care for Feldspar, to train him or to walk him.

By default, caring for Felfy fell to Mossy, who had never had a dog. I tried to instruct her about the basics, explaining to her about housebreaking and the need for walks every day to keep the dog happy and the house clean. She looked at me in absolute horror.

"You mean you want me to go out there on the street alone, with just Rebecca, to walk the dog?" she asked, with considerably more emotion than was usual for her. "We are in New York. This is Greenwich Village. There are drunks and drug users and muggers and people who will attack a woman and a child that they find alone on the street simply because they can. And even if they were not there, you are asking me to bundle up our daughter twice a day and drag ourselves out every day—twice a day—whether there is rain or cold or whatever, just to empty out a dog?

"I expected that this would be like keeping a cat. Cats learn to use a litter box. You don't have to walk a cat twice a day on dirty and dangerous streets to keep the house clean. I was told that you can do something like litter box training for dogs. They call it paper training. You throw some sheets of newspaper in an unused corner and teach the dog to use them. All you need to do is to pick up the papers when they are messed and put down new ones. Either you paper train the dog or you arrange your schedule to be home twice a day to walk the dog. I am not walking any dog."

With that, she got up, went to the kitchen, and put the teakettle on the stove, so I knew that this discussion was finished and I had lost.

I sighed and asked, "Which corner would you like him to use?"

Paper training Feldspar actually turned out to be easy. The use of papers as his toilet became so ingrained that on days when I would take him outside for a walk, he would refrain from eliminating until he found a piece of paper to do it over.

The piece of paper could be the size of an envelope, but that was enough. He would sniff it, and then place his head over it before letting go, often completely missing his tiny target. Eventually I got into the habit of always carrying a sheet of newspaper folded in my pocket when he and I were walking to speed matters up.

Training Mossy to clean up after the dog was not as easy. I don't know whether it was a holdover from her anger at my expectation that she would take care of Felfy, or that she simply did not like housework (things like dirty dishes and unwashed laundry often piled up to crisis levels), but whenever I came home, there were always soiled papers in the corner. Making an issue of this unsanitary problem would have only brought a further chill to our relationship, so I kept silent and replaced the soiled papers with clean ones when needed.

Felfy did what he was supposed to do as Rebecca's dog, she loved him dearly, and she often sat and babbled to him about everything and nothing at all. She invented games, like "touch noses," which involved more time spent laughing than nose touching, and "airplane ears," where she would bend his pricked ears down to make them look like airplane wings and then make airplane engine noises while turning his head this way and that as if she were flying him.

He was a pleasant dog, and I wanted to bond with him, too, and to give him a voice, but because Feldspar belonged to Rebecca, I did not feel that I should compete for his attention, although I can now look back and recognize my stupidity. My deliberate holding back of the affection I wanted to share with him sometimes made it painful for me when I was around Felfy.

🐾 🐾 🐾

I was channeling all of my ardor and enthusiasm into my research and writing, building a name for myself, and developing a good reputation among my colleagues. Yet I was still young and beginning to miss the passion to be found in a close relationship. The results were probably inevitable as I became quite fond of one of my graduate students who was incredibly bright, creative, and sociable. After she got her degree, she continued to do research and write articles with me and we made some significant scientific breakthroughs together. Clearly, I had chosen a personal relationship that would not interfere with my obsession with science.

Mossy announced to me one evening that she was pregnant again, this time with my son Benjamin, who is one of the true bright spots in my life. When he arrived Rebecca was delighted to have a new brother. One day she took two stools and put them next to where Benn was sleeping. She then sat on one of them and had Feldspar sit on the other. Then she carefully explained what the baby was to the shaggy gray dog. As she spoke, she would first point to the baby and then look back to Feldspar to make sure that he was listening.

Rebecca carefully explained what the baby was to the shaggy gray dog.

Feldspar observed Rebecca carefully, playing his part in the conversation exactly the way that dogs are supposed to. I wondered how this conversation might have gone if Rebecca had been older. What would she talk to her dog about? Would she have given the dog a voice to answer her the way that I had always provided a voice and silly answers for each of my dogs? Would she have the kind of therapeutic and self-revealing conversations with her dog that I had found so valuable?

❧ ❧ ❧

With two children I felt committed to stay in the marriage for their sakes and also decided that New York City was not the place that I wanted them to grow up. In the early 1970s violent crime was rampant there and the newspapers had published a series of stories exposing the sad state of the public school system. I soon came to believe that if I could move my family to a quieter, more civil locale it would better for my children. A new place and a new home might also help my relationship with Mossy.

In November 1972 I gave a well-received talk at a conference held by the Psychonomic Society, an organization dedicated to experimental psychological research. While there I let it be known that I was thinking about leaving New York. Even though I was young, my reputation was very good and within three months a dozen institutions had made queries, and six had brought me out to visit them and talk about my research. All six eventually offered me a job in their psychology departments, but one institution really caught my interest: the University of British Columbia, in Vancouver, Canada.

One reason I was attracted to UBC was certainly the department chairman, Peter Suedfeld, an intelligent, cultured, and highly productive researcher. His attitude toward science was similar to mine, and I felt comfortable around him. At one point in our first discussion I told him that my research interests tended to change continually. At the time, I was working on problems involving perception and cognitive processes but would soon be starting some research in neuropsychology and behavior genetics. I asked if that would be a concern. His reply was exactly what I wanted to hear.

"Stanley, it doesn't really matter what areas you do research in. As long as you do good work, publish in good journals, and bring honor and respect to this department, you can do anything that you like," he said.

UBC also seemed like a good choice because of the core of extremely bright and productive faculty members already there or newly hired. Finally, I was attracted to the city itself. Vancouver is beautiful, with its incredible vista of water and mountains, well-kept parks and recreational areas. Most residential areas outside the downtown city center have quiet, tree-lined streets. A zoo, an aquarium, a symphony orchestra, and a fine arts museum contributed to its cultural life, and major popular entertainers made Vancouver a regular stop on their tours. At that time there had not yet been a big influx of people and the population of Metropolitan Vancouver was around 1.5 million, so housing was still affordable. As the third largest city in Canada, it had all of the services and facilities that one would expect of a large Western metropolis. That year in New York City there had been more than 52,000 violent crimes of which around 600 had been murders, while Vancouver was concerned that their murder rate had just risen to an all-time high of 12 for the year. This seemed like the perfect place to raise my children.

At the end of the spring semester in June, we packed up and moved to Vancouver, buying a little house with birch trees on the front lawn and a fenced backyard. It was located only about 10 minutes from the university. Once we moved in, we started what was supposed to be a new life.

❖ ❖ ❖

As a psychologist I should have known better. Psychological training recognizes that long-established behavior patterns and well-established habits of social interaction do not change simply by changing the place or setting where a person lives. So before long Mossy and I had reestablished all of the same patterns of interacting, or not interacting, that we had hoped to leave behind in New York, and I again sought meaning and feeling in my life by throwing myself into my research and writing.

To fill the emotional void in my life, just as had happened before in New York, I again became involved with a graduate student, Clare, who, after completing her doctoral work took a faculty position at the University of Victoria, about four hours travel from Vancouver. We did a significant amount of important research and published together for around 16 years.

Mossy and I continued to drift apart, and our personal exchanges became shorter and more distant. Despite the fact that we now lived in a safe city and a quiet neighborhood, and even though we had a large backyard that was fenced and safe for a dog to be in, Mossy continued to put out papers for Feldspar. Nonetheless, Feldspar had turned out to be the companion for my kids that I had hoped that he would be. I had helped Rebecca and Benn train him to do the basic "sit," "down," "come," and "stay" commands and then also trained him to do some other activities that were simple and practical. I also taught him some ways to entertain and play with the kids.

One of the things that I like to teach my dogs is to find family members. This is especially useful if you have small children who tend to disappear from sight when something is happening that they are not interested in, like baths, nail clipping, or cleaning up a room. The basic command that I teach is "Where's" followed by the person's name. Thus "Where's Rebecca?" would cause Feldspar to immediately run to where he had last seen her and bark furiously when he got there. Teaching this is a lot of fun because the person to be found gets to play a part in teaching the command while the dog gets to do some running around and receives lots of treats and praise.

When we taught Felfy to do the "Where's" command, I would first say, "Where's Rebecca?" Rebecca was standing across the room and would enthusiastically call out "Felfy come!" When he arrived, she would wave a treat at him until he barked and then give it to him. Then we might repeat it with "Where's Benn?" and Benn would call the dog and again wave a treat until he barked. After a while the kids could hide just out of sight or in the next room. I would say "Where's Rebecca?" in a voice loud enough that she could hear it, so that she knew it was time to call him. Repeated over a period of days, we finally got to the point where the kids no longer had to call Feldspar and he would hunt them down and begin to bark to earn his treat on command.

The "Where's" command came in particularly handy whenever we used to play hide-and-seek, with the role of "it" usually falling to me. When it came time to find my son, I would ask, "Where's Benn?" The little terrier would run to his hiding place and bark, usually eliciting screams of "Felfy, go away!" followed by howls of "Daddy, you're cheating!"

Terriers are not as scent-oriented as many other breeds, but they appear to be very attuned to the location of things. Once they have found something interesting in a location they will immediately check out that place the next time they enter the area. Watching Feldspar convinced me that he was basing his responses on some kind of spatial memory or mental map, rather than simply searching around randomly until he found the child. He only resorted to searching when something that he wanted had actually become lost. This became clear when Rebecca learned how to outsmart both her father and her dog.

She would let Feldspar see her hiding place and wait until I called him back to me. Then, when he was out of sight, she would change hiding places. Thus Feldspar might return to the closet where she had first hidden and bark to indicate this, but in the meantime Rebecca might have switched to the bathroom across the way. She was still easy to find, though, because she could not keep from giggling at how well her deception had worked. By using Feldspar to do my advance scouting I was clearly not above cheating, but the idea was to enjoy the playing of the game, so in those cases when Rebecca had been so creative, I would pretend not to know where she was, just to reward her for her cleverness.

One day I also tried to teach Feldspar how to square dance, which didn't turn out so well. This human-canine square dancing actually involves a simple set of moves, but it results in what looks like a complicated musical routine done to traditional country dance music. I usually chose from two or three Irish jigs or reels played with a fiddle, banjo, guitar, and double bass. All of these had a similar sound, and I believe that the nature of the music serves as an extra reminder to the dog as to what he is expected to do.

First, I taught Felfy to heel, which is just to stay by my left side when I walk. That allowed us to perform some dance maneuvers like "promenade," where couples walk side by side around in a circle. Then there is the "forward and back," where I call the dog to face my front and then he and I move a few steps back and then a few steps forward to face each other again. There is also the "dosado," where the dog starts in front of me again and we pass right shoulders as we circle around and return to the starting place. Finally, there is the "sashay," where, starting from the heeling position, the dog and I circle each other and return to our places. When you string together these four simple actions in various combinations, you provide the illusion that the dog is square dancing. The fact that all of these maneuvers are in response to subtle hand signals makes it look as if the dog is spontaneously performing his part of the complex dance routine on his own.

Felfy was well on his way to learning his steps, so I decided to teach him one little additional trick that heightens the illusion that the dog has a sense of rhythm and is truly dancing. This involves having the dog stand still and alternately lift his right and left front legs as if he were keeping time to the music. My hand signal was simply waving my index fingers up and down, which looks much like I am keeping time as well. The first stage of teaching this was to use that same motion of my index fingers to lightly touch Feldspar's front paws so that he would reflexively lift the paw, for which he would be rewarded. Of course, with a small dog this involves a lot of bending down as if trying to touch my toes.

No one was home that evening, which was how I had planned it, because I wanted to surprise my kids with a performance after Feldspar had learned the entire "dance routine." The music was playing loudly and I was bending over touching Felfy's front legs and getting little paw lifts as planned. Suddenly I felt a tremendous sharp pain in my back and found myself lying on the floor. My back hurt so badly that I was unable to get up again.

I lay there on the floor in a state of rising panic, afraid that I had lost my ability to stand and walk. Feldspar seemed to recognize that something was wrong and came over to lick my face. I told him, "I really should have taught you how to dial the 911 emergency line."

After what seemed like hours, but was probably more like thirty minutes, the pain subsided enough that I could drag myself over to a chair and use it to pull myself up. I sat there hurting, and felt around to my lower back, where my fingers encountered an area of quivering muscles. Feeling these muscle spasms actually was reassuring, since it suggested that muscles were the problem, not a more devastating spinal problem.

The next day my doctor confirmed my suspicions and announced, "Welcome to the low back pain club. You now have a lifetime membership."

He then paused and asked, "Now, what exactly were you doing when you hurt your back?"

As soon as I said, "I was teaching my dog to square dance," he gave me a look that we save for people who are too stupid or unbelievable to warrant any attempt at further communication.

I tried to add some information to make my previous statement seem less outrageous, but he waved his hand dismissively at me and said, "Well, whatever it was, don't do it again."

Thus ended Feldspar's dancing lessons.

🐾 🐾 🐾

My life could have easily continued in the same vein that it had been going for many years. I was completely immersed in my work, which gave me a focus and a sense of accomplishment. I had earned a lot of respect, honors, and accolades for my research. On the other hand, my marriage was now pretty much in name only. For the sake of my children, whom I love dearly, I still thought we should stay married, at least until Rebecca and Benn were in their teenage years and could understand and deal with a divorce.

Over a period of a month or so, however, I began to notice that I was becoming more easily fatigued. It was becoming difficult for me to maintain my concentration when writing or doing data analysis over the long sessions of work that I had become accustomed to. I was also emotionally less responsive, and fewer of my usual activities interested me. I had had an infection a few months earlier that had produced some of these same symptoms and began to wonder if it had come back. The doctor didn't seem to be very concerned, but he sent me off for a number of tests. A few days later he called me and told me to pick up a form from his nurse, because he wanted some additional tests. I did, and then spent some time in a medical lab giving blood, and then in the hospital for a battery of other tests.

At the end of the week I found myself sitting in my doctor's little examination room. He was holding a manila folder and looking at its contents. The concerned look on his face and the fact that he avoided eye contact suddenly had me worried.

"The tests came back positive," he started.

"Positive?"

"Well, that's actually negative for you," he said, still looking down at the folder.

"Negative?"

The doctor took a breath and then seemed to gather his composure as he remembered what he had been taught in those medical school courses with titles like *Bedside Manner 101* or the more advanced course *Bad News 202*.

"Your immune system does not seem to be working well, and you have developed a systemic infection."

"Systemic?" I was beginning to feel that I was just an echo following his statements and turning them into questions.

"That means that the infection is pretty widespread. It is not something where we can isolate the affected region and cut it out. I have concerns about using more antibiotics, at least any that we've used before, because your reaction to them may be part of the problem."

"The problem?" There was that echo again.

"Look, the infection is advanced . . . There has been some organ damage . . . Under normal circumstances this might be reversible, but your body doesn't seem to be cooperating. I will do what I can to make you comfortable, but our course of action—if any—is not clear. I will contact some people that I know in the Centre for Disease Control and at the Medical

Schools here and in Toronto and Halifax. Maybe one of them may have an idea. But for now I would suggest that you get your affairs in order."

"Affairs in order?" came the echo.

"It is really difficult to put a timeline on this thing. However, if we don't find a method of treatment that works, you have around eighteen months at most. The good news is that with pain management, you should be able to function pretty much as normal up until around the last two months."

Normal? How could anything be normal when I had a death sentence hanging over me? I wanted to talk to someone about this—to vent my emotions—but who? I had no intention of telling my friends, family, or Clare about this. When people know that a person is dying, everything that they do around that individual changes. Human beings do not like to confront the idea of death, so when we know that someone is dying we tend to stay away from him and choose to not interact, because every contact with a dying person reminds us of our own mortality. If I had had a dog of my own, we could have talked . . . But the only dog that I lived with really belonged to my kids and, although I was fond of him, I did not feel close enough for that reliable talking cure.

Later, as I stood in the pharmacy waiting for three little bottles of pills, my mind was racing as I tried to sort things out. Eighteen months—what could I—should I do in the remaining eighteen months? Did I want to remain in my cold, loveless marriage for the last eighteen months of my life? Did I want my children to watch me waste away in front of them? The answer to these last two questions was clearly "No."

I pocketed my pills and went to a newsstand. I prowled through the "Apartments for Rent" section of the classified ads. I had to find one that was close to the university and my kids. It had to be one that I could afford, since if I ended my marriage I would be using a good chunk of my salary to pay for family support. The second apartment that I looked at appeared to be acceptable. It was on a quiet street, and it had a tiny but functional kitchen, a big living room, and a small bedroom. It was completely empty, so the landlord told me I could move in on Friday, which was only two days away, and he would not charge me for the four days before the new month began.

Over the next two days I scrounged around to find furniture. The building that my office was in was being renovated. Bookshelves had been broken down and piled up for disposal, free for the taking. Furniture from the wing that had been gutted was available from the university's surplus center and being sold for a pittance just to clear things out. For a few dollars I managed to buy some wooden chairs, a table, something that could pass for a sofa, and so forth.

I asked for help from a close friend and colleague in the psychology department, Lawrence Ward, who was sworn to secrecy for the moment. I only told him that my marriage was breaking up, which he understood. I did not tell him about the ultimate reasons having to do with my failing body and a ticking life clock. Lawrence and I have done a lot of research together over the years and coauthored six books. We also share a love of science fiction novels, music, and films. Lawrence was also originally from Pennsylvania, which gave us a feeling of kinship so that when I was struggling to put together my new living space, without any hesitation he volunteered to help me move my few new belongings into my apartment.

On Saturday morning I told Mossy that I was leaving. I momentarily thought of explaining my medical condition to her as some partial explanation of my decision, but it had been so long since we had shared confidences that I had to stop to consider how to tell her. Before I resolved the matter in my head, she simply walked away.

Telling the kids was much more difficult. Even though Rebecca was only 9 and Benn 7 years of age, they seemed to know that something significant was happening, and the two of them huddled together on the sofa with Feldspar sitting between them. Rebecca had a handful of his fur clutched in her hand and seemed to draw strength from having her dog nearby. Benn simply leaned his head against the dog and listened. I don't think that they understood that this was going to be a longer separation than for a scientific meeting or research trip or that I wouldn't be living in the house any longer. I gave them a kiss and Felfy a pat and told them I would be back in a couple of days.

When I returned two days later to pick up some of my personal belongings, my side of the bedroom closet was bare. I asked Mossy where my clothes were and she answered, "They are your clothes—how would I know?" My collection of relatively rare books in the psychological and biological sciences, which I had put together over more than ten years of hunting in used book stores, personal library, and estate sales, was also gone, as were a number of other small personal items.

I left and returned to my apartment to look in my closet. I had three shirts, two pairs of pants, two sport jackets, a sweater, and a couple of scarves. It looked like I would have to get some new garments.

When I went to get some funds to replace my missing clothing, however, I found that our joint savings and checking accounts had not only been emptied but closed. All of my credit cards had been jointly held with my wife, and she had run them up to their maximum in just a few days so I had virtually no money to live on until my next paycheck. It was then that I went to a lawyer to have her draw up a formal separation agreement.

Living quietly in my new apartment actually turned out to be a comfort to me. I missed the kids and the dog, but I got to see Benn and Rebecca twice a week. We would make dinner together in my little place while I tried to teach them how to cook. They would work on their stamp collections, play games, or just talk a little. Although my health was failing, I actually felt more at ease by myself and closer to my children.

Just after our interim divorce had been granted, I left the city to do a short speaking tour that had been arranged before I knew about my medical problem. While I was away, Mossy secretly tried to sell the house. Her attempt was unsuccessful because the house was one of the few things that was in my name and not held jointly. The divorce agreement had stipulated that she could live in that house as long as she wanted to, and if she decided to move out, it would be sold and the proceeds divided equally between us.

A short time later, in defiance of her promise to the judge during our divorce hearing, she took the kids and moved back to Philadelphia. There she had the support not only of her family but also of mine. My parents never questioned me about the divorce and never blamed anyone for the dissolution of our marriage. They were saddened by it, but they always provided love and assistance to Mossy and the kids whenever they could and virtually never spoke to me about our breakup.

I had now lost contact with my children. Whenever I would call to try to speak to them, I was always told that they were not at home. Letters or birthday cards I sent never seemed to make it into Benn and Rebecca's hands. I suppose that I could have sent them to my parents to deliver personally, but I did not want to involve them in a way that might poison their relationship with Mossy or affect their ability or inclination to help my kids.

With my children gone, all that I had left of real importance to me was my work. I wanted to finish as much of it as could before my time ran out. I saw Clare less often, and other than spending time with my friends Peter and Lawrence, I did not do all that much socializing. I was slowly closing in on myself—isolated, sick, and lonelier than ever.

My doctor was monitoring me more closely but was offering little in the way of long-term hope.

"Things are going pretty much the way that we expected," he would say. "Don't give up yet. I've arranged for you to see a specialist in a few weeks, and I've sent your records off to some other experts in the field to see if they have any ideas."

"Are there any changes in the timeline?" I asked.

"I can't really say," he replied.

❧ ❧ ❧

I had always assumed that Mossy had taken Feldspar with her when she left Vancouver with the kids. Approximately 10 weeks after she had gone, I received a bill in the mail. It was from a local veterinarian whom I did not know. The cover letter read something like:

"As per your instructions, the Cairn terrier, Feldspar, was kept in our kennel for two months. You had specified that you were going to attempt to have him adopted within that time frame, but if he was not picked up by the designated date, he was to be euthanized. Enclosed you will find a bill for his boarding, euthanization, and body disposal."

I was stunned. Felfy had been on death row for two months and I hadn't known it. I still don't know if not telling me about Feldspar's whereabouts was an oversight, since the dog was never important to Mossy, or whether it was an act of cold, deliberate vengeance to kill my dog—I mean, the kids' dog—and send me the bill.

I sat there at the table in my little apartment looking at the veterinarian's demand for payment. I was in a state of shock. After a bit I was surprised to see that my right hand was gently stroking the piece of paper, much the way that I habitually stroked the head of Feldspar on those rare occasions when we were alone together.

I felt swamped with emotions. I should have bonded more closely with Felfy. I should have given him a voice. I should have checked up on where he was. I should saved him from his cruel fate. I should have . . . I should have . . .

I looked back down at the table. There were wet spots on the veterinarian's invoice. I was crying. For the first time since the doctor had given me the bad news, for the first time since I separated from my wife, for the first time since my children were taken from me, I was crying. Feldspar, the dog that I would not permit to become mine, was gone. Felfy was dead and I was dying, too.

CHAPTER 6

CONVERSATIONS WITH WOLF

ometimes, miracles happen and restore your faith in God, science, kismet, or dumb luck. Eight months into my death sentence, I was still trying to carry on as if nothing had changed except my living arrangements when I got a phone message from my doctor asking me to come to his office as soon as possible. I had a flash of panic. Had one of the seemingly millions of tests that I had been taking shown up worse than expected? Was the clock now ticking faster? Was my time shorter than I thought?

A few hours later, I was sitting in front of him. He had a legal-sized envelope in his hands and the postage on it indicated that he had received this in the mail from someplace in Canada. He pulled a few sheets of paper out of it, glanced at them, and then made full eye contact with me (a good sign?).

"Stan, I've been in touch with a few people about possible courses of treatment for you. I haven't had anything promising come out of those inquiries, but something else has turned up. A medical researcher in Toronto is doing research on the effectiveness of a fairly radical method of treatment for certain rare but serious problems. He is looking for people suffering from those conditions who might become participants in his research study. Specifically he is looking for individuals with broad, systemic infections that are unresponsive to normal treatment, or that can not be treated for some reason. Because the course of treatment itself has not been tried before, and it involves massive, but controlled, doses of pharmaceuticals that can be toxic, he is looking for cases that are very serious." He paused, and looked down, then said quietly, "Actually, he is looking for terminal cases."

The doctor looked up at me then and made eye contact again. "Listen, I don't have anything better to offer and this is at least a chance. You don't have to go to Toronto. His team has sent me their treatment materials and testing protocols, and you can stay here in Vancouver. I will monitor your progress and send them reports. It looks like there might be side effects from this treatment regimen. It might even accelerate your decline. On the other hand, it is the only thing that I can see that might make a dent in your problem. I took the liberty of sending him copies of your medical records, and he has already told me that you are an acceptable candidate to be in the study if you agree."

Science makes progress and often comes to the rescue in times of need. I thought of Max Theiler, who discovered the cause of the deadly disease, yellow fever, which is transmitted by mosquitoes and was a major killer in tropical areas and around port cities. In the 1920s, Theiler was working nonstop on his research because he, like me, was also working under a death sentence. In his case it was diabetes, which at that time was untreatable and usually ultimately fatal. However, Frederick Banting and Charles Best discovered insulin as a treatment, just in the nick of time. Theiler became one of the early recipients of this new cure while it was still considered experimental and potentially dangerous. He took this experimental drug as part of an unproven treatment regimen, and ultimately lived to receive the Nobel Prize for his work on yellow fever some thirty years later. Perhaps, as in Theiler's case, I too might get lucky.

✿ ✿ ✿

My enrollment in the research project first required that I sign a long, involved consent form, typical of those used in most medical research. I had to indicate that I understood that the procedures used might not cure me, that I might be placed into a "control group" that received placebos rather than active drugs, that there might be side effects, that if I died (even if the cause of death could be traced back to the nature of the treatment), the researchers could not be sued because I had agreed to this process. I had to agree that I understood and consented to the fact that the specifics of the treatment, drugs, and procedures would not be indicated to me in advance. Lovely—I was signing away the rights to my body and they weren't even going to tell me what they were doing.

My treatment took me to the clinic on a regular basis for administration of the drugs and testing. I was given a checklist to indicate any side effects, of which I had a ton, including nausea, headaches, diarrhea, ringing in my ears, and occasional dizziness, but they usually became tolerable enough for me to continue living "normally" a few hours, or at most a day, after each treatment. I had to tough my way through the discomfort without knowing if it would be worth the effort, since I had also been warned that it might be several months before they knew if the treatment was working. Actually, the side effects were comforting because they confirmed that I was getting the actual treatment, not the placebo that the "control group" was getting.

At least 4 months after I'd started the experimental procedure, on one of my office visits, my doctor entered carrying an envelope that looked suspiciously like the one that had contained the consent form, but when he pulled out a small sheaf of papers, he smiled. That was the first smile that I had seen from him since before my initial diagnosis.

"Good news. Very good news! Your tests look wonderful. The team in Toronto wants you to continue the treatment for another six weeks, just to be sure, but it is beginning to look as if the infection has stopped spreading completely, and its severity has been brought down to a level where your own immune system can mop up what remains. Nevertheless, to be on the safe side they want those extra few weeks of treatment."

Then he smiled again. "Well, you took a gamble and you won a life!"

He gave me a pat on my shoulder as I walked out of his office. I felt like this should be a musical moment, and I should run through the clinic singing "Oh, What a Beautiful Morning" while a camera circled around me and a troupe of dancers appeared from all sides twirling in their sparkling costumes and holding their arms high while they sang along with me. I restrained myself from any sort of display until I was sitting in my car alone, where I clenched both of my fists, looked up, and threw my hands forward and shouted loudly enough for God to hear, "Yes! Thank you, Boss!"

🐾 🐾 🐾

Suddenly I had plans to make, and a life—a real life, hopefully, even a long life—to map out. I wanted to tell someone, anyone, about how happy I was, that I had beaten the odds and had been given a second chance. But I couldn't, because I had not told anybody about my illness. I didn't even have a dog in my life to share my joy. I glanced at my wristwatch. I had a class to teach in an hour, so I couldn't revel in the moment in any case.

As I drove toward campus, my mind was whirling. I had started no new projects and had avoided even close friends for nearly a year. I really did not know how I was going to restart a life that I had been carefully closing down ever since my death sentence had been announced. Should I try to do something to reestablish my family, perhaps fight for custody or at least more access to my kids? Should I consider some of the tentative job offers that I had been receiving and perhaps move to Philadelphia or to another university and start my life over again in a new place? Should I . . .

The endless possibilities that were open to me and the decisions that I needed to make were still racing around in my mind when I parked my car and started to walk toward the psychology building to gather up the material that I needed for my lecture. As I neared my office, I heard a voice call out, "Stan!"

I turned and saw the familiar face of Lou, a member of the education faculty who had been on several committees with me, and whose husband, Arnold, I knew from a boxing club that I occasionally used to work out in to try to maintain some semblance of physical fitness before my illness. We had all been together at a couple of social events, and I liked Lou's friendly, open manner, and the blue of her eyes reminded me of the color of my daughter Rebecca's eyes.

"Stan, if you've got a minute, I need some information. I know that you had a dog and I wonder if you know of any good boarding kennels where a dog can get some extra care. My husband and I have to go home—back east—to take care of a family matter. It's all very short notice since we have to leave the day after tomorrow, and we'll be gone around six to maybe eight days. The problem is that our dog, Wolf—a golden retriever—has a medical problem and needs a shot every morning and evening. Most kennels don't do that for you, and if we leave him at the vet's it will not only be expensive, but he will basically be confined to a kennel crate for the whole time, since my vet doesn't normally do boarding. We thought of getting a house sitter, but none of them is willing to give Wolf his injections."

I stopped dead. What was happening here? I thought of a quote from the nineteenth-century French poet, philosopher, and revolutionary politician Alphonse de Lamartine, who said, "When man is in trouble, God sends him a dog."

"I'll do better than give you the name of a kennel," I replied. "If you want, I'll house sit for you. I know how to give dogs injections, and, to be honest, I'm feeling more than a little bit dog deprived since I am now living by myself in an apartment building with a 'no pets' policy. My services come really cheap. Leave a bit of food in the fridge and a couple of bottles of bourbon and we can call it even."

Lou was delighted, so we arranged that I would drop by late in the afternoon the next day to meet Wolf and to make final arrangements.

The house was only minutes from the university on a short, twisting street with the odd name of Newton Wynd in an elegant neighborhood with big, expensive homes. I parked my car in a port at the rear of the house, and as I got out of it my friend opened her back door and waved. Rushing past her was a mountain of blond fur—Wolf—that bounded over to me as I opened the gate to the backyard. Big for his breed, he weighed about 95 pounds and his head was much broader than most golden retrievers', giving him an appearance more bearlike than wolflike. Like all goldens, however, there was nothing wolflike in his behavior. If dog breeds each had a motto, then motto for golden retrievers would be "You've got a face. I've got a tongue. I know we can work something out."

I ran my hands through his sand-colored fur and felt my muscles relax. Wolf turned and led me back to his mistress and into the house. Lou showed me around her home, which was bright, well-furnished, and stylish. She showed me the box in which she kept Wolf's medication in the refrigerator—insulin for his diabetes. She indicated where the syringes were kept, then showed me the guest room where I would be sleeping. As she was giving me a tour of the house, Arnold arrived.

"Stay and have a drink," he said. He turned to his wife, "Do we have enough food to set another place for dinner?"

Lou said she could throw another steak on the grill, which sounded quite inviting to me. I sat down and we sipped some scotch and worked out the rest of the details, such as how to contact them while they were away, who their veterinarian was, where the key to their liquor cabinet was, and where the freezer was located (which was filled with steaks and other expensive cuts of beef).

The next day, a few hours after Lou and Arnold had left for the airport, I came back. When I opened the door, Wolf bounded forward to sniff my hands and the small suitcase containing a few clothes and personal items. Then, in the manner of golden retrievers, he accepted me as if I had lived with him all of his life, inviting me into his home with his tail wagging.

🐾 🐾 🐾

The home that I found myself temporarily living in had big windows and was only a short walk away from a strip of parkland that overlooked the water. I grabbed a ball from Wolf's box of toys and we went out for a bit of a walk and some play. I knew that I should be at work, since this was a Friday and there was no excuse not to be doing my research and writing. I could have easily left Wolf for a few hours, and it would have been sensible to do so since my lab was only about five minutes away. On the other hand, this was also only the second day after my reprieve. I had phoned the lab and confirmed that only routine testing had been scheduled for the day, which I knew that my laboratory assistant, Wayne, could handle. After all, the reason that I was here sharing this great house with this sweet dog was to provide me with a few days of meditation or therapy. At the very least I was here to establish the fact that I was no longer bound to a lifestyle where my main concern was a clock quickly ticking away the short time that I had to live. Since I now had time on my side, I just relaxed and tried to get to know Wolf a little better.

Around seven or eight years of age, Wolf still had a lot of energy and, being a typical retriever, he loved to chase a ball. I found myself thinking about what Roger Caras, the author and former head of the ASPCA, wrote in one of his books, "Try throwing a ball just once for a dog. It would be like eating only one peanut or potato chip. Try to ignore the importuning of a golden retriever who has brought you his tennis ball, the greatest treasure he possesses."

Watching Wolf charge across the grass to catch a ball that I had thrown was a joy. He was not sleek and elegant because he was so large, and rather than bounding around, he sort of galumphed, his ears flapping like the wings of a bird. Looking at him happily retrieving his toy somehow made the sunshine a bit warmer and the day a bit brighter. It was only when the ball became too dirty and soggy to be pleasant to handle that we went back to the house.

After a light lunch I took a mug of coffee and wandered into the front room and settled onto a large wooden rocking chair while Wolf lay down on a woolen rug at my feet. It brought back memories of the times that I used to sit in my room and talk to my boxer Penny when I was still in college.

"Well, Wolf, I have a problem that perhaps you can shed some light on," I began.

I knew what voice Wolf would answer in since it had come to me as I watched his heavy movements and his way of sometimes running past the ball he wanted to fetch in his enthusiasm. He reminded me of a character named Deputy Dawg in a televised cartoon show that my youngest brother Arthur used to watch in the early 1960s.

Deputy Dawg was an overweight yellow dog with floppy ears much like Wolf. He was a deputy sheriff with a grandfatherly voice who lived in a fanciful version of the backwoods of southern Mississippi, where bayous abound, and phrases like "dag nabit" and "gosh darn" are commonplace. More concerned with napping than catching bad guys, he was not very bright, but he often got the better of his adversaries due to dumb luck or some far-fetched plan that somehow succeeded, though never the way that Deputy Dawg had anticipated.

When Deputy Dawg's voice answered me with, *"Well, dag nabit, don't beat around the bush. Just tell me what your problem is,"* I laughed. I had gotten out of the habit of having these conversations with dogs in the years since Penny and I had parted. Nonetheless, though it was silly, it was also comforting. Out of a long forgotten habit, I quickly glanced around to make sure that no one was watching.

"You know, everything just changed so much when I got the diagnosis—my death sentence. I ended my marriage, and I threw myself totally into my work to the exclusion of everything else."

"That's not true," said the Deputy Dawg voice. *"Your marriage ended a long time ago and you just let it drag on—maybe for the kids or maybe because it was just easier not to take any action. And about your work—you know that your research and your writing are addictions. You need to do it. You live for it. But, gosh darn it, you've also used your work as a hiding place—when things got tough at home or in any of your relationships you hid in your work. Your work was always something that you had under complete control so you could be safe there."*

This oration was a lot longer than any I remembered coming from any other of my dogs' mouths. Still, it did appear to be a clear summary of the facts. Now that they were lying out in the open, my situation seemed to be quite clear. Wolf was still resting on the rug but had his eyes open just a slit, allowing him to look at me. Apparently, he enjoyed the attention or at least the sound of my voice. As Deputy Dawg he had just put into words a set of truths that I had refused to acknowledge and had ignored or repressed for too long. Nonetheless, I said to the dog, "Really? Aren't you being a bit harsh in your evaluation of my situation?"

"Dang it! If you wanted some kind of sympathetic Sigmund Freud, you should have given me a German accent! What I said was true and you know it. Think about it."

Suddenly tired, I didn't want to continue talking, so I moved over to sit on the sofa and a short time later fell asleep. After an hour or so, I awakened to find that Wolf had climbed up beside me and was resting his heavy head on my lap. I shook myself awake and wandered out onto the sunlit rear deck of the house and sat down. Wolf followed and sat looking at me.

I looked at him and said professorially, "Did you know that the first dog in Sigmund Freud's life was named Wolf?"

I asked him, professorially, "Did you know that the first dog in Sigmund Freud's life was named Wolf? He wasn't a golden

retriever, but a German shepherd. Freud got Wolf as a companion for his daughter Anna, who was still living at home. Anna
liked to take walks, especially in the evening, but the streets
of Vienna were not considered safe for a woman walking by
herself—especially a Jewish woman during that anti-Semitic era.
Freud felt that Wolf's size and his wariness of strangers would
help to keep her safe."

The Deputy Dawg voice answered, *"Dang! I could have
been Sigmund Freud's dog! So now that you've had your beauty
sleep, have you decided anything?"*

"Well, I will try to make sure that Mossy gives me more
access to the kids. I've been missing Rebecca and Benn a lot. I'll
see my lawyer next week and find out what can be done."

*"Yeah, but that don't solve nothin'. You would be better off
living with someone. How about Clare?"*

"No, that's over."

*"Okay, then, I'll give you some advice. Think of it as great
wisdom coming from the reincarnation of Dr. Freud's dog. Don't
get personally involved with another psychologist and certainly
not one who you are doing research with. You always get the
research and the personal relationship knotted together and
when choices have to be made, you always choose the research
and get hurt when the relationship goes down the drain."* Wolf
rolled over and seemed to be asking for a belly rub. I scratched
at his underside and the Deputy Dawg voice continued.

*"Find yourself a nurse, or maybe an elementary school
teacher. These are professional, intelligent women who have a
caring attitude. They would understand what you are talking
about whenever you decide to talk about your work, while they
would still have the inclination to try to be supportive when you
act like a big child—the way that university professors always
do. Keep whoever you find out of your research life. Your
research and writing will never stop being your passion, but you
need to have passions outside of your career."*

I asked the big shaggy dog, "You want me to pick my life mate based on her profession? I think that all of this therapy is melting my mind. How about some supper?"

The 6 or 7 days that I spent with Wolf were quiet and relaxing. I taught my classes and did some laboratory work, but I kept my hours closer to a 9 to 5 normal workday, rather than the usual 12 to 14 hours I had been working. I would dash back to the house to let Wolf out at noon and play with him a bit. Nobody noticed, or at least nobody commented that I was not working as many hours. Yet the research and writing were still getting finished on time.

In the evenings Wolf and I would spend an hour or more talking. That Deputy Dawg accent was becoming so easy and natural that, at one point, when I spilled a cup of coffee in the psychology lounge I was surprised to hear myself saying, "Dang, what a cotton pickin' mess I've made!" My professional colleagues who were sitting with me laughed, thinking that I was trying to be funny.

During one of my conversations with Wolf, I made another major decision. We had been discussing the first steps that I had to take to get my life back on track.

"Well," the Deputy Dawg voice said, "one thing that you've got to do is to get yourself a dog. You need a dog to keep you sane, and I don't make no gosh-darn house calls."

"I can't, there is a 'no pets' policy in my apartment building."

"Then buy a house."

"They are way too expensive here in the city."

"Dag nabit, then be creative. You've got some money left over from paying off Mossy and settling up your debts when you sold the other house. You can teach summer and evening courses in addition to your regular teaching and salt all of that money away. You can also do some consulting work, some more writing . . . I figure that if you do all that, then in less than two years you could have enough to put a down payment on a small house—and a small dog."

The moment the words were out in the air I knew that this was the course of action that I needed to take.

🐾 🐾 🐾

Wolf and I worked out other small decisions over those days we were together. In the end I felt as though I knew where I was going and what I would be doing. It was as though I had undergone an extensive round of psychotherapy and had achieved the insight, comfort, and guidance that clinical psychologist strive to bring to their patients.

In a way, I had blundered inadvertently into what today is known as *pet-assisted therapy*. In North America the number of pet-assisted therapy programs was under twenty in 1980, but by the year 2000 more than one thousand such programs were in operation. We probably owe the origin of using dogs as part of psychotherapy to Sigmund Freud (funny how often that name comes up when a psychologist is writing or talking), who often had one of his dogs with him during therapy sessions. He first noticed that the presence of the dog seemed to be beneficial for patients who were children or adolescents. They seemed more willing to talk openly when the dog was in the room.

Later, Freud noticed that having the dog in the room also had a positive effect even if the patient was an adult. He thought that this might be due to the fact that patients often worry about whether what they are saying might seem unacceptable to a listener—even a psychologist. However, nothing the patient ever says will shock the therapist's furry companion, who continues to stay close and pay attention. Freud suggested that this gave the patient a sense of safety and acceptance. Clearly, this was what had been happening between Wolf and me.

Although Freud carefully recorded his observations and interpretations in notes and journals, they were not well known or readily available until the 1960s. The first formal presentation of pet-assisted therapy came about quite independently, more than 20 years after that great psychologist's death. Boris Levinson, a clinical psychologist associated with Yeshiva University in New York, was working with a very disturbed child and noticed that when he had his dog Jingles with him, therapy sessions with this child were much more productive. Other children who had difficulty communicating also seemed more at ease and actually made real attempts at conversation when the dog was close by. Levinson presented a scientific paper describing his results at a meeting of the American Psychological Association. Other psychologists were not impressed by his results, and many ridiculed his work—some even asked him what percentage of the therapy fees he paid to the dog.

Freud's influence reached out from beyond his grave to help rescue Levinson's work and reputation. Shortly after Levinson's case studies were reported, Freud's journals were translated and published. New insights into Freud's life also came from books published by people who knew him and who mentioned his therapeutic use of his dog. With evidence that a scientific icon such as Freud was willing to entertain the value of animal helpers in psychotherapy, the laughter stopped and some serious research began.

As I sat on a rocking chair talking with Wolf, it was 10 years before any new convincing scientific confirmation of the therapeutic value of interacting with a dog would be published in scientific journals. I just knew that it dang well worked for me, dag nabit!

CHAPTER 7

THE ARRIVAL OF JOAN

There is an old saying, "Every journey begins with a single step." The real truth is that every journey begins with an intention or a plan to go somewhere. Having benefited from what seemed like a miracle, I was starting a new journey and a new life. My 6 or 7 days of meditation and therapy with Wolf had given me my plan. I now knew what I had to do. First, I had to get a house or some sort of living space that would allow me to have a dog. It could be a little house, since I was planning on sharing it with a little dog. Next, get the dog. Along the way I wanted to control my addiction to work and research and reestablish and strengthen some friendships that I had neglected during my illness. It would also be nice to find a life partner to share my new home.

I went to Peter, who was still head of the department, and explained that I wanted to earn a bit more cash, so he signed me up to teach an evening course and two additional courses in the summer. It was a lot of extra teaching, but it was the same subject matter that I had been teaching since I arrived at UBC. Over two years my savings grew to the point that I had enough to finally put an initial payment on my little house.

❧ ❧ ❧

This heavy teaching load was often exhausting, but I enjoyed working with the interesting range of students that populated the evening and summer classes. In my large evening sections of Introductory Psychology, there are always a few mature students— individuals who are clearly older than the average undergraduate, people who had to delay completing their university education because of financial, family, or work-related concerns.

The stories of these mature students are often quite interesting. I once had a pair of adult students taking my course, one of whom was a convict on parole who was trying to get a college degree to start a new life, while the other was his parole officer. The parole officer enrolled in my section of the course initially to monitor whether his client was actively working on his education. He also seemed a little upset by the fact that the convict was earning higher grades than he was.

Another mature student in my class was a thin brunette woman who seemed to be around my age. She appeared to be quite dedicated to getting good grades but also less than perfectly organized. Since my classes are large, with the smallest being around 200 students, my examinations are made up of multiple-choice questions, and the scoring is done by machine. As part of the testing process, students must know their university identification number, because grades are entered and sorted using that code. This number is listed on students' registration materials and library cards. Usually for the first test in each course I make sure that I have the class list with me just in case someone forgets his number, but after the first test I assume that everyone knows it. Immediately before the first examination this woman came down to the front of the class because she did not know her student number. Her name was Joan, and I searched the list and found her number. Just before the second test, however, she appeared before me again, this time quite embarrassed.

"I know that you'll think that I must be ditzy, but I forgot my student number again," she said.

I didn't have the list with me that time, so I told her to bring her materials to me directly at the end of the test period and we would walk to my office to find the list that had her number.

On the way to my office I noticed that Joan had very pretty eyes, a sort of greenish-blue with some light brown flecks, and so transparent that I felt as if I were looking through the water to see the bottom of a clear mountain lake. She also had a sweet sort of half smile when she was relaxed. She was also wearing a wedding ring.

Joan seemed a bit shy around me, almost as if she were a little frightened, and for some reason I got the impression that she had been undergoing some rough times—or she may have just been uncomfortable being the only student in the class who did not have her student number for this second exam. Walking to my office, she explained that she had been trained as a medical laboratory technician and worked for several years in a hospital in Yellowknife, the capital of Canada's Northwest Territories. Now that she had moved to Vancouver she was returning to the university because she wanted to become a primary school teacher. It didn't cross my mind then that Wolf had suggested that a good partner for me would be a nurse or grade school teacher, and now I was talking with someone who was a kind of hybrid of those two professions. It would be a couple of years before my relationship with Joan developed beyond professor and student.

🐾 🐾 🐾

My friend Peter Suedfeld is quite brilliant in many ways, and much of his life reads like a plot for a book. He was born in Hungary, and his father was a concert cellist. His life fell apart with the onset of World War II, when most of his family became victims of the holocaust. As the Nazis clamped down on the Jewish population, their living conditions became more brutal and dangerous. After the Russians liberated Budapest, Peter and his father managed to sneak into Austria and ultimately found their way to New York, where Peter was reared by an impoverished great-aunt. However, he made it through school based on hard work and native intelligence, served in the army as a sniper stationed in the Philippines, and returned to complete his university training as a psychologist.

Peter reads or speaks four languages. He is a creative researcher and good writer. One of the most exciting aspects of his research has to do with his studies of extreme and unusual environments. This research has taken him into the high Arctic and the North Pole and down to the Antarctic and the South Pole. In the process he became the head of the Canadian Antarctic Research Program. He has consulted with NASA and worked with astronauts in both the American and Russian space programs. During all of this he still had time to serve as head of the Psychology Department for twelve years, dean of the Faculty of Graduate Studies for six years, president of the Canadian Psychological Association . . . well, you get the idea.

One evening we sat in my apartment eating one of our favorite comfort foods, spaghetti with marinara sauce and sausages. After I had poured some red wine, I told him I wanted his advice on dealing with my research addiction. He smiled and said, "You know, as addictions go, being addicted to research and writing is not so bad. If you think about it, no scientist who was historically significant was casual about his research. You have to have a compulsion to spend the time and effort to make progress in science, and it is hard to turn your brain off when you are struggling with a problem or a manuscript.

"I'll tell you what I think your real problem is—time management! You do virtually everything in your lab by yourself.

You have one research assistant and a couple of part-time students doing the testing, and everything else you do by yourself. You end up doing a lot of the data coding and routine analysis. You even stuff envelopes when you are sending out sets of research surveys. Do you really think that that kind of work requires a full professor with a PhD degree?"

Peter's advice was to obtain some additional grant funding and put it all into paying for lab personnel to do the routine work. I did as he suggested, and it freed up a large amount of time for more creative work and writing. My rate of publication went up, and several theoretical breakthroughs emerged from the research. I was still coming into campus early, but I could leave at a normal hour and had time to spend my evenings in more relaxing activities or with friends.

If I were ever to be able to have that dog and that regular family life, I would have to be comfortable with the idea of spending a little more time at home. So I set up something more like an office in my apartment and began to work at home two afternoons each week. To my surprise, working at home actually seemed more efficient, since I had few interruptions and could concentrate fully.

During this transitional time, Joan had taken a second-year course that I was also teaching. After completing her second-year work, she came to my office to ask for some advice about future course work. It was an early spring afternoon and I felt in need of a cup of coffee, so I invited her to come with me while we continued our discussion.

The Bus Stop was the closest place to get coffee, an old-style diner with counter service for customers who sat on pedestal-style stools. As the waitress, a Chinese woman in her midfifties, placed our coffee on the shiny white counter, I asked her about her dog. The waitress had recently adopted a mature dog from the SPCA that turned out to not to be fully housebroken. I had suggested some things that she might do to remedy the situation. She patted my hand and told me that the dog was behaving much better and thanked me.

Joan said, "Everybody feels comfortable talking to you. That's why I felt that I could come to you for some advice."

I never know how to respond to compliments, especially when I am not sure that they truly reflect my nature or accomplishments. Fortunately, I didn't have to search for something to say, since Joan continued telling me about her concerns. In addition to her course of study in the Faculty of Education (with an aim to become a primary school teacher), she was taking a minor in psychology. Because she had a husband and family to care for, she was not taking a full course load and expected that it would take an extra year or so to complete her studies. She was considering several different courses in psychology and wanted to know who the best teachers in our department were.

Most of her questions were easy to answer. With the business part of the conversation completed, and since there was still coffee in our cups, we continued talking and the conversation became more general.

Eventually I looked at my watch and told her that I was leaving campus to work the rest of the afternoon at home. She also glanced at her watch and said that she had to leave campus shortly as well, since she had to drive her kids to the swimming pool. Her three children, Kevin, Geoff, and Karen, were all competitive swimmers. Joan's part in their training was rather dull, involving spending several hours in the afternoon at the pool sitting and waiting for them to complete their practice sessions. Because the pool was only a few minutes away from my apartment, I mentioned to her that I usually worked on Tuesday and Thursday afternoons at home, and if she got bored watching the kids some time, she could give me a call and come over and talk. Then I gave her my home phone number.

I winked deliberately and added, "Who knows, I might even offer you a glass of sherry along with the conversation."

She looked down and, with a sweet, half smile she said, "I might just take you up on that."

A few weeks later I was working at home when Joan called. She was at the pool and wouldn't be needed for a couple of hours and wondered if she could drop by. I was surprised but not displeased.

A short time later we were sitting on my sofa sipping dry sherry. We talked a bit and eventually our conversation became more personal. Over time her visits would become more frequent and soon I could expect that once every week or so she would come to visit for a few hours. During these visits I learned more about her life, her history, and her children. Her marriage was in trouble, and she dropped a lot of small clues that suggested that she was being ill treated by her husband. Ultimately, she revealed that she was contemplating leaving him.

I did not press Joan for details. Talking about that aspect of her life made her uncomfortable, and she was quite happy when talking about any other topic. I liked talking and interacting with her when she was smiling and her eyes were sparkling. I expected that our relationship would end when Joan finished her education and started to work as a teacher. I had no idea that I would fall in love with her, so at that time sherry, smiles, and friendly company in the afternoon were all that I was seeking.

I sometimes wonder if I should have explored her consciousness more deeply in order to better understand her. It would have been easier to do that in those early stages, since there still was some distance and a clear status differential between us— important components for psychological analysis. However, it is likely that had I done such an analysis, we never would have formed the affectionate bond that we did. Once that bond was formed, my doorway to her past would remain locked, and after more than 30 years of knowing Joan, it still is. I have no desire to awaken those past feelings in her, since I still enjoy that half smile and find it difficult to endure her discomfort. Knowing the past is not a requirement for living well and happily in the present. This is one place where Freud and I part company.

🐾 🐾 🐾

Joan did leave her husband. After she moved out of her house, we began to see each other more frequently, not just in the afternoon when the kids were swimming, but for dinner and for various social occasions involving my friends and colleagues. She was intelligent and dedicated; on her graduation, she was awarded the provincial silver medal for being the best student in the primary education program.

By now I had accumulated enough money to buy the house that I would need for my dog. After a lot of searching, I found a small bungalow that I could afford, with only 835 square feet of floor space divided into six rooms (if you count the bathroom as a room). Above each of the drafty, ill-fitting wooden-frame windows was a beautiful stained-glass panel. Dark wood trim, ceiling beams, and window frames gave the main rooms the look of an old hunting lodge. In the dining room, which was the largest room in the house, there was a fireplace. The lot that the house sat on was very small, 30 by 70 feet. The backyard was only 12 feet wide but could be fenced for a dog. I felt comfortable in this little house. It seemed like sort of a freestanding apartment with its own little yard, and I knew I could live here quite easily with my dog.

The house was built in 1916, during the era when mail-order catalogs were a primary source of obtaining goods. Sears and Montgomery Ward, in the United States, and Eaton's, in Canada, were the big suppliers of mail-order goods: work pants for Dad, a new dress for Mom, special gifts for the kids, and almost everything you needed for your house. Between 1910 and 1930, you could also purchase the whole house from the catalog. According to the Eaton's 1915 catalog, the style of house I was looking at had a starting cost of $925, plus $150 for indoor plumbing and $90 for hot air heating. The special stained-glass window trim cost an additional $70. Thus the total cost would have been $1,235. It cost me a lot more than that some 60 years later, but it was still affordable.

🐾 🐾 🐾

Lawrence once again volunteered to help me move my belongings to my new residence. I think that I assured him that this would be the last time his services would be needed. The next day Joan visited me there. She sat on a high stool in the doorway of my new little kitchen while I unpacked my dishes and cookware. She was sipping red wine from a coffee cup. She laughed when I told to her that the coffee cup was really a stemless wineglass that would doubtless be extremely fashionable in the future. She would spend many hours over many days on that stool talking, while I fussed around cooking dinner. I liked the idea of having her there in my home and began to think that I wanted her to be there all of the time. Clearly, I was falling in love.

Not too long after that, I asked Joan if she wanted to live with me. She had graduated from the university and was now working as a first grade teacher. She had been caring for her daughter Karen, but Kari had finished school and now had a job and a boyfriend with whom she was living. That meant that there was really nothing to keep Joan from joining me. A week or two later she parked her old orange Ford Mustang with its black racing stripe next to my house. She unpacked her rocking chair, sewing machine, some clothing, and a few boxes of books. Those were the only possessions that she cared about, and that was all that she ever brought into the house—except for the love that she carried with her.

❧ ❧ ❧

Too quickly it was the end of August and both Joan and I would be starting our new teaching year in a few weeks. There was just one more task I had to finish before the end of the summer—to fence the backyard. As Joan helped me build the fence, she and I chatted happily about the dog that I would get. During her marriage she had had two dogs: a dachshund named Max and later a Shetland sheepdog named Dusty. As I had felt about Feldspar, she believed that those dogs really belonged to her children, especially her daughter, Kari, who was fond of animals and had a good rapport with them. When it came to the dogs, Joan's job had simply been routine maintenance, and her bond with them had not been very strong. Truth be told, she liked sporting dogs—big sporting dogs like Labrador retrievers, the kinds of dogs she'd grown up around. But she understood that I would be selecting the dog, and perhaps a big dog would overwhelm this small house.

As we finished the fence and tested the gate latch, she asked, "So now are we ready for a dog?"

I certainly was, or thought that I was. Joan didn't know that she would soon be sharing her life with a hurricane—not one surrounded by gray clouds, but one enveloped in gray fur. Before this year ended, life in my little house would change.

CHAPTER 8

THE NEW PUPPY

I t was time for a new start. I had my little house, the woman I loved was living with me in that house, and my work was under reasonable control. I now needed a dog.

I knew that I wanted a Cairn terrier. A clinical psychologist might have suggested that a new start would require a new and different breed of dog so that I would have no bad memories associated with my previous life. But in my mind the pup that I was getting was to replace Feldspar, only this time the dog would be mine.

Even before Feldspar, I had an emotional connection to Cairn terriers. I suppose it began when I was still a child and saw Toto in my favorite film, *The Wizard of Oz*. Some say that the film starred Judy Garland, as the orphan adventurer Dorothy, but every child knows that the real star is Toto, a gray brindle Cairn terrier. If you doubt me, let me refer to a colleague of mine in the Film and Theatre Department, who did the hard number-crunching and found that Toto is in more scenes and has more screen time than Judy Garland does (although Judy has more close-ups). Dorothy also addresses more lines to Toto than to anyone else in the film. The fact that the state of Kansas features prominently in the original story recently led a resident of Wichita, Kansas, to start a movement to make the Cairn terrier the state's official dog. Notice that no one has suggested that Judy Garland be the official actress of Kansas.

Toto was really a dog named Terry who belonged to the famous dog trainer Carl Spitz. She was brought to his dog training school by her owners, who felt that she was uncontrollable and needed training. The owners never returned for the dog, so Spitz trained Toto along with his other acting dogs, and she went on to star in 10 Hollywood films including *Bright Eyes* with Shirley Temple.

Toto was a valued member of the *Wizard of Oz* cast and was paid a weekly salary of $125. In comparison, the little people who sang and danced as the Munchkins received only $50 a week. However, like most stars, or at least like most Cairn terriers, Toto had her quirks and terrierlike outbursts. During the cornfield scene when Dorothy meets the Scarecrow for the first time, the shooting had to be stopped while Toto was reprimanded by director Victor Fleming for trying to chew on the costume of Ray Bolger, who was playing the Scarecrow. Carl Spitz explained to Fleming that the straw around the Scarecrow's legs was flopping around so loosely that it was irresistible for a terrier. Something moving erratically on or near the ground triggers the genetic predisposition in a terrier and tells its brain, "Here is a thing that must be chased." A quick costume repair was needed to tighten the pieces of straw at Toto's eye level so they would be less appealing. While the crew waited for the costume modification, the director fumed, "Must dogs be just as temperamental as actors?"

In a second incident, an actor playing one of the witch's guards stepped on Toto's paw. At first everyone feared that it was broken, but it was only bruised. To give her a bit of rest, however, they decided to use a stuffed toy, the same shape and size as a Cairn terrier, to stand in for lighting and camera checks.

The moment that Toto saw her replacement, she leapt off her chair and raced across the set with teeth bared and began to rip her stuffed double to pieces. The director Fleming sighed and asked, "Must dogs be as jealous and insecure as actors?"

As a child I loved the way that Toto scampered around Dorothy, the Scarecrow, the Tin Man, and the Cowardly Lion as they danced down the yellow brick road, but it was that scene where Judy Garland sings "Over the Rainbow" to Toto that was the clincher. It would be wonderful—heavenly—to have a dog who gazed so lovingly at me when I talked to him.

🐾 🐾 🐾

So, whether to replace Feldspar or to find my own version of Toto, I was getting a Cairn terrier. I had recently learned about the Melita line of Cairns, which had been established by the late Mrs. L. M. Wood, who lived in nearby Victoria, British Columbia. Her dogs were quite handsome, and she had bred them to have a milder, more sociable temperament than most terriers do. She would not breed any animal that showed aggressive tendencies, since her dogs lived together in large open kennel areas and fighting could not be tolerated. Because Mrs. Wood had died only a few years earlier, and her dogs had been so successful in the show ring, it was relatively easy to still find dogs that were only one generation away from the Melita line. I eventually discovered a litter of pups that would be available for pickup the second week of December.

Joannie decided to present the new dog as her Christmas gift to me. She and I were not yet married, and she felt morally obligated to contribute something toward our living expenses. As a teacher, she was at the bottom-rung starting salary and was still paying off debts associated with her education and things that her kids needed or wanted but her husband would not cover. I refused her offers to pay what she called her "room and board."

Even though I was still paying child support and alimony, as well as a mortgage, I was earning enough for both of us to live on (albeit modestly), and believed that she would feel happier and less stressed if she had fewer drains on her financial reserves. Still it bothered her that she did not appear to be contributing to our household, and although the dog would be an expensive gift, she wanted to buy it. She put her arms around me and whispered in my ear, "I know how good that dog will make you feel, and I want to know that I'm part of making you happy."

We couldn't have known that the new dog would become a high point of my life and a low point of hers.

🐾 🐾 🐾

A few weeks later we took the ferry to Vancouver Island to pick up the pup. The breeder was a pleasant older woman named Margaret who had been breeding Cairn terriers for more than four decades. Margaret offered us mugs of sweet mint tea and explained that the new litter had been small, only three puppies, and she had already reserved a female to keep for herself. I looked at the two remaining pups, a gray brindle and a brown brindle, and knelt down and began to get to know them better. Their mother, an almost black dog with a bit of light gray brindling, had a good temperament; she appeared to be friendly, self-confident, and independent as she bustled around her pups and then explored the visitors before settling down for a nap. A dog's temperament is under a strong genetic control, and pups will usually grow up to be their sire or their dam or something in between in personality.

Today there are several popular systems of puppy temperament testing, but at that time nothing formal had been developed, although I knew of some tests that were emerging as reasonable ways of determining what a puppy's personality might be. I started by seeing how sociable the pups were. I knelt down, placed my mug of tea on the floor and off to the side, and called, "Puppy, puppy, puppy!" in a friendly tone. The gray dashed over to me immediately, and the brown followed somewhat more slowly.

I gave each a little pat on the head, then stood up and started to walk away again calling "Puppy, puppy, puppy!" and slapping my leg as I moved. Again the gray was most enthusiastic and the brown lagged behind. Pups that willingly come to people and follow them are usually sociable and friendly.

I asked Joannie to hold the brown and sat on the floor with the gray. I flipped him on his back and held him there for about 30 seconds. He gave a quick attempt to free himself, but then lay there quietly and licked my hand. When I did that with the brown, she struggled and then tried to bite me. Next I lifted each pup and held it up for a few seconds with its legs hanging down and got much the same results: the gray first struggled, then accepted the situation, while the brown continued to try to bite me. These tests both indicate whether a dog will accept human control.

Next I asked Joan to stamp her foot as loudly as possible on the wooden floor. She winced a bit at my request. Joan's philosophy is that a person should never do anything to draw attention to herself, nor do anything that anyone might consider impolite, unusual, or eccentric. Stamping your foot to make a loud sound in the home of a complete stranger violated her idea of proper behavior.

"Joannie, please! I need a loud sound coming from a direction that the pups are not looking."

Joan sighed and glanced at Margaret, who simply smiled pleasantly. So she stamped her foot hard enough to produce a loud clapping sound. The brown pup looked startled, jumped backward, and then growled, while the gray pup gave a quick snap of his head in Joan's direction and than took a few steps toward her as if he wanted to investigate the source of the noise. This is a crude test of sound sensitivity and response to an unexpected stimulus.

Next I took a piece of paper and crumpled it into a ball. I waved it in front of the pups and then threw it. This test is based on the suggestion of Clarence Pfaffenberger, one of the most important figures in the development of training and selection programs for guide dogs for blind people. Although he used a variety of different tests to select dogs, he claimed that a young puppy's willingness to retrieve playfully thrown objects was the best single indicator of whether it would grow up to be a good working dog.

In this case the brown dog simply looked at the paper ball and then moved a few paces away from me and sat down. The gray pup ran out after the paper ball and nosed at it. I repeated the test for the gray, and again he raced out after the crumpled paper ball and this time picked it up and looked at me. Then he dropped down on his belly and began to tear it apart.

As I watched him I thought, "Typical terrier." As a follow-up I took out my key ring and jangled the keys. The gray looked up, dropped the paper ball that he was dissecting, and trotted over to inspect the shiny tinkling object in my hand. When he drew close, I tossed the key ring into the middle of the floor. He immediately dashed over to it, grabbed the keys by biting the plastic identification tab on the ring, and began to shake it back and forth as if he were killing a rat. This was a true terrier—brave, energetic, and with a hunter's instinct. At that moment I knew that the gray was going to be my dog.

The little pup continued his battle with my keys, but his puppy teeth were not strong enough to hold on as he snapped his head back and forth trying to kill them. As a result, the ring full of keys slipped out of his jaws, flew across the room, banged into my mug of tea, and spilled its contents over the floor. The pup was not fazed by this outcome at all, and merely sauntered over to lick at the sweet liquid. Joan was very embarrassed by the outcome of my testing, however. She began apologizing to Margaret and offering to clean up the spill, glaring at me as I sat on the floor laughing at the pup's antics. She could not understand why I was not upset by my role in making a mess.

So it began. A bouncy dog acting like a classic terrier, my laughter, and Joan's distress—this would become the pattern of our life for years to come.

Of course, Margaret was not bothered by the pup's behavior any more than I was. If you choose to live with terriers, you either have to be very accepting and tolerant or you have to have a good sense of humor.

I told Margaret that we would take the gray and call him Flint because of his color. She nodded but pointed out that the brown was the more handsome of the pair and would grow up to be good enough to do well in the show ring while the gray "doesn't have classic Cairn proportions."

"I know," I told her, "but I don't intend to put him in confirmation shows. If we ever enter a show ring, it will be in an obedience competition."

Margaret looked a bit nonplussed at my comment and said, "Cairn terriers really aren't designed for obedience work. They're more catlike and independent. In my forty years or so of breeding, only two of my dogs have ever earned an obedience degree. Terriers don't like taking orders." She paused for a moment as if considering whether she had been too negative and then added with a smile, "They do learn their names very quickly."

Joannie looked at me as if to ask whether this new information would make me reconsider taking this hyperactive little gray thing home. I repeated, "His name will be Flint and we'll just have to see what he can learn."

Long before I'd signed the paperwork and officially purchased him, Flint had cleaned up all of the liquid on the floor and was now nosing the mug around, pushing it noisily across the floor. Joan glanced back and forth between me and the pup, looking a bit apprehensive.

❧ ❧ ❧

The trip home with Flint was relatively uneventful. Although I had brought a secondhand wicker-and-wire kennel crate, and padded the bottom with some bath towels, Joan had decided that it would be "cruel to cage him" and had piled the towels on the space between us and put Flint on top of them. He curled up there, and she stroked him gently, softly smiling in the way I had grown to love.

Once at the Swartz Bay ferry terminal, we had nearly an hour's wait ahead of us. So I clipped a leash onto Flint's new little collar. In my house, from the moment a dog enters my life until the day that it dies, it wears a collar. My father had been quite adamant when he had said, "A dog with a collar is an owned dog and he wears that collar with pride."

I lifted up Flint and said to Joan that we had time to wander around and let him explore a bit of the world. Although it was a nippy December day, the sun was shining and she agreed that a walk would be nice.

I carried Flint over to the nearest patch of grass, and, as puppies usually do when they first wake up, he squatted to eliminate. Then we strolled down toward the edge of the water, Flint inquisitively shoving his nose into everything that he encountered. Occasionally he'd stop and twirl around in a full circle, apparently trying to get his bearings.

At the edge of the berth where the ferry would moor, Flint became quite fascinated with the water. Perhaps it was the smell of the saltwater and its contents, or maybe the sparkling caused by the sun glinting off the ripples on the surface. In any case, he climbed onto a wide, flat wharf support and began staring down, moving his head up and down like a bobble-head toy on the dashboard of a car.

At that moment a seagull landed a couple of feet away from

Flint. I was amazed at the size of the bird, which seemed to tower over my tiny puppy and looked as if he clearly outweighed him as well. Flint turned to face this feathery visitor, showing no fear at all. He looked at the gull carefully, took one step in his direction, and then sat down as if to consider what to do next.

The bird eyed the pup carefully and then looked to the side and squawked "Grock! Grock!"

Flint jumped to his feet and answered in his high-pitched puppy voice, "Ruff! Ruff!"

The pup matched the gull's squawks.

The two animals stood watching each other, and the bird announced loudly "Grock!" to which Flint responded "Ruff!"

The bird nodded its head then gave its wing a cursory stroke with its beak. The gull then stared directly at Flint and screeched, "Grock! Grock! Grock! Grock!"

Flint stood and responded "Ruff! Ruff! Ruff! Ruff!"

The bird then shook itself and flew off with Flint staring after it. I turned to Joannie and asked, "Did did you notice that he was counting?"

"What do you mean by that?"

I was fairly excited. "When the bird squawked twice, Flint answered with two barks. When he squawked once, Flint answered with one bark, and finally when the bird gave four squawks Flint answered with four barks. He was counting and matching the number of sounds that the bird was making."

She looked at me as if I had just said something remarkably stupid or impolite. "Dogs can't count. Kids have to be taught to count, so dogs can't be born with the ability to count, and he is not old enough to have learned to count on his own. I hope that this doesn't mean that you are going to brag about your genius dog from now on."

I quickly did the math in my head. Suppose that the dog and the bird have a vocabulary consisting of 1, 2, 3, or 4 barks or squawks. Then the chance that the two animals would make the same number of sounds in any one "conversational exchange" is 1 out of 4. That means that the chance that the gull and my pup would match the number of sounds they were making 3 times in a row turns out to be less than 4 chances in 1,000. Those are pretty long odds.

It would be 3 or 4 years later that I would have a better demonstration that dogs can count. I would be back on Vancouver Island with Flint at a dog obedience competition held a few miles from that same ferry terminal, in a town called Saanich. We had completed our time in the ring, which had been a disaster, since Flint had been in a playful mood and had decided to dash out of the ring to "visit" with some kids who had been watching and waving at him. Nonetheless, he had made people laugh, and I would rather have a friendly and not fully obedient dog than a standoffish but obedient animal. At the end of our performance I took him out of the building to enjoy the spring afternoon. One of the other competitors had finished for the day and was in a large field near the parking lot with his small black Labrador retriever named Poco. He was tossing orange plastic retrieving bumpers. The bumpers were about the size and shape of a small loaf of bread and each had a cord on the end so that you could whip them around quickly and throw them quite a distance. As we watched, he casually mentioned to me, "She can count to four quite reliably, and to five with only an occasional miss."

"She must be a really smart dog to be able to count," I replied.

"She is, but all retrievers have to be able to count to three if you want to compete in high-level hunting competitions. Look, I'll show you how it works. First, you pick a number from one to five."

I chose the number 3, and while the dog watched, her owner tossed 3 bumpers out into the field in different directions and at different distances. All disappeared from sight in the high grass. I got down on my hands and knees at the dog's eye level to verify that she couldn't see the bumpers from the starting position. Then, without pointing or giving any other signals, the man simply told the dog "Poco, fetch."

Poco immediately dashed out to the most recently thrown bumper and brought it back. He took the bumper from the dog and repeated, "Poco, fetch." The dog quickly moved out into the field and started to cast about and search for the next one. After the second bumper was returned, he again commanded, "Poco, fetch," and she quickly retrieved the remaining lure. Removing this last bumper from the dog's mouth, he continued as if he believed that there were yet another object out there to be retrieved and again gave the command, "Poco, fetch." At this, the dog simply looked at him, barked once, and moved to his left side, to the usual heeling position, and sat down. He smiled and gave Poco a pat and murmured, "Clever girl!" He then explained to me, "She knows that she's retrieved all three, and that is all that there were. She keeps a running count. When there are no more bumpers to find, she lets me know with that 'They're all here, stupid' bark that you just heard, and then goes to heel to let me know that she's ready for the next thing that I want her to do."

Although Poco's performance was impressive, I was still a bit skeptical. In the end we spent the better part of a half hour, varying the number of bumpers up to 5, with me and another dog handler tossing the bumpers and sending the dog to fetch. We reasoned that this would serve as a sort of a check to see if something in the way the items were placed or the way Poco's master gave the commands affected the dog's success. None of these changes seemed to matter, and even with 5 objects, the dog never missed the count once. If I had conducted a similar experiment with a young child, by tossing toys behind items of furniture, and they had performed as well as Poco, I certainly would have taken that as proof that they could count from 1 to 5. Some 20 years later researchers would confirm that dogs not only have the ability to count, but may even have a primitive ability to add and subtract.

However, all of that was in the future, and on that day I simply suspected that Flint could count. I had never seen any mathematical ability in my previous dogs, so maybe this puppy was really clever, or maybe I should start observing dogs' abilities more closely. I had to smile at the puppy teaching the professor of psychology new tricks.

🐾 🐾 🐾

When we got home, Joan carried Flint into the house and I brought the kennel crate inside and placed it in the bedroom next to my side of the bed. I went back out into the living room, where Flint was sniffing around, took the very light nylon show leash that I had just purchased and attached it to Flint's collar. Then I put a spring clip on the other end and attached the leash to my belt.

Joan gave me a puzzled look. "He's in the house, so he really doesn't need a leash now," she said.

"I'll leash him in the house for the first few weeks. He'll have to stay close, but clipping the leash to my belt leaves my hands free for normal activities. Obviously, he can't sneak off and get himself into trouble while I'm not paying attention to him. Young puppies are always chewing on inappropriate things and some of those, like electrical cords or even knitting yarn, can hurt them. But I'll be close enough to see everything that goes into his mouth. It also gives me a chance to start house-training him since I'm likely to notice when he stands and indicates that he wants to go to the potty."

This training method has psychological benefits as well. Dogs don't instinctively understand that they've been adopted and are beginning a new life with a new family. Having the pup by your side continuously teaches him that he is now supposed to be with you rather than off on his own.

It was also a great way to teach Flint to pay attention to me so that he could learn his name. Every time I would get up to go someplace, I just said his name. Soon he'd learned that the sound of his name had a special significance and meant that something concerning him was about to happen. Before long, whenever I said, "Flint," he would look at my face to see what was going on.

I explained to Joan that the leash is a kind of umbilical cord connecting the pup to me, the human who was going to be "his person." Even though the natural umbilical is cut when the dog is born, the puppy in a new home needs to be reborn as my dog and also reborn into new behaviors. Flint would have to be at least a minimally well behaved and house-trained dog before I removed this umbilical house leash.

Joan asked, "You mean you're going to drag him around with you every time that you move?"

"No. He'll learn his name and walk happily beside me."

To demonstrate I said, "Flint!" in a happy voice and looked at the pup who was dozing beside me. He didn't move or respond, so I repeated his name "Flint!"

Joannie snorted, "Like I said, you're going to drag him around every time you move," and then left the room as I was gently nudging the pup to awaken him.

Applying psychological principles is not the same as applying the principles of physics or engineering, in which you create an apparatus, turn it on, and get instantaneous, predictable results. Chemists know that mixing the same set of chemicals will always produce exactly the same compound. Biologists know that each seed or fertilized egg is programmed to produce only one, completely predictable species. Behavioral psychology, however, is different. Even when psychological principles are sound, their application does not always produce exactly the predicted results, and even when it does, those results are often not immediate. While a physicist or chemist may have the ability to control reality and force it into the shape that he or she desires, psychologists are often in the position of *negotiating with* reality, since they are dealing with living beings who can behave unexpectedly. Each living thing has its own agenda, motives, and history, which are often unclear to those around them. So psychologists have learned to apply the principles that have the highest probability of working. Then they must be patient and adaptable, modify procedures to fit the current circumstances, and respond to changes as they occur. It would take a few days before Flint would learn the routine, but he quickly learned to pay attention because each time I said his name it meant that I was about to move. I used the umbilical for only around 2 weeks (with occasional returns to it during his housebreaking period), but the effects were lifelong. Every time I said Flint's name, he would pause in what he was doing and look at my face.

❀ ❀ ❀

Using the umbilical leash indoors was not completely free of momentary difficulties. One day when I was not paying really close attention to Flint while I was working on the computer, I needed something from my bookshelf and stood up to walk across the room to get it. As I said "Flint," he looked up in time to watch me topple over onto my face. I had not noticed that he had looped the leash around my ankles. I managed to avoid falling on my puppy as I hit the floor and suffered no permanent damage.

Another time, I had to change out of the light cotton work pants that I wear when writing and into some more respectable clothing because some visiting colleagues, whom I knew only professionally and wanted to get to know better, were coming for dinner. When I slipped into the bedroom to dress, I forgot to unclip Flint's umbilical. When the doorbell rang, Flint dashed out of the half-closed door to the bedroom to investigate, dragging my trousers behind him. Flint arrived at the front door at the exact moment that Joan opened it to formally greet our guests. Their first view of my home was of my beloved Joan standing next to a little gray dog attached to a pair of my pants. My two colleagues broke into an amused smile at the sight—Joannie did not.

CHAPTER 9

CIVILIZING FLINT

In many homes house-training a pup is a major issue. The top three reasons that dogs are given up to shelters or abandoned are (in order): aggression, noisy barking, and soiling the house. Before she moved in with me, Joan had lived mainly with dogs that were kept outside, so her tolerance for indoor "accidents" was low. Certainly, paper training was out, since she wanted no evidence in the house that my dog even owned a rear end.

There are many ways to house-train a pup. Actually the easiest is to already own an adult dog that is house-clean and knows the routine. The puppy observes the adult dog's activities and in only a couple of weeks you have a pup that never soils indoors. Obviously, that solution would not help me now.

The traditional method of house-training involves establishing a routine and paying attention to time. Puppies don't have full control over their sphincter muscles until they are 5 or 6 months of age, but certain things predict when they need to pee or poop. Eating or drinking starts a wave of rhythmic contractions along the length of the digestive tract that results in elimination. Waking up from a nap and becoming active also triggers this response, and a bout of vigorous play can do it as well. Within 5 to 15 minutes after each meal, nap, or round of playing, you can predict that the pup will need to empty its bowels or bladder. So the direct method of house-training involves taking the puppy outside a few minutes after each of these events.

To simplify the house-training process, I use a kennel crate. Dogs and their wild predecessors, like wolves, are den animals. In the wild, canines are born in a den, a small confined space, or a burrow. The pups enter the world already equipped with the instinct to keep their den and sleeping area clean. If they cannot leave their den, they will instinctively try to avoid relieving themselves until they can. This den instinct is the reason dogs can be house-trained, while cows and horses cannot. Ultimately, the dog comes to view the whole house as part of his den that must be kept clean. Usually, dogs will generalize this to include all indoor areas, whether your home or someone else's. Before that happens, however, it is extremely helpful to provide the pup with an artificial den, and that is a kennel crate.

The value of the crate is that when you can't keep an eye on your pup, such as when you are sleeping or out of the house for a few hours, you can leave the puppy in his crate. If he views the crate as a den and his sleeping area, then his instincts will cause him to try not to mess in the area. Your dog should be comfortable in the kennel so that he considers it a sort of nest.

I placed Flint's kennel crate beside my bed so that he could see me and hear me breathing, which is reassuring to young dogs. A bath towel on the floor of the crate made it comfortable and was also easily washed in case of an accident. To make the kennel crate a pleasant place for the puppy, I gave him a treat each time I put him into it. A 3- or 4-month-old pup should sleep cleanly through a 7- or 8-hour night. A younger one, like Flint, will start to fidget or whimper when he feels he can no longer hold it, and I expected that those sounds would wake me in time to get him out of the crate and outside.

Flint's crate—his den and his sleeping area.

The size of the crate is also important. The kennel needs be large enough so that the dog can stand up in it and turn around easily. But a kennel crate that is the proper size for an adult dog will probably be too large to be effective for a puppy, because the pup can sleep in one end and eliminate at the other end and still believe that he is keeping his den clean. For this reason, I blocked off part of Flint's kennel by putting a cardboard box in the back half to temporarily make the space smaller.

Joan was not familiar with this method of house-training or with the idea of using kennel crates indoors. She observed, "First, you leash your dog in the house, then you cage him, and then—just to make sure that he knows that he's caged—you take away half of his floor space. Maybe you should have gotten a parakeet, rather than a dog. How long does this caging thing go on?" she asked.

"Maybe until he is around 6 months old. At least he should be in his kennel when we go to bed. After that, we can leave the door to the crate open and see if he is clean overnight."

I could see that she was not buying into my reasoning, but she let the matter go with what would become a frequent refrain: "Well, he's your dog . . ."

🐾 🐾 🐾

As is often the case with shaping behaviors, there were a few glitches.

That first night I placed Flint in his crate next to my bed, I added a second towel next to the one he rested on, one that I had rubbed over his mother when we had picked him up. I had kept it in a plastic bag to hold her familiar scent. Before I crated Flint, I wrapped that scented towel around a windup alarm clock whose ticking would mimic the sound of the heartbeats of his mother and littermates to help him adjust to being away from his litter.

My preparations seemed to have worked, since Flint slept soundly and only began to stir at around 5 A.M. I got up and opened his crate. The towels were dry, so I attached the leash to his collar in order to walk him to the back door. Bad move. Flint took fewer than 10 steps, then squatted on the bedroom rug and left deposits of both types before what was happening had registered in my sleepy brain. I grabbed the still damp pup and rushed him outside to the place that I still hoped he would learn to use for elimination, but it was already too late.

A short time afterward, I was on my knees with a roll of paper towels and a bottle of white vinegar cleaning up the mess. It is important to kill the smell of urine quickly, because the pup will be attracted back to places that have that smell and will ultimately decide that that particular location must be the toilet. I don't know whether it was the noise that I was making or the smell of vinegar that awakened Joannie. She rolled over and looked at me.

"Dog mess?"

I grunted an agreement.

"Crate works well, huh?" she replied and turned back and dozed off again.

🐾 🐾 🐾

On the second morning with Flint, I operated on the assumption that walking him out to the backyard wouldn't work until he was a bit older. So when I woke up I opened the crate. I tousled the pup for a moment to make sure that he was awake and would not be startled when I lifted him, then I picked him up to carry him outside. Another bad move. I was about 10 feet from the back door when I felt something warm and looked down to see the stream of yellow fluid running from the puppy in my arms down the front of my pajamas.

Sometimes psychologists fail to see the natural connections between correct theories and everyday activities. I knew that after a period of sleep or rest, any increase in activity would trigger elimination in the pup. I had simply forgotten that walking after a night's sleep was activity and so was playing with the pup for a few moments before taking him out of the crate. So on the third morning I quietly took Flint from the crate, carried him out to the yard, and we had our first morning elimination outside, rather than on the rug or me.

Following the first success, Flint's progress was fast. After a week he was sleeping until 6 A.M. without fussing, and by the end of a month he was sleeping for 8 hours, allowing me the luxury of staying in bed until 7 A.M. if I wanted to.

❀ ❀ ❀

Since Joan and I both worked fairly long hours away from home, we kept Flint confined by a baby gate in the kitchen during the day, although eventually, when he was housebroken, he would have the run of the house. I spread some newspapers near the door to the backyard. These were initially marked with a bit of Flint's urine, to attract him to that spot if he had to go during the day. After a couple of weeks I would generally come home to dry newspapers. I believe that he learned to keep from messing inside because it was never rewarded. On the other hand, he knew that when I arrived home, I would immediately rush him out to do his business and he would get a treat for doing it outside.

There were a couple of "accidents." One weekend, both Joannie and I were at home but attending to household chores. Suddenly, I heard Joan's voice raised in anger. I rushed to see what was wrong and found her bent over Flint. She had pushed his face down to the floor an inch or so from the edge of a suspicious puddle and was yelling "Bad dog!" at him.

"Joannie, just let him go. I'll take care of it," I said.

"He's got to learn not to go in the house. He is so arrogant. He looked right at me and peed on the floor," she replied angrily.

"Punishing him isn't going to work. He'll just learn that he can't go in front of people, so he'll find hidden places to mess. It might create other problems, like making him reluctant to go when he is being walked, because he feels he might get punished for being seen when he's peeing."

"Look," she said, "this is the way people have house-trained dogs for centuries. If the dog makes a mess, you show it to him or push his nose in it, and punish him. That way he learns not to do it in the future."

"Do you remember Anne—she works in the library on campus?" I asked. "She and her husband Angus have a Labrador retriever named Trixie. Anyway, I ran into her a while ago and she told me that she was having trouble with her dog. It started out as a simple housebreaking situation. If the pup peed on the floor, Angus would grab Trixie, shove her nose in the urine, yell at her, give her a swat on her rump, and then throw her out of the open kitchen window into their yard [which is where they want her to go when she needs to eliminate]. Angus is a big man and the whole procedure was probably pretty traumatic for the dog. So instead of stopping her from urinating, this procedure actually produced a different kind of urination. When Angus would first come into the house after being away for a while, Trixie would look at him, cringe down, and pee. Animal behaviorists call this submissive urination, and dogs sometimes do this when they are frightened by somebody or some situation. Angus insisted that he would solve her behavior problem the traditional way and continued his routine of yelling, slapping, shoving her nose in it, and then tossing her out the kitchen window.

"According to Anne, it really didn't work at all and now they have a new problem. Whenever Angus enters the house now, Trixie runs over to him, pees on the floor, and then jumps out the kitchen window."

Joannie looked at me as though I had been speaking a foreign language and replied, "I never even thought about throwing him out of the window!"

🐾 🐾 🐾

A couple of months after Flint had come home with us, he was on the window seat barking as quickly and as loudly as his puppy lungs would allow. The house must have been under attack from a breath of wind or some similar threat, and I was admiring this early display of watchdog instincts with some amusement.

Joan stopped her reading, looked up at the pup and then

back to me, and asked, "Isn't it about time that you trained your dog how to live in harmony with a civilized society?"

"I'm working on it," I replied.

"Really?"

"Sure. He's already housebroken well enough to give him the run of the house, and I've already taught him some advanced first-grade material to take advantage of the early arithmetic ability that he's shown. Watch."

I called Flint's name, and courtesy of his umbilical training, he immediately stopped barking and turned to look at me. I called him over and had him sit in front of me.

"Now watch this, Joannie. Flint, how much is two plus two minus four?"

The little gray dog sat looking at me not making a sound or a movement.

"That's absolutely right! Nothing. What a clever and well-trained dog."

I glanced in Joan's direction and saw that she had pursed her mouth in a pained little smile and was shaking her head. "I'm living in a situation comedy program," she sighed.

But she was right that it really was time to begin to train Flint for his life in a world of humans.

🐾 🐾 🐾

For someone who lives in North America it is often a revelation to see how well dogs behave in Europe, where they appear to be much better trained and under control. The truth of the matter is that the average European spends less time training his dog than does the average North American. The dogs in Europe are not better trained, but they are better socialized and thus have become much more civilized.

Consider the life of an average North American pet dog. His family awakens in the morning and, after a few moments of greeting, they either put him out in the backyard or give him a 15- or 20-minute walk. Then back into the house while family members disperse to work, school, or to do chores. In the evening there might be a few minutes of play with the dog and another walk. Then, a few hours later, it is off to bed. The only time the dog may get any extended experience with the outside world and new people might be on weekends when the dog is taken to the park or on an outing with the family. Even then, his experience might include many hours of staying in the car while the family goes to a restaurant, shopping, or to some public event simply because many public venues ban dogs from their premises. This means that the dog has limited experience with new people and with how to conduct himself in new places.

Europe places fewer restrictions on dogs. In many countries, a dog can accompany his family when they go downtown, on public transit, into cafés and shops, and to many different events and activities. Thus, from early puppyhood, the dog is constantly encountering new people and new places, so these events become more routine and less exciting or stressful. European dogs appear to be better trained simply because they are more self-controlled and more responsive to their masters under a broad variety of conditions.

If you look at the notebook of any dog behavioral consultant, you will see two large categories of difficulties that people have with their dogs. The first set has to do with fear-based problems. We can list these as something like "Lassie is _____," where the blank is filled in with "shy," "timid," "skittish," "easily frightened," "afraid of men with hats (or beards or glasses)," "frightened by the sound of trucks (or vacuums, thunder, or crowds)," "uneasy around children (or large dogs or flickering lights)," and so forth.

The second group of problems has to do with aggression and runs something like "Rover is _____," "dominant," "pushy," "snappish," "suspicious of men in raincoats (or dark-skinned

men or men smoking)," "aggressive toward children (or puppies or any other dogs)," "hard on the fingers when he takes
treats," "barks violently at everyone who enters the house (or
is seen across the street)," "doesn't tolerate being touched (or
approached or even looked at)," "tends to frighten people with
his jumping (or snarling or staring) behaviors." While at first
glance this looks like a mass of many different behavior problems, each of which must have a separate reason or cause, all of
these difficulties can stem from a set of experiences that the dog
had, or didn't have, well before he was 6 months of age. Most
of these problems can be avoided with a little bit of work when
you first get a puppy, namely, with "socialization."

Socialization is the process by which a dog (or a person)
learns what his "society" expects of him and learns the rules and
behaviors that will allow him to become a functioning member
of that society. For wild animals this is straightforward: a wolf
pup only has to learn that he is a wolf and then to learn how
to act around other wolves in a wolf society. Because dogs are
domesticated, however, and live their lives with humans, their
socialization is more complicated. A dog must socialize to dogs
in order to learn that he is a dog and how to function in a canine
society, but he must also learn how to act and behave in the society of people. Dogs must welcome both dogs and humans (and
sometimes cats) as acceptable members of their family or pack.

The importance of socialization for dogs was first demonstrated by John Paul Scott and some of his associates, including
John L. Fuller. Their research was done at the Jackson Memorial
Laboratory in Bar Harbor, Maine, and continued for 13 years. It
resulted in a book entitled *Genetics and the Social Behavior of
the Dog,* which was written for a scientific audience and unfortunately is not an easy read for most dog owners.

Scott learned that there is a very early window of time during which it is vital for the puppy to have adequate contact with
people and dogs. If there are not enough of these social interac-

tions, fear and aggression problems may develop that can be very difficult to correct later on. Similarly, part of the process of learning to adapt to the world involves exposure to different places, objects, and events.

Scott was the most significant twentieth-century researcher on dog behavior and deserves to be as well known to the public as Sigmund Freud and B. F. Skinner. His many discoveries include the difference between competitive aggression (over an item of value) and social dominance–based aggression in dogs (competing for a higher rank in the pack). He provided the first descriptions of a number of common canine behavioral problems, including separation anxiety. He even coined the term *sociobiology* to describe the field that he was opening up—namely the study of the social behavior of animals and humans and how this is related to genetics, early experience, and the survival of species.

Scott did not appear to be distressed by the lack of public recognition of his accomplishments. I once was with him at a meeting of the International Behavior Genetics Association in Boulder, Colorado, when somebody asked if he was bothered about his lack of renown outside of scientific circles. He casually explained, "So much of what I've done has become accepted as 'common knowledge.' No one realizes that someone had to document such basic facts as when puppies first open their eyes. Someone had to be the first to notice that the social behaviors of pups around people or other dogs don't come fully packaged in their genes, but that the pups have to learn how to interact with others. It's actually gratifying that so many people are familiar with my results today, even if they don't know who first recorded them."

That's the way science works. Sometimes your name is lost if your results are too widely and well accepted. Usually, it is the people who are clever enough to apply fundamental research to common problems who tend to get most of the credit. The best known name in dog socialization has become Ian Dunbar, a veterinarian with a doctorate in psychology, who has turned such research findings into practical procedures. While I chatted with Dunbar at a meeting in Saskatoon, he reminisced, "I can still picture myself sitting in the library at the Royal Veterinary College of London and reading *Genetics and the Social Behavior of the Dog,* by Scott and Fuller. It caught me and I thought, 'That's the kind of work that I want to do.' I wouldn't be who I am today if it weren't for Scott."

Dunbar went on to establish guidelines for socializing puppies and to introduce the concept of puppy kindergarten classes, which are all about socializing rather than training very young dogs. He recommends that every puppy should meet at least 200 different people and be exposed to at least 50 distinct places by the time it is 6 months of age. I intended to follow his advice and intensively socialize Flint.

🐾 🐾 🐾

The essence of my plan to socialize Flint was to take him to work with me at the university. I already had the agreement of my department head Peter Suedfeld (whom I had designated as my puppy's godfather). I set up my office to accommodate the puppy with a wire kennel crate, which I wedged between the side of my desk and the wall to provide a "den," and which also allowed me to leave him there when I was out of the office teaching, at meetings, or in the lab. I threw a large beach towel over the tiny two-cushion purple sofa in my office to keep it free of dog hairs. A water bowl in the corner finished the modifications.

In a recent survey, the American Pet Products Manufacturers Association, a nonprofit organization that conducts an annual survey on a variety of topics associated with pet ownership in the United States, reported that 1 out of 5 large companies allows pets in the workplace and that it seems to produce tangible benefits. Workers seem happier and are less stressed, more cooperative, and there is even a marked decrease in absenteeism in companies where pets come to work with their owners.

Taking Flint with me was a daily confirmation of the positive effects of dogs at work. Walking into the psychology building and stopping at the departmental office and mail room on the way to my own office became a social occasion. People would smile at the sight of the gray puppy beside me. Others would come over and fuss over him. For the first time in all of my years at the university, I got to know virtually all of the graduate students in my department, as they would veer away from whatever route they were walking to say hello to Flint.

Being the effervescent terrier that he was, Flint was not one to remain still and unresponsive. He would dance around and jump up to greet people that he liked, so he occasionally left some muddy footprints on clothing. Being a dog, he was also always on the lookout for something to eat, so one day when a female graduate student put her mug of coffee down on the floor when she knelt down to pat the little dog, he marched over to it and stuck his tongue into the hot liquid. It was too hot, and he gave a slight yelp and jumped back, dumping the mug over and pouring the coffee onto the floor. The cold floor quickly cooled the coffee so that now he could safely drink it, and he mopped the floor dry with his tongue. From that day on, if someone put a mug of hot liquid on the floor near him, he would knock it over with his paw or nose and then drink the cooled fluid from the ground (unless it was on a carpet which, of course, defeated his strategy).

Once, while visiting the departmental office, Flint found a sandwich that one of the secretaries had left in her open-topped purse on the floor. The sandwich was nearly gone when I reached him, so of course I felt compelled to buy another for her. However, from then on, when I entered the office I would announce, "All food off of the floor! The scavenger has arrived." Everyone was good-natured about it, and the secretaries still greeted the shaggy gray dog with smiles.

Occasionally, when I was working in my office, faculty members, staff, and students would wander by just to say hello to Flint. He thus became socialized to virtually every type of human being and became remarkably friendly and controlled in the presence of strangers. Our wandering around campus had also let him become familiar with a variety of different places, and so he became quite unflappable.

Flint was also a comfort to me. Whenever I felt a bit stressed or pressured, I would run my hand over his dense coat as he lay on the little sofa. Touching him eased my mind, which was the same result that I had experienced from every dog that had gone before him. The power of dogs for healing sore minds became even more salient to me one Saint Valentine's Day.

I was working on the statistics for a scientific report when I heard a tap at my door. I looked up, and one of our clinical psychology students, Jan, was standing there. A pleasant girl who had grown up in Ontario, which is where her family still lived, Jan liked Flint and had told me a little about her family life and growing up with a series of dogs, several of which had been small terriers. On this day her face looked puffy and her eyes were red, as though she had a cold or had been crying.

"Hi, Jan," I said. "What's up? You look like you're a bit under the weather?"

"I was wondering if I could spend a little time with Flint this morning," she said quietly, and rubbed at one eye with her hand. "My boyfriend is leaving me. Could you believe that he'd tell me that on Valentine's Day?"

Jan bit her lower lip and looked down at the floor. "Anyway, when I was home and had problems, I would sit with my dog and talk to her until I felt better. This time my dog is two thousand miles away, and I was wondering if I could just spend a little time with Flint?"

Flint, heartbreak therapy.

"Sure," I said, and she crossed the office and dropped heavily onto my little purple sofa next to Flint. She swept my puppy up into her arms like a teddy bear and pressed her face against his fur. I continued talking to her as though I expected that she might be listening—which I doubted, "I haven't taught him to speak yet, but he's a good listener—trained in Rogerian Therapy. [Carl Rogers was a clinical psychologist who introduced a method of therapy which involves, at least for the early stages, a lot of listening and very little speaking on the part of the therapist.] Anyway, I have a couple of errands to run, so I'll leave you here. When you want to go just pull my office door closed if I haven't returned yet."

I grabbed my empty coffee cup and left the office, quietly closing the door behind me. I wandered down to the mail room and then with a handful of unopened envelopes went into our little lounge, which had a coffee urn. After about 20 minutes I had gone through my mail and finished my cup of coffee. As I stepped back into the hall, Jan approached me. Her eyes were still red, but she was visibly less tense.

She put her arms around me and gave me a gentle hug while whispering in my ear, "He is a good therapist. Thank you."

As I watched her leave, I thought to myself, "Not only has bringing Flint to work socialized him, but it has also certified him as a clinical psychologist. How's that for early dog training?"

CHAPTER 10

PRIMARY SCHOOL

Whether it's fate, destiny, karma, chance, or predestination, certain events at some times in our lives seem to foreshadow later ones. Events separated by thousands of miles and decades of time often appear to be connected. Of course, as a scientist, I recognize that sometimes things are linked by random chance with no real connection or bond beyond accident or happenstance. But in the intimacy of my own thoughts, a fluke or a matter of luck can cause me to wonder about cosmic influences. And so it was when I decided to begin to train Flint formally.

Dog obedience classes are almost a necessity if you really want a well-trained dog. It is certainly possible to train a dog to respond to basic commands at home, simply using a book as a guide, but classes with multiple people and dogs work better. Class not only continues to socialize your dog, it also teaches the dog that, even when many things are going on in his environment, (including the presence of other dogs), his master is still in control of his behavior.

Now, before a sensitive, feeling reader gets bent out of shape by my use of the word *master* in this context, I think that an explanation is in order. My dogs are my companions and friends, but for a dog to be civilized and under control, the relationship between the dog and his owner cannot be equal. When you tell a dog to "sit" or "come," you expect the dog to execute those commands. It is not a matter of equals discussing alternate courses of action. "Come" means that the dog is supposed to return to you. It is not a request that the dog can choose to evaluate and then decide whether or not he wants to respond to you or whether something else is more interesting. The old-fashioned word *master* works in describing this relationship, since one individual (the master) gives the commands and another (the dog) responds to them. Other words describing this relationship don't seem to work as well. Referring to a dog and his "general," or a dog and his "boss," or a dog and his "king" sound silly and inappropriate. So until someone gives me a term that works better, I will stick with the traditional *master*.

🐾 🐾 🐾

By the time he was 4 months old, Flint had found his voice. One day, I spoke to him and for the first time gave an answer in his voice. It imitated that of Bert Lahr, the actor who played the cowardly lion in *The Wizard of Oz*. I asked Flint, "Do you want to go to school now?" and answered myself with a *"Lemme at it. I've never been so ready!"* My imitation of Lahr's voice was so bad that it made me laugh, and that in turn excited Flint, who then danced around as if he had actually said the words.

Locally, the Vancouver Dog Obedience Training Club was highly recommended, and several dogs trained in that club had gone on to become top competitors in national dog obedience competitions. The classes were held in a church, in a large room that also served as a children's day care center. Although I had called ahead to preregister Flint in the beginners' class I did not know much about the club and certainly had no idea that I would ultimately come to be associated with it for more than 30 years. I eventually learned that I also had a sort of karmic link to its past.

The Vancouver Dog Obedience Training Club (which we usually call "The Club") is a nonprofit dog training club that has no officers and no written constitution or set of bylaws. It gives classes for dogs and owners at all skill levels. All of the instructors are unpaid volunteers who have earned titles for their dogs in national kennel club competitions. Some have even placed in the top 10 of national rankings for dog obedience competitors. Each instructor has full control over his or her classes and decides on the methods of instruction that he or she feels work best. Three or four instructors may be present at each class, and they are always willing to step in to help a student who needs more personalized instruction. They also often playfully provide their own viewpoints and suggestions from the sidelines, which keeps the classes light and informal.

The club actually owes its existence to a housewife named Jean Lyle who had become interested in showing purebred dogs in 1948. Her boxer hadn't been doing very well in the show ring, so she had decided to try her out in obedience competition. Since there were no obedience classes around at the time, she ended up using Blanche Saunders's *Training You to Train Your Dog*, the same book that I had started training dogs with when I was 9 or 10 years of age. A few other people who wanted to train their dogs for competition joined with her. Each had a copy of the book, and they shared equipment and tried to support each other. Other people found out that they were training dogs and asked if they would be willing to run some beginners' dog classes for pet owners.

Jean found out that Blanche Saunders would be doing some workshops and judging a series of shows in Washington State in May 1952, so Jean wrote to her and invited her to Vancouver to show them how to run an obedience class. Saunders agreed and arrived with a car full of jumps and other obedience equipment as well as some of her poodles to use as demonstration dogs.

Jean told me, "She was a great teacher and a real showman, but at the same time she was gentle and reserved. I remember that at one point she stopped and looked at us and said, 'We know a lot more about dog behavior and dog training than has ever been known before—but we have only scratched the surface. I would like to come back in fifty years and see how much more we will have learned about dogs and training then.'"

Shirley Welsh, my first instructor in the club, was a nurse whose infectious humor and friendliness made her a valued asset in a clinical setting as well as in training classes. In another unexpected connection, I later learned that Shirley and my Joannie had been longtime friends and their children had grown up together.

Training an exuberant Cairn terrier pup can be exhausting and, if you lack a sense of humor, frustrating. For the first 2 weeks or so, Flint was a little whirlwind, twirling at the end of my leash. Being surrounded by so many dogs and so much activity revved him up. He wanted to touch noses and play with all the dogs in the class. One of his classmates, a large black Newfoundland dog named Admiral, generally ignored Flint until one day Flint walked under the big dog, looked up at his belly, and barked at him. Admiral's response was to quickly drop into a down position. Flint was not fast enough to get completely out of the way, so when Admiral hit the floor, he landed on Flint's leash a short distance from where it attached to his collar. It pulled Flint to the floor where he lay flat, looking much like the pelt of an otter that had been stretched out to dry. Flint struggled for a moment to get up, but quickly gave up and lay there helplessly.

Shirley observed the scene and announced to me, "You might learn something from this. Admiral has no problem teaching Flint the down command."

Actually, Admiral had taught Flint to go down very effectively. Now whenever Flint and Admiral would meet, Flint would automatically drop into a down position for a few moments and the cowardly lion voice would announce, *"Yes sir! If you want me down, I'm down,"* much to the class's amusement.

I wanted to teach Flint the basic commands that would allow him to live in civilized society, but I also wanted to learn applied dog training. So I did not mention that I was a psychologist and a professor at the university because I did not want any of the instructors to be looking over their shoulders at the "professional." I was at the club to learn from them.

My years as a researcher have taught me that many intelligent and well-educated specialists understand high-level theories but have great difficulty applying them to practical problems. The classic example is the brilliant mathematician Albert Einstein, whose checkbook was always out of balance because of simple addition and subtraction errors. A highly respected chemist I know can't follow a recipe well enough to bake a cake. I also know a successful developmental psychologist whose young children are totally out of control, and there is another psychologist who specialized in conflict resolution but who suffered the embarrassment of having his neighbors call the police because an argument with his wife had gotten too loud. Since I wanted to know the practical steps that brought the club's dogs to their high levels of performance, and not a theoretical discourse on how they *should* be trained, I kept my mouth shut, observed, and followed instructions.

I was particularly interested in watching the two Barbaras, two senior instructors in the club, to see how they worked with different breeds of dogs. Barbara Baker seemed to have a magic touch when training terriers. She trained her Staffordshire bull terrier, Mori, to perform obedience exercises with such precision that she would ultimately rise to become the fifth-ranked dog in all of Canada, well ahead of many border collies and golden retrievers who are acknowledged to be brighter, more trainable breeds. Barbara's young Staffordshire puppy Nutmeg seemed to watch the proceedings as closely as I did. Nutmeg would later surpass her housemate by becoming the number-three dog in the country. Barbara Merkley worked with her little Shetland sheepdog Noel, who darted from one exercise to the next and seemed to have an almost psychic ability to divine exactly what Barb wanted her to do. These dogs worked with such a happy enthusiasm that I wanted them to be role models for Flint.

🐾 🐾 🐾

Since the early writings of Blanche Saunders, some advances had been made in training, but the dogs were still wearing metal slip collars that tightened around their throats when you pulled the leash, and dog training, especially for the basic commands, still involved physically manipulating the dogs into the required positions. The command to sit was followed by a tug up on the leash while you pushed down on the dog's rear with your other hand. Once the dog was in a sitting position, you said, "Good dog," which was supposed to be the reward. The wonder is that this actually worked—at least for some dogs—but it was not working well with Flint. Practicing at home, I would try to place him into a sit and he would fight back, popping back into a standing position the moment my hand was off him. Watching me work with Flint looked more like a wrestling match than a training session.

This was before today's era of positive dog training, which involves lots of food rewards, so it took me a while to stumble upon the real teaching value of food. Flint loved to eat and, if I had let him have all the food he wanted, he would have ballooned into a very chubby terrier. One day, I was offering him a treat and noticed that his head and body were following every movement of that treat and my hand. As an experiment, I passed my hand and the treat over his head. In order to keep sight of it Flint raised his head, rocked backward, and assumed a sitting position. I had an epiphany! Instead of continuing the tug-and-pull technique, I could use food to lure Flint into a sit.

Quickly I grabbed another treat and said, "Flint, sit!" and moved my hand with the food over his head, toward his rear, and in a straight line between his ears. His eyes were glued to the treat in my hand, and as he tipped his head back to keep it in sight, he sat again. Yet another piece of treat and another perfect sit. After two more tries, I left the treat in my pocket and simply moved my hand in the same motion that I had used when holding the treat, and when I said "Flint, sit," he sat. At that moment the voice of the cowardly lion announced, *"Hey, stupid, why didn't you think of this before? This is fun. We don't need no wrestling match."*

I had inadvertently stumbled upon what is now called *lure training*, using food as the lure. People like Ian Dunbar would later independently formalize this concept and give it a name. With their insightful refinements, lure training became a mainstay in positive dog training methods. For me, however, it was a private miracle. I could easily lure Flint into a sit, a down, or a stand position by moving the food in an appropriate path. After the initial training, I could phase out the food lure and replace it with an occasional treat as a reward.

The following week, we showed up for our dog class and Flint was a star. Shirley came over and asked me what I had done to improve his behavior, and I explained my lure training to her, demonstrating the movements for each command.

"That's just bribery!" she objected.

"I look at it as well-earned wages for doing the work that I want him to do," I replied.

Later that same session, the lady with the Newfoundland, Admiral, was having trouble getting him to lie down on command. He was way too large and strong for this small woman to simply push him down. Shirley walked over to me and, smiling, took Flint's leash and said, "Show her how to use food to get him down."

I did and Admiral followed the treat in my hand as I moved it in a downward arc toward the floor and said, "Admiral, down!" The moment that his belly touched the floor he got his reward and followed it with a large happy thump of his tail, that rang off the wood floor.

That interaction with Shirley really shows the essence of the club. I was there to learn how to train my dog, but the instructors were willing to watch and adopt any techniques that seemed to work well, without worrying about the theory behind them or who had first suggested them. They were always attending workshops and seminars from successful dog trainers to learn new methods. In this way, the world of dogs was very different from my academic life, where eminent colleagues would defend an abstract conjecture simply because it was their own personally derived theory, without much concern for whether it worked in the practical world.

❧ ❧ ❧

I don't want you to misinterpret either my skill at training or the ease of training Flint—even with food and lots of positive rewards. Lure training has its limits, and I have never figured out how to use it to keep a dog in one place for a long time. The "stay" commands in obedience competitions require a dog to sit or lie down in a given place while his handler moves a distance away from him. The dog then has to remain sitting for a minute or remain in the down position for 3 minutes until the handler returns. At a distance of 40 feet or so, you can't effectively use food lures and rewards to keep the dog in place, especially if other interesting stuff is going on around him. So the training reverted back to the old-fashioned procedure of simply manipulating the dog into position and correcting him every time he moved. I got a lot of exercise doing this.

"Flint, sit and stay!" I would command and then walk 40 feet away. When I turned, I would see him prancing over to April, a poodle he loved. Racing back 40 feet to retrieve my dog, I put him back in the starting place. "Flint, sit and stay!" Walked 40 feet. Turned to see him walking away to check out the Labrador retriever sitting next to him. Raced back 40 feet to retrieve my dog. Put him back in the starting place. "Flint, sit and stay!" more forcefully this time. Walked 40 feet. Turned to see him tentatively walking toward me. Raced back 40 feet and again, put him back in the starting place. "Flint, sit and stay!" with the best imitation of a British sergeant major's voice that I could muster. Walked 40 feet. And repeated these corrections until the instructor decided to move on to the next exercise.

Although I could get frustrated at times, I tried to keep my sense of humor, knowing that Flint would learn eventually. Not so for one woman in my class who had an Australian cattle dog named Mate. One evening when the dogs were in a long line practicing their sit-stay exercise, Flint and Mate were sitting next to each another. Flint got up and wandered over to say hello to Mate. The cattle dog also stood up in a friendly manner and wagged his tail. His owner shrieked at me, "Get your animal away from my dog!" Her loud shout startled Mate, who had been happily getting acquainted with Flint. He slicked his ears down and raced to the far end of the room with his owner in hot pursuit, seething with anger. She dragged the dog back to his original position and continued ranting at me.

"You are ruining my dog's training! Your dog should be expelled from this class! He's a juvenile delinquent!" As her voice rose in anger, Mate cringed, obviously assuming that her hostile tone was aimed at him. From that moment on, the cattle dog, who had been working quite well, became unreliable in his sit-stay and down-stay exercises. He would watch his owner intently and, whenever she became tense or upset, he would break from his position and run. There were lots of opportunities for this fearful behavior because his owner became hypervigilant. If Flint would simply look in Mate's direction, without moving, she would raise her voice at me again, "Stop your dog now before he does it again!" which would cause Mate to break from his position, immediately followed by his owner chasing after him and grabbing his collar and dragging him back to his place.

Shirley decided to separate Flint and Mate to calm the situation. Flint was at one end of the line and Mate at the other with eight dogs between them. Nonetheless, when Flint would start to fidget or squirm, Mate's owner would shout at Shirley, "Do something about that nasty dog! He's making Mate nervous! Does he have to be in the same room with civilized dogs?" At the sound of his mistress's angry voice, Mate would then break from position again.

I did learn something from all of this. Clearly, Flint was no threat to Mate, who was twice his height and weight. Mate's real problem was his owner's anger. As her anger grew, Mate began to feel that something in the situation was unsafe, and the last thing that a dog wants is to be a stationary target in unsafe circumstances. The wild ancestors of dogs always preferred to run away from danger if that were an option, and so Mate expressed his discomfort by breaking from his sit or down position.

Observing the situation with Mate caused me to rethink what I was doing when Flint moved away from the place where I had told him to wait. As I repeatedly placed him back in position, I would order him to stay with an ever more forceful tone of voice. After he'd break several times from position, I probably sounded like a marine training officer putting the fear of God into a platoon of raw recruits. Perhaps I was making Flint insecure by my voice tone. If he couldn't run, then he was probably reasoning that the safest place in a time of potential trouble was by my side rather than across the room lying still.

So I changed my strategy, carefully giving all of my commands in a calm, businesslike tone. If Flint broke from position, I would simply put him back and repeat the command in as bored and emotionless a tone of voice as I could manage. Eventually, he learned the exercise well enough to allow us to move on to the advanced beginners' class, and after repeating that class only three or four times, Flint had graduated to the point where he would stay in position perhaps four out of every five times. On that fifth time, however, he would happily prance off to explore the world or to greet the other dogs in the class, as if he had never been trained at all.

🐾 🐾 🐾

Flint was not fully reliable, but I was feeling better about his performance, so we took the opportunity to move into the novice class, joining dogs who really understood what was expected of them. Apparently, the club's instructors were also feeling good about Flint's performance, because Shirley and Barbara Baker came up to me one evening and said that Flint was doing well enough that they thought I ought to put him into competition.

I glanced down at my dog, who was spinning around at the end of his leash trying to convince a Shetland sheepdog to play with him, and asked, "Really?" There must have been something about the tone of my voice, or maybe Flint was just escalating his request to play, but at that exact moment he barked happily.

Shirley said, "You see, even Flint agrees," and the decision was made.

CHAPTER 11

BARKING TO SAVE THE WORLD

Day by day, Flint was behaving more like a classic terrier. The root *terra* in *terrier* means "earth" or "ground" and is associated with a genetically wired set of behaviors to follow game into its burrow and to either flush it or kill it. Old-time breeders often say that what a terrier needs is "coat and courage." His heavy, hard, or wiry coat protects the dog from abrasion as he plunges through rocky areas and down into the lair of a fox or badger. His courage allows him to work completely alone when entering a burrow after his prey, where all is in darkness underground and retreat is difficult, if not impossible. Here the dog's life might depend on his fighting ability. Many terriers have died underground, locked in a final struggle with their quarry.

Flint's courage was undeniable. The size of his opponent or the severity of the threat made no difference. One day we were having a new refrigerator delivered. I opened the door to find two men negotiating a hand cart loaded with the refrigerator wrapped loosely in plastic sheeting that was flapping in the breeze. Flint interpreted this as some huge beast that was invading his home territory and started to bark. When the plastic-wrapped monster did not back up or stop its flapping, he charged it, leaping into the air and hitting the appliance hard at a height of around 3 feet, and sinking his teeth into the plastic wrap. Unable to free himself, he hung with his hind legs several inches off the ground and his upper jaw entangled in the plastic, growling angrily.

Imagine the courage needed for a dog that stood 13 inches at his shoulder to take on a flapping monster 5 feet taller than him. As I gently worked his jaw out of its entanglement with the plastic wrapping, I spoke reassuringly to him.

"It's all right, Sir Galahad," I said. "This dragon won't hurt us." I then clipped a leash onto his collar and invited the men into the house.

Flint quieted down and watched as they unwrapped the refrigerator, accompanying their activities with low, rumbling growls. His eyes flitted back and forth between the pile of plastic sheeting on the floor and the big white rectangular thing that now stood in our kitchen, until the men exited with the old appliance and the plastic wrap.

When I had closed the door on the departing crew and unclipped his leash, Flint immediately dashed back into the kitchen to stand in front of the new refrigerator, staring at it and softly growling. Then he barked twice and waited for a response. When none came, he eased his vigilance (perhaps the monster was dead), but for several days afterward he would occasionally glance at the new refrigerator and give a little threatening growl that seemed to say, *"Stay dead, you big beast!"*

🐾 🐾 🐾

Then there was the first time Flint encountered the great dog beast in the sky. In Vancouver, electrical storms with lightning and thunder are relatively rare, and Flint must have been around a year and a half old when he encountered his first. I was sitting at my dining room table surrounded by many sheets of data from a research project when suddenly Flint froze. He spun around, looked up, and then dashed toward a window with such fervor that I stopped my work to watch him. A moment later, my own less-sensitive human ears picked up the rumble of distant thunder. Flint was growling and making a low throaty sound much like the sound of thunder. Suddenly, there was a bolt of lightning followed by a burst of thunder to which Flint responded with angry barking.

Many dogs have a fear of thunder, which sounds to them like the ferocious growls of an enormous dog or similar animal that is threatening to attack them and that is far too large to fight off or defend against. The idea that thunder was the sound of dogs growling has made its way into a number of myths. My favorite comes from a tribe of Plains Indians in the Northwestern United States who told stories of the Fire Cat, a puma who is the Sun's pet. When the Sun is shining, Fire Cat sleeps and absorbs some of the Sun's fire and heat, but when the Sun disappears because it is obstructed by storm clouds, Fire Cat becomes angry and unleashes the fire he has stored in the form of bolts of lightning. If not stopped, he could burn out great forests and plains and destroy everything on Earth, so the Great Spirit created the Thunder Dogs, whose job it is to chase away the Fire Cat before he does too much harm. That is why every lightning bolt is followed by the clamor of growling Thunder Dogs who have come to drive off Fire Cat. It also explains why the noise of the Thunder Dogs' warning growls can be heard long after there are no more lightning bolts—they are making sure that Fire Cat has run away to hide and will stay away until the Sun returns.

After another flash of lightning and burst of thunder, Flint barked angrily again. Instead of cowering from the great dangerous dog growling in the sky, like any sensible dog his size might, my courageous little terrier had appointed himself a member of the Thunder Dogs, Guardian of the Earth, Enemy of the Fire

Cat who was raining lightning upon the helpless denizens of this world. I got up and went to the window just as another lightning bolt struck.

Flint barked again and I joined in, shouting, "Get away, Fire Cat! There are too many brave and strong dogs here, and we will bite you if we catch you! Ruff-ruff-ruff! Get him, Flint. Ruff-ruff-ruff!"

Flint barked again at the thunder, and I joined in, shouting, "Get away, Fire Cat!"

Flint looked at me with his eyes alight and his tail straight up in the air and then ratcheted up the level of his barking and growling. Then Joannie came into the room.

"What's going on here?"

"Flint and I are helping the Thunder Dogs chase away the Fire Cat before his lightning can do anybody any harm," I replied with a smile.

"You're teaching him to bark at lightning and thunder?" she asked.

"It's the sacred duty of any brave and noble dog."

"Is it the sacred duty of their university professor owner to bark at the sky as well?"

"In times of danger every citizen must contribute what he can."

Joan looked at us and asked, "I can accept living in a madhouse, but does it have to be such a noisy madhouse?"

"We'll stop as soon as Fire Cat has gone away," I reassured her.

For the rest of his life, Flint would growl at the sound of thunder and bark at the window. I was not as brave as my dog, however, and rather than upset the woman I love, refrained from helping the Thunder Dogs—at least not when Joannie was within earshot.

🐾 🐾 🐾

In addition to coat and courage, terriers need to bark. A functional terrier must bark when the least bit excited or aroused. Because the earliest terriers didn't bark very much, hunters would attach bells to their collars to help them locate their dogs underground so they could dig them out if they got stuck in a burrow. A lot of terriers choked to death when their collars caught on snags or because the hunters could not hear the bells underground, so hunters bred terriers to bark whenever they were excited.

Unfortunately, the excited barking of a terrier is a behavior that would not endear a dog to Joan, who prefers dogs that pay attention to humans, are strongly inclined to do what they were told, and work silently. Joan cherishes quiet, order, reliability, predictability, and unobtrusiveness in her own life and expects these qualities in dogs, so she was completely unprepared for a terrier like Flint who barks at any change in his environment or at anything that has raised his excitement level. Joan was certainly not amused when he created what would become his favorite game, *The Barbarians Are Coming!* It always began with him leaping into the air with a furious round of barking explosive enough to be heard throughout the entire house. He would then rush to a door or window or leap onto the highest surface he could reach, the bed or sofa, where he kept up the cascade of noise until I did the modern equivalent of grabbing bows and arrows and rushing to the ramparts to defend the realm. The game always started when the house was quiet—when Joan was reading, sewing, or napping. It could also be played in the dead of night when Joan and I were sleeping. Careful investigation would often reveal that the triggering event was something like the wind brushing some tree branches against the house or a noisy vehicle traveling down the nearby street.

When Flint's barking one night awakened us at around 3 A.M. Joan turned to me angrily and hissed, "Why must he do that?"

"Joannie, terriers are bred to bark. They have to bark so that when they are underground in a burrow the hunters know where to dig them out and uncover the fox or badger they've cornered."

My historical explanation was lost on her. Joan bolted from the bed and stood glaring at me, then turned and angrily shouted at Flint.

"Stop your damned barking. There is no badger under this bed—look for yourself! And if there is a fox or a badger under there, you just keep that information to yourself. This is a bed-room—not a burrow!"

Over the next few days I tried to reduce the tension between my wife and my dog as best I could. I even bought Flint a silly little doggy cap with the motto "Born to Bark" embroidered on it and a collar tag that said "Woof!" Joan was not amused.

"Why didn't you tell me all this before we got him?" she grumbled and turned away, muttering about "nice quiet dogs, like golden retrievers and Labs." She then stopped and, hands on her hips, said, "Promise me that the next dog that you bring into this house will not be a terrier—will not be genetically pro-grammed to bark—will not be anything more than a standard, quiet, unassuming dog!"

🐾 🐾 🐾

There actually were a few times when Flint's barking proved to be useful. Since Flint's barking was communication—specifically an attempt to call his pack leader over to check to see if there was some threat—the easiest way to quiet him when he was barking at a window or a door was to get up, make a show of looking out at where he thought the problem was, and then give him a little pat.

"Good watchdog," I would tell him. I would then call him away, back to where I was sitting or working. Generally, he would calm down because the leader of his pack had indicated that there was no problem.

One night, I was awakened by Flint's barking and, as I nor-mally did, I went to the bedroom window to see what he was barking at. Joan's car was usually parked along the side of the house and in full view from the bedroom. When I looked down to the street, I saw a man with what looked like a screwdriver appearing to pry at the car door. I opened the window and shouted, "Get away from there! I'm calling the police!"

The man immediately ran down the street.

The next morning I checked Joan's car. There were scratch marks on the door on the driver's side, so it appeared that the man had been trying to open the car, no doubt to steal it.

As I poured Joan a cup of coffee and told her what I'd seen, I asked, "Doesn't Flint deserve a bit of thanks today? After all, his warning probably kept your car from being stolen last night."

Joan glanced at Flint, who had started wagging his tail at the sound of his name, then shook her head.

"Why not?" I asked.

"Too many false alarms," she replied.

CHAPTER 12

THE DEVIL IS IN THE DNA

I f you read the genetic code of a terrier it would say, "bark-eat-bark-dig-bark-chase-bark-grab-bark-hunt-bark-kill it (if it is little, furry, and moves quickly)-bark-growl-bark-tug-bark-shred-bark-ignore sounds from two-footed creatures-bark-bark . . ."

Flint was clearly growing into his genes. He was not only barking more, his hunting instincts were beginning to emerge. Every terrier carries the genetic ability and desire to kill rats and other vermin. People who don't know terriers tend to think that the most efficient rat killers are cats, who certainly are efficient at killing mice, which requires stealth and patience. Rats, however, are a different matter. Today's modern cats are smaller on average than those that were first domesticated some 7,000 years ago, but even at their original size, adult rats were often too large and vicious for cats to handle. This fact ultimately encouraged the breeding of terriers to keep down the population of the larger rodents.

Terriers are not stealthy in their hunting of vermin. Their technique simply involves sighting and chasing anything small that is moving swiftly. They dispatch their prey by grasping the rat or other small mammal by the neck and giving it one or two swift shakes to break its neck. In our relatively rodent-free cities today, it is difficult to appreciate just how efficient terriers can be at rat killing; however, back in the Victorian era, the terrier's abilities were turned into a sport that attracted enthusiasts like the young girl who later would become Queen Victoria of England. In this type of "sporting event," terriers and rats were placed in a pit to fight to the death. Side bets were often taken on the survival of dogs or rats, while other bets were taken on the amount of time that some of the better dogs might take to finish off a particular group of rodents. A number of records have survived describing some of the "superstars" of the sport. For instance, we know that one champion rat fighter was "Tiny," a bull terrier who weighed only 5½ pounds. On one particular night he killed 50 rats (some of which were nearly as large as he) in 28 minutes and 5 seconds.

🐾 🐾 🐾

Cairn terriers are no different from other terriers, and their desire to chase vermin, whether rats, mice, rabbits, or squirrels, is built in. Basically, any small thing that moved erratically could trigger Flint's genetic programming to hunt.

One morning Joan announced, "Flint has finally flipped out. Look at him."

As we turned to watch him, he made a mad dash across the room, stopped and stared at something, then dashed in another direction. I looked more carefully at what he was doing and noticed that he was pursuing some glints of light on the floor. I finally figured out that these moving flashes were coming from the sunlight reflecting off a large heart-shaped cut-crystal pendant that Joan was wearing around her neck. I had gotten her that bit of jewelry specifically because I liked the way it reflected light in many colors. Now, as the sunshine bounced off the crystal, it scattered into tiny points of light that randomly moved around the room, turning on Flint's vermin-hunting behaviors. I pointed this out Joan, along with my version of Flint's voice saying, *"Hey, Mom, if it moves I'll chase it!"* The woman I love responded with a large theatrical sigh. Looking back and forth between me and my dog (who was still chasing miniature points of rainbow-colored light), she plaintively asked, "Do I have to now start taking the way Flint's brain is wired into account before I get dressed in the morning?"

🐾 🐾 🐾

Flint was one of the few dogs that I have owned who spontaneously watched television. You can get dogs to watch televised images, but you have to attend to certain details. To be most effective you have to lower the TV set so that it is about at the dog's eye level and use images that are shot from the a dog's point of view—say, a foot or two from the ground. Images taken from a dog's eye level that have a lot of motion can capture a dog's attention, especially if the soundtrack contains lots of exciting sounds. I recently created a series of videos with these characteristics designed for dogs to watch. The dogs do seem to enjoy them, but the videos don't make a whole lot of sense or have much entertainment value for humans viewing them.

Most dogs tend to ignore TV images designed for human viewing, but Flint was in hyperdrive all the time, always scanning the environment for something that moved and might be chaseable. My spunky dog first became interested in television when I was watching a program called *The Littlest Hobo,* a low-budget series about a German shepherd who wandered around the countryside befriending various people and getting them out of trouble through his heroism and cleverness. Then, like an errant knight, after each good deed Hobo would wander away looking for his next adventure.

Flint spontaneously watched television.

Flint's attention was immediately captured by this dog moving across the TV screen. He stood up on his hind legs, as he often did at the windows to watch other dogs go by. When Hobo disappeared from the screen, Flint would get closer and look slantwise in the direction that the dog had gone, trying to catch a glimpse of the disappearing furry star. From then on, he would always check the TV screen as he passed. If a dog or another animal were visible, he would often stop to watch; sometimes his tail would tremble as he studied the images, sometimes he would let loose an excited whimper or a quick bark.

None of this caused any problems until the attack of the giant rats. A film whose title I don't remember involved scenes in which rats were occupying an abandoned structure or tunnel. When close-ups of the rats filled the TV screen, Flint froze. A low territorial growl started, and he began to quiver with excitement. At that moment in the movie, the rats became frightened, massed together, and dashed madly toward the camera and past the hero of the film. As the rodents swarmed, with all of the accompanying frantic rat sounds, Flint could contain himself no longer. He launched himself off the sofa and attacked the wooden stand on which the television stood. Growling, barking, slashing, chewing—desperately trying to grab the table leg and shake it to death. In moments the wooden leg was gouged and splintered, the rat squeals stopped, and the rodents were gone. Flint backed off and looked up. He snorted once or twice, and then with tail erect and legs stiff, proudly walked out of the room, pausing only once to glance quickly at the screen to make sure that his job of saving us from the onslaught of vermin had been well done and was truly finished. *"And stay away!"* his voice said.

At first I chuckled at his fury, but once I saw the savage gouges he left on the wooden television stand, I stopped laughing and rotated the TV stand so that the damaged leg was against the wall where it would not be visible. I really didn't want to have to explain this new episode of genetically generated terrier behavior to Joan. Over the next several days I surreptitiously sanded, stained, and varnished the chewed piece of furniture, and Joan never noticed the initial damage or the subsequent repair. Flint watched me at work and that silly voice assured me *"Those rats aren't coming back, but if they do I'll finish the job this time."*

🐾 🐾 🐾

Later that winter I got to see more of Flint's terrier hunting behavior. It doesn't often snow to any significant degree in Vancouver, but that particular winter we had a massive snowfall that piled up to nearly 2 feet. I dragged a snow shovel up from our basement and opened the front door of the house with the idea of clearing snow from the stairs and walkway. As I opened the door Flint dashed past me and disappeared into a drift of snow. For a moment he stopped, startled, then glanced back at me and started to dig.

Flint rapidly threw plumes of white behind him as he dug a tunnel through the snow. In total defiance of the known laws of physics and engineering, the snow did not cave in on Flint during his excavation. He simply disappeared into the snowbank, leaving an open channel behind him. I could mark his progress by the sound of his intermittent barks and his heavy breathing which, muffled by the snow, sounded like the distant chugging of an old-fashioned steam engine. Minutes later, a foot or two in front of the trunk of a pine tree, his head popped up through the snow, looking for all the world as if he were part of a Whack-a-Mole–type carnival game.

At just that moment a woman and her young daughter came by, trudging through the snow. The little girl, dressed in puffy pink winter clothes, caught sight of Flint's head rising through the snow. She started to laugh, with a high-pitched attractive little-girl laugh sounding like the tinkling of crystal. At the same time she pointed her pink-clad little arm at Flint. The woman contrasted sharply from her child both in terms of the gloomy look on her face and somber, colorless clothing she wore— dark coat, dark scarf, and dark knitted cap. But she clutched a brightly colored purse that had two rows of large, multicolored, woolly fringes gathered in bunches at its top and bottom.

By the time her mother looked where the girl was pointing, Flint had already disappeared back under the snow. This time there was virtually no evidence of his presence or progress through the snow except for the faint sound of that invisible steam engine. He was probably moving toward these pedestrians, because Flint always found the sound of laughter—especially that of children—irresistible. Whenever people gathered he would single out and hover around the people who giggled and guffawed the most. Sure enough, only moments later, Flint's head popped up again, only about 2 feet from the mother and daughter. The girl burst out in a loud peal of laughter, but the mother seemed not to know what to make of Flint's snow-covered head, pointy ears, dark eyes, and black nose suddenly emerging in front of her. She yelped in alarm and held out her purse defensively in front of her.

Of all of the things the woman could have done, this was probably the one thing most likely to trigger the final step of Flint's dig-hunt-kill sequence of behavior. The fringes flapped vigorously in the winter breeze. The woman's high-pitched squeal could well have sounded to him like a frightened or wounded rodent. In any event, Flint launched himself from the snowbank toward the purse as if he had been hurled by a catapult, arcing up in the perfect trajectory to reach his target. The instant he made contact with the purse, the woman dropped it and turned to clutch at her daughter protectively. I watched in horror while Flint "killed" the fringed monster by whipping it back and forth in his mouth. As he did, the contents of the purse flew out and disappeared in the high snow.

When I got over my original astonishment, I shouted at the top of my voice, "No! Stop it! Get away!" and dashed toward my little dog. As I hurtled down the steps, I lost my footing and toppled forward into a large snowdrift.

Because I do not usually yell at my dogs or charge angrily toward them, Flint was taken aback by my behavior and broke out of his frenzy. In his mind, I must have looked as if I had just gone berserk, and he most likely concluded that the safest place for him might be the interior of the house. As I toppled forward

I caught a glimpse of a grayish object scooting past me toward the stairs and into the open front door.

The woman had turned away to gather in her daughter and had not seen Flint's exit. To her it seemed that I had dashed forward to save her from the attack of some monster. She looked around fearfully.

"What was that thing?" she asked in a shaky voice.

It dawned upon me that she had probably not gotten a clear view of Flint during the incident. He'd poked his head out of the snow for only a second before leaping at the purse, and she had immediately dropped it and turned away toward her daughter.

I struggled out of the shabby indentation I had left in the snow, which appeared much like a bad attempt at a snow angel, and started helping her retrieve the contents of the purse. The purse itself was undamaged and no one was hurt but me. Later that day I would find that my impact with the snowy ground had left me with a long, painful bruise down my body. I was worried that if I admitted that the whole distressing situation had been caused by my little terrier, I would soon see an animal control officer on my doorstep. But just then the little girl solved the problem.

"It was a raccoon, Mommy," she said. "I saw his pointy ears and he was all gray except his face, which was mostly black. My teacher says that we should stay away from them because the ones that live in the city aren't afraid of people anymore and they might bite."

The mother nodded, as if accepting that explanation, and thanked me for chasing the animal away.

"I'm glad no one was hurt," was all I said as I picked up her car keys and some cosmetics for her. A few minutes later she and the little girl in pink were safely trudging down the street again.

I returned to the house, where Flint was sound asleep in his crate, and poured myself a hot cup of coffee with a slug of whisky. I sat down to warm my hands on the cup as I sipped and gratefully felt it warm my belly and relax my muscles a bit. At that moment, Joan appeared.

"I thought that you were going to shovel snow," she said.

"I was," I replied. "However, I just learned that an applied genetics experiment that I am fond of has the potential to go dangerously awry."

"I didn't know that you were doing genetic research again."

"I'm not," I said. "I just watched the results of someone else's genetic manipulations."

Flint's head was resting on his front paws and I could imagine an artist adorning that image with a halo of complete innocence, but Flint opened his eyes just a crack and his voice in my head completed my thoughts: *"The devil is in the DNA."*

CHAPTER 13

HUNTER AND HERO

Joan and I had been living together for a few years by now. It was a good and comfortable relationship. That is not to say that we never had any friction. Two people living together for any period of time without having an occasional spat suggests a lack of spirit and independent thinking that would not be admired even in sheep. Flint was the cause of more of Joan's harsh words than any other single source, but she recognized my feelings for him and would usually end any dispute over him with her by-now-traditional, "Well, he's your dog!"

Late one afternoon, my friend Peter and I were sitting in the Faculty Club with some male colleagues sipping scotch and musing about life. Somehow the conversation turned to our personal lives and the merits and shortcomings of our wives, lovers, and the concept of marriage.

One of the people in the group was the well-respected personality theorist Jerry Wiggins. Someone turned to him and commented, "Well, Jerry, you should know a lot about marriage. After all, you've been married four times."

Jerry laughed. "I suppose that marriage is just one of those things that you have to keep doing until you get it right." He took another sip from his drink and then added philosophically, "Marriage is a lot like a circus. It is not as colorful and as exciting as is represented in the advertising, but there is still enough pleasure to be had to justify the cost of admission."

At that moment Peter leaned over to me and said, "Well, Stan, your Joannie is a good, sweet person. She certainly deserves a good husband. Maybe you should marry her before she finds one!"

It was a light conversation, but it left me thinking. Joan craved stability, tradition, and conventionality. She had difficulty describing our relationship to other people, and she would be much happier if we were married, since the role of "wife" is more easily understood and accepted than the role of "woman living with . . ." Joan's mother was still alive, as were both of my parents, and they all seemed to expect that sooner or later Joan and I would get married. Because of the hurtful nature of my divorce I had been avoiding remarrying, but my more rational side knew that neither of us was inclined to be anywhere else.

One evening Flint was resting next to me and I turned to him and said, "I've been thinking about getting married again."

The voice that still had faint traces of the Cowardly Lion answered, "*I believe that it was Lord Byron who observed, 'All tragedies end in death, and all comedies end in marriage!'*"

"Since when have you become a philosopher?" I asked. "Anyway, do you think Joannie and I should make our relationship respectable and get married?"

Once more that silly voice responded, this time giving the opinion "*Seems like a good excuse for a party—as long as I don't have to be respectable, too!*"

🐾 🐾 🐾

A few days later I asked Joan if she would like to marry me. She threw her arms around my neck and kissed me as her eyes filled with tears. "I never thought that you would ask me," she said. "I would love to marry you, but there is one condition: I don't want Flint to be part of the ceremony in any way!"

"Oh," I said, "you must have seen the note from the theological seminary that I had enrolled him in. I was planning on having him read us our vows!"

Her pretty eyes twinkled and she hugged me again. "If he is not already ordained as a minister, then he is not any part of the ceremony!"

The following August we were married. Joan made her own wedding dress and looked lovely. Our far-flung families converged on the city, and a group of our friends gathered for the event. Peter arranged for a bagpiper to play as Joan and I entered the hall. I did momentarily wonder to myself how Flint would have reacted to the sound of bagpipes, but after that we just had a good and fun party.

I actually made two promises to Joan when I asked her to marry me. In addition to agreeing that Flint would not be part of our marriage ceremony, I promised her that as soon as I could pay off the mortgage on my little house in the city I would find her a tiny bit of farmland within easy driving distance. Coming from the prairies, she wanted her own bit of land with a garden where she could plant flowers and grow vegetables. If things went well, she also hoped someday to have a house large enough so that we could have visitors stay over—particularly her children and the grandchildren she was longing for.

Less than a year later, Joan's brother-in-law, Cameron, managed to find a small piece of farmland that he thought might work for us. A bit more than an hour's drive away from the city, the 5 acres were being offered at a very low price because the property had been on the market for a long time in an area that was not very prosperous then. The owners wanted to get rid of it and accepted the low bid that I could afford. In addition to the land, there was a small shack of a house heated only by a woodstove in the main room, although electricity and indoor plumbing made it livable. There was also a structure that was supposed to be a barn—an empty shell of a building that was propped up on the east side while the wind kept it up on the west side. Joannie was ecstatic and set about clearing overgrown sections and planting her flowers and vegetables and trying to save some fruit trees that were already growing there.

We spent most of our weekends and a good chunk of the summer out on the farm. I set up a little office space and began to work on my next book, for which the quiet of the farm was conducive. In between bouts of writing, I would take Flint out into the field and work on obedience exercises with him. Come the fall there would be a lot of pressure from members of the club for me to put him into competition. Joan seldom came into the house during daylight hours unless the weather was too inclement to garden. The little shack was rather ramshackle, and bits and pieces occasionally seemed spontaneously to self-destruct, but Joan soon had constructed a trellis with beautiful roses over the door. The windows of the house were too warped to open and close easily (or sometimes at all), but when you looked out of any one of them you would see the pleasant array of flowers and shrubs that she had planted and nurtured.

🐾 🐾 🐾

Out at the farm Flint showed his prowess as a hunter. As with most farms, lots of vermin were around: rats, mice, moles, rabbits, opossums, skunks, and raccoons. All seemed intent on doing some form of damage. Some raided Joan's little vegetable patch, some chewed on the trees, tore at the siding on the walls, tore holes in the roof, or worked their way into the house and cupboards and ate their way into boxes of crackers and other foodstuffs. It was a real problem trying to keep things safe from these pests.

Soon after moving in, however, we began to find dead rats and mice in corners of the house or near Joan's garden. At first Joan was upset because she thought that I must have set out poison, but I assured her that I would never do that because it could hurt Flint. Then one afternoon, as I stopped work and stepped outside with Flint to look for Joan, an opossum dashed across the grass, heading for a nearby tree with a carrot from Joan's garden in his mouth. Flint, who had been walking beside me, immediately streaked forward, grabbed the opossum by the neck, and swung the animal in a violent snapping motion. The result was instantaneous death for the vegetable thief.

Once again the marvels of genetics brought me to a halt. Suddenly the source of the dead rodents that we had been finding became clear. My dog—who had lived in the city all his life and had never been exposed to the situations for which terriers had originally been bred—followed his instincts the moment he was in the appropriate environment. Flint had become a formidable vermin hunter. I marveled at the dead opossum, which has more teeth than any other land mammal and can be ferocious when cornered—they don't always play possum. Compared to my little dog, it certainly looked large and dangerous.

Flint was happily prancing around and his proud voice boasted, "Call me Bwana, the great hunter! I am stalker and killer of all things with fur that enter my domain." Then he simply left the site of his adventure, not even looking back at the body of his victim.

When I told Joan about it, she smiled and replied, "Well, if that is true, then perhaps he's not completely useless." She then got a faraway look in her eyes and continued, "I wonder how he would be in the city."

We had a recurring problem with mice in our little old house in town. Due either to its age or to the fact that it had been put together quickly from a mail order catalog, it was never quite as well sealed as it should be, especially around the basement.

Every year, as the autumn rains began to fall and the weather started to turn cold, mice got inside. They started in the basement, eventually reaching the kitchen where they would chew at food containers and leave their droppings. Mice had also damaged some of Joan's favorite books and torn holes in some bolts of cloth that she'd stored in our basement. It was an unpleasant situation, but neither of us was comfortable using poison, and traps were inefficient, so it had seemed that we had to put up with them.

When we returned to the city, Flint had the opportunity to shine. Joannie began to leave the basement door ajar and some of the floor-level cupboard doors open to allow him to find and catch the mice. Flint was great. He hunted rodents the way that terriers were bred to do and with a degree of patience and dedication that would make cat owners envious. He was a fabulous biological mousetrap.

Joan was quite pleased with Flint's proficiency. Typically, when he would kill a mouse he would leave it on the floor where it fell just as he had done for the larger vermin out at the farm. Joan gladly disposed of the small carcasses and would gratefully praise Flint for his efforts, giving him a friendly pat and sometimes even a treat. She seemed to be warming toward my little dog, and I had high hopes that the cold war between them had ended.

Perhaps Flint saw this as his opportunity to make amends with Joan, that other human that he lived with, or perhaps he just reverted to being a terrier with a sense of humor. In any event, one morning Flint decided to make a peace offering to Joan. It was quite early, and Joan had awakened in bed to the gentle pressure of Flint's front paws resting on her. She looked down at him only to find that he had deposited on her chest a mouse—still warm but quite dead. I fear that the gift was not accepted in the tender and accommodating spirit with which it was offered. She jumped up with a startled shriek and Flint began to dance around happily. He knew that he had done something truly great and grand, since it was causing such a commotion on her side of the bed and such convulsive laughter on mine.

One morning Flint decided to make a peace offering to Joan.

Joannie was upset. "You put him up to this, didn't you?"

I protested, "Of course not. Flint was just trying to please you, not insult you." But Joan glanced back and forth suspiciously between us. Even as I tried to regain my composure and look innocent and reassuring to my wife, I could hear Flint's voice in my head, *"My motto is, if two wrongs don't make a right, then try three!"*

For the next several days, Joan would wake up in the mornings and automatically sweep her hand down over the covers to make sure that Flint had not deposited any more "gifts" for her.

Although Flint's hunting instincts were useful, there was one instance in which his behavior could have gone wrong. I had taken Flint to work with me, as I often did, and since I had nothing scheduled for the next hour or so and it was close to lunchtime, I decided to take him for a short walk around the campus.

The university was in an expansion phase, with new buildings being erected and new wings added to existing buildings. Older structures were being torn down, most of them "temporary" wooden buildings that had been built as barracks and office spaces for the military personnel stationed on campus during World War II. When the war ended and many returning soldiers accepted the government's offer to pay for their university education, there had been no space in the existing buildings for the sudden surge of returning veterans who were becoming students. As a result those temporary buildings were adapted for use as classrooms, offices, and labs. After a while these old, weathered wooden structures simply came to be accepted as normal campus facilities. Some new departments had been born and housed in these old structures for all the years that they had been functioning.

Several wooden barracks were located behind the education building and now, some 40 years after the war's end, were finally being demolished to allow the construction of a new wing. The wooden edifices disappeared one at a time. Each one would be knocked down, the debris cleared, and then the next one razed. This orderly work pattern made activity predictable, and on sunny days education students would sit outside their building and watch the demolition of these old structures while eating lunch or sipping coffee. Flint and I wandered in the direction of the building scheduled to be pulled down that afternoon.

Two large bulldozers were parked next to the doomed building. I'd taken Flint to this area to allow him some sport with the large population of mice, rats, rabbits, and squirrels. The university sits out on a peninsula and is completely surrounded by woods that continue down to the shoreline. A lot of wildlife call this area home. Three main groups of predators hunt the small animals. The largest group is the predatory birds: hawks, owls, and eagles. There are also a small number of coyotes, which are seldom seen except after sundown when much of the human population has gone home. There are a number of cats, too, both domestic (which are allowed to roam by owners living in nearby campus residences) and feral (which live and breed in hidden spaces, under older structures, or anywhere else that they can find). Like the coyotes, feral cats are seldom seen unless they are out hunting. We could now add to these groups one gray Cairn terrier who got to explore the terrain at the end of a 25-foot extendable leash.

Flint loved to sniff around as we walked. He seldom managed to catch anything on campus, although he occasionally flushed out a rabbit or rat, or got to dash madly after a squirrel. At least once, he did startle a large rat from cover. It made a wrong turn in its attempt to escape and Flint caught and dispatched it in his efficient terrier style. Mostly, however, he simply got to chase his prey out to the end of the long leash, at which point he could not actually make contact with his target. Nonetheless, just finding and pursuing vermin seemed to give him pleasure. Near the empty building, a cluster of students was standing or sitting, ready to watch the initial phase when the walls and roof would be brought down—the most exciting part. As we got closer to the structure, Flint got excited. These old buildings had been intended to be used only for a short time, so they had only minimal foundations and no basements, with the floors raised 2 or 3 feet off the ground. An open lattice of wood slats had once surrounded the crawl space, but over the years pieces of lathe had broken or rotted out leaving large holes that allowed access to the area under the floor. I assumed that Flint must have caught the scent of some rodent hiding in the crawl space and wanted to go after it.

The situation seemed safe, so I moved near one of the larger holes in the understructure and let him run ahead on the lead. He raced inside with a happy bark. Some of the students wandered closer to see what I was doing.

"He's a terrier," I explained. "He thinks that there is something in there to hunt. Maybe he'll catch a mouse or rat. I have him on this long leash so that he won't get lost under there."

"Really?" asked one of a knot of young coeds standing off to the side, and she bent down to try to look through the hole that Flint had disappeared into.

I could feel an occasional tug, so I knew that Flint was near the end of the line. Then there was a quick slackening and tightening causing several jerks. He's actually caught something, I thought. I assumed that the tugs on the leash were from Flint grabbing some rodent and giving it the shake of death. Shortly I would know for sure, since Flint was bound to come out and present me with his prize.

The leash went slack and a few moments later Flint emerged from the shadowy subfloor area. Sure enough, he was carrying a gray furry object, which hung limply from his mouth. He was carrying it by the scruff of its neck, its tail dragging on the ground. When the sunshine hit him, I saw to my horror that he was carrying the body of a young kitten that couldn't have been more than about 6 weeks old.

My heart sank. One of the feral cats must have chosen to have her litter under this building. But unfortunately, my hunter-killer terrier had discovered them, and now in a moment or two, when we would be standing surrounded by dozens of student witnesses, my dog would prove to the world that he was a murderer of helpless, cute little kittens. There was a gasp from the group surrounding us when they realized what my dog was carrying.

Flint dropped the limp carcass and gave a bark that seemed a request for praise for his hunting skill. As I bent over the kitten's body, it suddenly twitched and rolled to its feet. Blinking at the bright sunshine, the kitten scanned the people surrounding it, then looked down and, seeing the dust and dirt that had accumulated on her fur from Flint dragging it around, began to clean itself. The assembled students oohed and ahhed.

When I looked up to see what Flint was doing, he was gone. The leash disappeared through the hole, so he was back under the building. A few moments later he emerged again, carrying an orange-and-white striped kitten that he dropped next to its littermate, also alive and unharmed.

I barely caught a glimpse of Flint's carrot-shaped tail, which was quivering with excitement, before he ducked yet a third time back into the gloom. Two or three minutes later he reemerged with a black-and-white kitten that was squirming a bit, as if annoyed by the indignity of being rescued by a dog. Once Flint deposited it next to its brother and sister, it began to make little mewling sounds. Flint then circled the group, as if to assure himself that all were present, but made no move to go back under the building.

Kneeling next to this collection of felines, I wondered, "What do I do next?"

I took a chance, and announced, "Well, gang, it looks like my dog has saved the lives of these three little guys. In an hour the bulldozers would have brought this whole building down on them. Now we have a problem. These kittens are going to need a home or I'll have to take them to a shelter."

I had barely stopped for a breath when one young woman with a Shirley Temple mop of blond hair rushed forward and asked, "You mean that we can take them?"

"I don't believe that they belong to anyone, and they certainly can't survive on their own. So if you want one of these kittens, feel free to take it home with you."

The girl bent over the trio of kittens and lifted the black-and-white one up to her face. It stretched its paws out and touched her nose. "I'm going to call you Patches," she announced, and then tucked the little animal into the crook of her arm and disappeared into the crowd.

A moment later another girl in a faded denim jacket picked up the little gray cat. "Hello, Shadow," she said to the cat, as she carried it away. "That's your new name."

A slim Chinese girl lowered herself to her knees next to the remaining orange-and-white kitten, which immediately got up and approached her. "May I have him?" she asked in a soft, tentative voice.

I nodded and she looked back at the kitten, gazed into its eyes, and said gently, "I will call you *Lao Hu*, which means 'tiger' in Chinese, if that is acceptable to you." The little cat rubbed against her outstretched hand as if to say that he was happy with his new name. She carefully lifted the kitten and hugged it to her chest. She looked at me and smiled, and said, "Thank you." Then she turned and looked at Flint and said in a quiet and respectful voice, "And thank you. If you were mine I would call you *Hui Shih*, which means 'gray lion,' because you are brave and noble and benevolent like the Celestial Lion."

Two Chinese girls who had been standing close to her overheard this and both shouted "Yes" and clapped their hands. The girl on her knees clutched the kitten tightly, gave a little bow with her head, then rose and joined the other two girls. The small group disappeared as they passed through the crowd of spectators.

About a half hour later the engine of a yellow-and-black bulldozer started. A few minutes after, the whole side of the building next to the place where Flint had emerged with the kittens collapsed. I looked at my little dog and marveled. Even though he was genetically programmed to hunt and kill small furry things, today he had gently retrieved three young cats and presented them to me as if he intended for me to take care of them. I looked at the growing pile of rubble that was once a building and observed, "You saved three lives today, my puppy. You are a hero!"

"*You can just call me the most honorable and respected Hui Shih,*" said a voice that I would never again equate with the Cowardly Lion.

That night I told Joannie about Flint's heroic deeds and mentioned that for a moment I had considered taking the orange-and-white cat home as a gift to her.

Joan looked directly at Flint, made eye contact, and announced, "Hero or not, you're lucky that Stan didn't bring that cat home. That would have put you out of business. Cats not only hunt and kill mice, they eat them. That means no dead bodies to clean up and no warm, dead carcasses left on a person's chest!"

"*But for now you still have the services and protection of the revered and esteemed Hui Shih,*" said the new voice of my lion dog.

CHAPTER 14

COMPETITION AND CHAOS

I n late September, I was standing near the entrance to a dog show ring, Flint next to my left side, twirling around in circles to watch the other dogs passing behind and in front of him. He always spins in a clockwise direction, so every few minutes I had to loosen the leash to let it unwind so that it didn't cut off the circulation to my hand.

Several people from the Vancouver Dog Obedience Club were sitting next to the ringside watching the competitors in the novice class. Both Barbaras were there, as were Shirley and Emma, all sitting on folding lawn chairs. Shirley, Joannie's long-time friend, had convinced Joan to come to view Flint's first obedience competition and was explaining to her what was going on. A woman was starting her competition trial with her Welsh corgi, and I was wondering why I was there about to display to the world and my wife the degree of control—or, I suspect, lack of control—that I had over my little Cairn terrier.

I was excited to share the legacy of Blanche Saunders, who had helped establish the sport of dog obedience trials in the 1930s. The exercises demonstrated what dogs could do beyond their usual jobs of hunting, herding, or guarding. The dogs that she showed were merely "companion dogs," and the first title that a dog can earn is the CD, which stands for Companion Dog.

Modern obedience competitions begin with *novice class* exercises that are designed to demonstrate that the dog is under control and has good manners. More advanced obedience degrees depend upon the owner's ability to train the dog to do more complex tasks, some of which may look more like "tricks," including fetching a thrown dumbbell, jumping different obstacles, obeying commands instantaneously whether the command is spoken or given by hand signal, and using his scenting abilities to find items that have been touched by his owner when put with other items.

When casually observing dogs performing, you may have the sense that most of the dogs are working well and virtually all of them are better controlled than a typical pet. But the standards in competition are much more rigorous than those that a typical pet owner would require of his dog.

Each time a dog enters the ring it is assigned a perfect score of 200 points. From then on, the dog can only lose points, which he does if any of his exercises is less than perfect. Judges deduct points for dogs that drift out of the perfect heeling position (by the handler's left leg) by lagging behind or forging a few steps in front as their handler moves around the obedience ring. Dogs lose points when they sit too slowly or not at all. Any dog that moves from the position that it has been commanded to hold, or even fidgets too much, whether standing, sitting, or lying down, loses points. A dog that walks away when ordered to stay or refuses to perform a task when commanded to do so loses all the points for that exercise. Any single exercise with a zero score disqualifies the dog for that trial. In order to qualify, you have to get a score of 170 or higher and you have to qualify three times, under different judges, to earn a title. Each qualifying score is referred to as a "leg," so a dog with an obedience title must have three legs.

Actually the "team" of dog and handler is being evaluated, which means that the handler can also cause points to be deducted. Judges deduct points for handlers who use the leash to physically guide the dog, such as when they keep the pressure too tight or tug at the dog. They lose points or fail exercises if the handler talks to the dog during an exercise (even to give a word of praise) or if the handler gives two or more commands for a single exercise. Some judges can be quite picky about this. One competitor's team was failed simply because the handler unconsciously nodded her head at the same time that she commanded "Come!" When asked about this, the judge simply said that the head nod "could have been an additional signal that the dog was trained to respond to."

In many ways the judging of a dog's performance is much like the judging of Olympic and high-level figure skating. According to kennel club rules, *"The judge must carry a mental picture of the theoretically perfect performance in each exercise and score each dog and handler against this visualized standard which shall combine the utmost in willingness, enjoyment and precision on the part of the dog, and naturalness, gentleness, and smoothness in handling."* That gives the judge a lot of leeway and certainly allows the judge's preferences, biases, and expectations to creep into and influence the scores they assign to particular teams. Among competitors, rumors abound about "good" and "bad" judges, and the prejudices that certain of the "bad" judges are believed to have. I had been warned away from competing under one particular obedience judge, for example, because I was told that he trained retrievers and "only retrievers and sporting dogs seem to get good scores in his ring."

This belief in judges' unfairness probably accounted for one particular joke around the dog show circuit. It began with the idea that God was looking for some entertainment and decided that having a dog obedience show might be fun. Since nearly all dogs go to heaven, the best competitors of all time could be found in paradise and God wanted to have them compete against each other in the same trial. So God turned to one of the archangels and told him to arrange it. A short time later Satan gets a phone call from that angel.

Satan is puzzled and asks, "I think that a dog show would be nice, but why are you calling me? After all, all of the dogs are in heaven."

"I know," replies the archangel. "However, you have all of the judges!"

🐾 🐾 🐾

Dog obedience competitors also have preconceived notions about the merits of certain dog breeds. Earlier that day, Joan and I had gone for a cup of coffee and were returning to the obedience ring with Flint walking beside me. At this show, there were several rings where dogs were being judged for confirmation (how well they looked and moved as representatives of their breed) as well as two rings for obedience trials. All of the obedience competitors had been assigned armband numbers that were 900 or higher, so we were easy to identify. As we passed by two women, we overheard one say, "That armband is in the nine hundreds. Who in their right mind would show a Cairn terrier in obedience?"

Both women chuckled. Unfortunately, Joan overheard them and asked me, "Do you really want to go through with this? He's not ready. I don't know if he'll ever be ready."

"It's just a dog show," I reassured her, "and the worst thing that could happen would be that we would fail to get a qualifying score."

Joan did not look reassured and was already uncomfortable feeling that people were staring at her because she was walking next to me and my "inappropriate" obedience dog breed.

❧ ❧ ❧

My attention was drawn back to the woman with the corgi. After she and two more dogs finished in the ring, it would be our turn. The judge said, "The first exercise is the heel on leash. Are you ready?" The woman nodded her head. In this exercise the dog is supposed to stay beside your left leg, matching your speed as you move quickly or slowly, turning when you do, and automatically sitting when you stop—all without additional commands. The woman was dressed stylishly in a skirt and knee-high boots, but the boots' high heels sank into the arena's sandy floor. Obviously uncomfortable walking under these conditions, she did not move very quickly or smoothly. The bouncy, energetic corgi appeared to be controlling its urges to run or play and all was going well.

In the next exercise, the *figure 8,* the team heeled around two ring stewards who stood in as posts about 6 feet apart while the team walked a figure 8 pattern around them. Afterward, the corgi was told to stand, and the handler moved a leash length away while the judge went over to touch the dog.

Then the heeling exercise was repeated, this time with the dog off leash. The woman responded to the judge's command "Forward," and the corgi immediately realized that there was no controlling leash attached to him anymore and decided to remedy the slow pace that his mistress was walking. Bred to drive cattle, corgis instinctively move them along by barking and nipping at their heels, so he dropped back a few steps, issued a couple of yiplike barks, and nipped at the woman's boots and legs. When she did not speed up adequately, he nipped again and barked more vigorously. When the woman stopped at the judge's command, instead of sitting, the dog circled her and continued to bark and nip. Some of the audience watching began to laugh, while several longtime competitors simply shook their heads and grimaced in sympathy.

The judge walked over to the woman, said something quietly, and then cut that exercise short. She had definitely failed to qualify. The woman reached down and brought the dog back to her side with a sharp command. Then they started the next exercise, the recall. The corgi was told to sit and stay, and the woman moved to the other side of the ring. On the command "Come!" the dog dashed toward her, barking all the way, and then sat perfectly in front of her. She then gave the command to send the dog around behind her and back into the heel position. The dog stood up, went around her, and gave a sharp bark and a nip when he got behind her, eventually returning to her left side and sitting down. The dog really seemed quite proud of its performance; the woman, however, was red-faced.

I looked down at Flint and quietly said, "At least you won't do worse than that."

"*Do you want to bet money on that?*" came his silly voice as he spun in another clockwise loop while trying to keep his eyes on the corgi leaving the ring.

The next competitors were a woman with a Shetland sheepdog and another with a golden retriever, both of whom produced picture-perfect performances.

When it was our turn, I told Flint to sit and gave him a treat. "There are more treats if you do well," I promised him. Treats are not allowed in the actual obedience ring, so he has just eaten the last one in my pocket.

We walked up to the gate and the steward showed us to the starting line. The judge, a middle-aged man in a business suit, came over to us, glanced at Flint and back to me, and asked, "Are you ready?"

"I'm ready," I answered, and looked down at Flint. "I hope that my dog is."

The judge smiled and said, "The first exercise is the *heel on lead*. Forward."

I said, "Flint, heel," and stepped out confidently. I didn't look down at Flint, but by the looseness of the leash and the flash of gray I glimpsed from the corner of my eye I knew that he was with me. Right turn, left turn, halt! Forward, about turn, fast, slow—all the while the leash was loose and Flint was heeling perfectly. I thought to myself, "This may actually work out."

It was now time for the figure 8 exercise. One of the two ring stewards acting as "posts" was a middle-aged woman in slacks and a pink sweatshirt with the image of a poodle on it. The other was a pretty young woman in her early twenties wearing an unusual wraparound skirt made of denim that was nearly floor length and had fringes running down its length.

The sight of the fringes gave me a flash of concern. Flint had already proved his attraction to fringes when he grabbed the woman's purse that day in the snow . . . Many people report that their terriers try to bite at their shoelaces if they are tied loosely and move when they walk. President Theodore Roosevelt had a terrier named Jock who was incited by the swishing of the tails of the French ambassador's formal dinner jacket when he visited the White House. Jock leapt up to bite at one of them but missed and instead tore out the seat of the ambassador's pants, nearly causing an international incident. I was hopeful that, since we were indoors, no wind would stir the fringes, and the woman was supposed to stand still. Flint was doing fine in his heeling so perhaps all would be well.

At the judge's command "Forward," I told Flint to heel and stepped out. The woman in the fringed wraparound skirt chose that moment to adjust herself, and while we were circling her I felt some tension on the leash and at the same moment heard some laughter from the sidelines. When I looked down and back, Flint had seized the fringed edge of the skirt and as he walked around the woman, he was unwrapping her. She was already displaying much more bare leg than she'd intended when she recognized what was happening and dropped her hands to her sides to stop her clothing from unraveling and so recover her dignity.

"Flint, heel!" I said sharply, knowing that this extra command and Flint's molestation of the ring steward had probably caused us to fail the exercise. He looked startled, dropped the skirt's edge, and returned to my side. As we began to circle the other steward, Flint did a clockwise twirl at the end of the leash, trying to keep watch on the fringes behind him. After a brief halt, we circled the girl in the denim skirt again, but this time she was prepared and her hands were straight down beside her. I was also prepared and made a very wide circle around with Flint, out of reach of the fringes. Unhappy about this, he did two more clockwise twirls in his eagerness to grab at them again.

In the next exercise, the *stand for examination,* I told Flint to stand, stepped a leash length away, and the judge came over to touch the dog, for which Flint was supposed to remain stationary. But being a very sociable dog, and a little bit excited after the figure 8, Flint was looking for someone to play with. He broke from the stand and danced over to lick the judge's hand, which was a clear failure.

For the next exercise, the *heel off lead,* on the judge's command I told Flint to heel and began to move. After a few turns and stops, we did an about turn and started to move toward the entrance of the ring. There the ring steward in the wraparound skirt was having an animated discussion with someone, waving her hands and moving a few steps so that the fringes on her skirt fluttered. I saw a furry gray form streak past my left side toward her.

I yelled, "Flint, heel!" The ring steward gave a little squeal of distress at the sight of Flint, dropped her hands down to protect her clothing, and at the same time tried to hide behind the woman she had been talking to. Flint spun to look at me, then looked longingly back at those fringes.

"Flint, heel!" I shouted with what I hoped sounded like authority, and my little gray dog made another clockwise circle and returned to my side.

In the final exercise, the *recall*, I called Flint from his sitting position across the ring, and he dashed toward me at high speed, coming to a perfect sit in front of me, and then returning to the heeling position on my command—a picture-perfect ending to a nonqualifying performance.

As I walked out of the ring with Flint, the ring steward with the fringes stood well to the side, hands on her skirt. A young collie was the last competitor, and he and Flint gave each other a playful sniff as we passed.

I walked over to my friends, and Barbara Merkley smiled and said, "That was interesting!" Joan had bent her head and was still covering her face with her hands.

The collie in the ring was very young, full of energy, and not under good control. As he left the ring, the steward with the pink poodle top called all of the competitors back for the group exercises.

We lined up with Flint and me near the end, followed by only the collie. We marched to the far end of the ring, where we sat our dogs and took off their leashes for the two group exercises. The first, the *long sit,* is really not that long—only 1 minute in duration—but it is done with the handlers all the way across the ring. The second, the *long down,* is for 3 minutes, and does feel very long when you are standing 40 feet from your dog, watching him fidget.

The dogs were in line and sitting when the judge said, "Leave your dogs." I told Flint to "Stay!" and strode across the ring. When I reached the far side and turned, Flint and the collie were standing and facing each other. The collie gave a little bow, lowered his front in an invitation to play, and then barked. Flint did the same, and before the judge or the ring stewards could do anything, the two dogs happily circled each other and then charged down the line gyrating and whirling around the other dogs and causing all of them—except the golden retriever—to break from their sitting positions. The judge hastily yelled,

"Back to your dogs," and the handlers rushed to retrieve their animals.

Once order was restored and the dogs were again sitting in a line, the judge took me and the collie's owner and our dogs over to the other side of the ring and told us to stay there while the long sit and the long down exercises were conducted without us. We remained in the corner, like dunces or misbehaved children. Joan was huddled down in her chair, looking as if she were searching for a place to hide.

We left the ring with the other, happier, and more controlled competitors. Near the entrance, Barbara Baker was standing with the small bag of treats I had left with her. As I bent over to give Flint one, she said with a smile, "He needs a little work, especially in the sit-stay, but you can't fault him for a lack of enthusiasm!"

🐾 🐾 🐾

On the car ride home, Joan was still upset.

"I've never been so embarrassed in my life. I was looking for a hole to crawl into!" she said, her voice quavering.

"Why should you be embarrassed?" I asked. "You weren't out in the ring, and nobody except the people from the club know who you are."

"I know who I am, and who I am with, and that is enough! You should be mortified by that performance. Aren't you the least bit bothered by what happened?"

I tried to explain, "Joannie, this was our first real competition. You can't expect a true novice at the game to start out with a championship performance. Besides that, I don't think that I did anything particularly wrong, and Flint was just being a terrier and a playful, friendly dog. Nobody was hurt, and the only loss is that I paid a fee to compete and failed to qualify. We'll do better next time, and if not the next time, then the time after.

Flint is still young and has plenty of time to improve his training and get better."

"Next time?" There was a note edging toward panic in her voice. "After that disgraceful performance, there is going to be a next time? Doesn't it bother you to know that your dog is a time bomb? I can't take this. I will never go to a dog show to watch you compete again!" She crossed her hands over her chest, slumped in her seat. I knew better than to continue the conversation.

In my pocket was Flint's score sheet. Out of the possible 200 points representing a perfect score my dog had earned 30. That was for his perfect recall exercise. He had managed to fail every other exercise. Later that evening, when Joan was soaking in the bathtub to calm down, I sat on the sofa sipping a large glass of bourbon. Flint was lying beside me. I unfurled his score sheet, held it up in front of him, and asked, "What do you think of that?"

He opened his eyes and actually seemed to look at it. Then his silly voice said, *"It could have been zero, you know. It was a brilliant recall, you must admit. Anyway, if the student has failed to learn, the teacher has failed to teach! You're the psychologist and I'm a dog—figure it out!"*

I laughed quietly to myself, making sure that the bathroom door was still closed. I didn't need Joan worrying about her husband apparently talking to himself.

I leaned over and tousled Flint's fur. "Thanks for the guidance," I said. "I think there is plenty of work ahead for both of us."

I just didn't know how much.

CHAPTER 15

KING SOLOMON'S RING

Earning obedience titles simply gets you ribbons and certificates, no monetary or substantive gain, and although you can hang them on the wall, ribbons and certificates really impress nobody except your children, grandchildren, and perhaps fellow competitors. Millions of people can easily name professional football stars or Olympic medalists in various sports, but I doubt that 1 person in 10,000 can name the top competitors in dog obedience.

Dog training for dog obedience trials, field trials, agility, or any of the dog sports is not a hobby but an obsession, an occupation, a disease, an addiction, a fascination, an absurdity, or perhaps a fate. People who spend time training their dogs *must* do it. Those who do not do it consider it a distant cousin of coin collecting or building model airplanes, or perhaps a brother of recreational swimming or skiing. In their eyes it is something that we do to fill time or in lieu of watching television. The reality is different. The dog that you work with is not a thing or an activity, it is a living being with whom you have a relationship. The dog's very existence in your home compels you to spend time interacting and training it. Working with the dog changes the nature and behavior of that dog and the nature of your relationship with it.

I wanted to train Flint to do well in competition because I wanted to prove to myself that I was a good enough psychologist to train a difficult breed of dog. Another reason was to prove to Joan that my dog was not "an empty-headed, unresponsive, and uncooperative beast." Flint was a handful, but he was also a happy, sweet little guy. He loved going to class and loved the busyness of weekend trials, of meeting new dogs and socializing with old friends. As I trained him, he did become more responsive— and of course it strengthened our bond. We both had fun.

But perhaps the most important reason that I wanted to train Flint could be traced all the way back to why I had become a psychologist in the first place. To successfully train an animal (or a person) you must first figure out what is going on in his mind. At a deep emotional level I wanted to understand what my dog was thinking, feeling, and trying to communicate.

When I was around 6 years of age, my maternal grandfather Jacob was listening to me babbling on about how I wanted to be able to talk to my beagle Skippy and have him talk back to me in a way I could understand. When I finished, my grandfather responded by lighting a cigar and telling me the story of King Solomon's ring.

"Most people don't know it, but King Solomon didn't have just one ring—he had three magic rings," he told me. "One was made of finely crafted gold and guaranteed him victory over all of his nation's enemies. The second ring was platinum and protected against djinni and evil spirits.

"As a reward for his early good deeds and his promise to build a temple to God in Jerusalem, the Lord came to Solomon in a dream and offered him a gift of anything that he wanted for himself. Solomon answered that he wanted a ring that allowed him to communicate with animals and understand their thinking. The Lord instructed that it should be made of silver and marked with the king's seal and the true name of God. To hold its magic, the maker of the ring had to start and complete it on one special night. The work on it couldn't start before the moon rose in the sky, and it had to be finished before morning. Because it was made so quickly, it wasn't as perfect as the other two and looked rough and unfinished. Yet this was the ring that Solomon most wanted.

"When Solomon died, God took back the two fine rings to hold them until another king as wise and devout as Solomon would need them. Because the silver ring had been a personal gift to Solomon, God felt that it wasn't right to take it back and so he hid the silver ring 'in a house with many doors.' They say that it's still there, and a smart person who loves animals might be able to find it someday."

I desperately wanted Solomon's silver ring, but the story suggested that Solomon's ring was hidden and might be lost forever. Then one evening, not long after my grandfather told me the story, my parents were listening to a radio program on which Albert Einstein, then a professor at Princeton University, was being interviewed. I no longer recall the main substance of that interview, but I remember Einstein saying that "Science is a house with many doors." Suddenly it was all clear to me. The folktale contained a secret code, and now I knew where King Solomon's silver ring was hidden. I formulated my future plans then and there: I was going to be a scientist so that I could search the house with many doors and find the ring that allowed me to understand animals. I was not searching for a physical ring, but rather a ring of facts and principles that could be held in my mind that would help me to communicate and interpret the behavior of dogs.

Whenever I am training a dog, I think about the tale of King Solomon's ring and its effect on my life choices. Training often requires me to study my dog's behavior closely and to try to interpret what he is thinking. Often these observations lead me to insights about canine behavior that had eluded me before. Of course, the mind-set of trying to understand is different from the mind-set of trying to control. Rather than a "dog trainer"—or as some have called me in the new vernacular, a "dog whisperer"— I view myself as merely a "dog watcher."

As I trained Flint seriously for competition, my observations of the feisty dog that I loved became another means of searching for the ring of understanding, much like the many animal behavior courses that I had taken and research that I had done in the library and in my own laboratory. Of course, there were also days when I felt that my little terrier was evidence that the pathway to King Solomon's ring was not only lost but forever blocked and barricaded.

Training for competition takes time, but except for the one evening each week that I spent in classes at the club, and weekends, when I would set aside a 20- or 30-minute session to work with Flint, we never had formal training sessions. Maybe I actually did, because training is not defined only by formal time set aside to work with a dog. Sometimes when I was taking a break from writing or research, I might spend a few minutes working with him on an exercise, or perhaps, if we were watching TV and I was not completely involved in the program, I might get up and do a bit of training off to the side of the room so that we did not annoy Joan.

Because my training sessions were brief and spontaneous, and because Flint was very motivated by food, I always had treats in my pocket, bits of dog kibble or broken dog biscuits. Who would have expected that these dog treats could have become a human relationship problem? Joan's major household chore was taking care of our clothes, but, because she was also working, she was often in a hurry and would sometimes forget to check the pockets of my pants before throwing them into the washer. During washing the dog treats turned into a soggy pulp in my pockets, which the clothes dryer then baked into a concretelike substance that effectively sealed closed the pockets.

When I tried to ask Joan to check the pockets in case I'd forgotten before putting them in the washer, it happened that she was having a bad day with Flint and was not in the mood to listen. Flint had extracted a ball of yarn from her knitting bag and, when she had tried to retrieve it (by running after him rather than calling him to her), he had decided that this was a great game and had run around the house until the ball of yarn had unraveled. Her response to me was, "I teach two dozen first-grade kids and I don't need to give them treats or rewards every time they do something right."

I could have reminded her about the principles of reward-based learning, or noted that she was teaching school in order to earn a salary and would be quite offended if the Board of Education said they were no longer going to pay her for her services. But I wasn't in the mood for an argument and it wouldn't have changed her mind about my dog. So I gently flexed the pockets of my pants to reopen them, and then cleared out the debris while making a mental note to check my pockets more carefully before putting them in the laundry bin. I try to train my dogs in a nonconfrontational way, and I should at least try to interact with the woman I love in the same mild, calm manner.

🐾 🐾 🐾

Training Flint *to do* things was not difficult as long as I did not require robotlike precision and reliability. Training Flint *not to do* things was another matter. He simply had too much energy and curiosity to stay in one place and not engage in random exciting activities. At obedience competitions, the difficult tasks for him were the group sit-stay and down-stay exercises. When he was a long distance from me Flint tended to fidget and eventually stand up and move across the room to me or try to socialize with other dogs.

Standard training practices for these stationary exercises are based on the idea that the dog must become aware that any body movement is inappropriate after he gets the "Stay" command. I was taught to watch Flint's behavior closely and anticipate his breaking from position. If I left him in a down position and he started to move his legs in or raise his rear end, I was to repeat the stay command ("using a firm but not threatening voice"). Or if he actually broke from his position, I would rush forward, return him to his position, and give the command to stay again.

During the early stages of his training, in a typical 3-minute down-stay exercise, I would end up repeating the "Down! Stay!" commands three or four times as he made small twitches and movements. After a good deal of practice, we reached a point where Flint would remain in place for the whole time (although this was sometimes supported by sharp glares from me when he moved a paw or shifted position). The confidence of everyone in the club was buoyed by our progress, and they encouraged me to put Flint in another obedience trial.

🐾 🐾 🐾

Never underestimate the ability of a clever dog to find a way to embarrass you in public and to make it look as if you had never spent more than a total of 5 seconds training him. At our next competition Flint had been doing remarkably well. His heeling on and off leash was fine and his recall exercise was spectacular. He did move his front legs a little bit when the judge came over to touch him on the stand exercise, but that would simply be some points lost, not a failure. Only the long sit and down remained.

Wonder of wonders, Flint sat rock still for the full minute during the group sit test. Now only the long down for 3 minutes remained, and we would be one-third of the way toward earning him his first obedience title.

I stood beside him and commanded, "Flint, down!" and he obediently dropped to the ground, assuming the lying position popular with statues of lions who grace entrances to many public buildings. "Stay!" I told him and then walked the 40 feet to the other side of the ring. I turned and he was still in position. I took a breath, thinking to myself, "This might really work."

Flint and I made eye contact and, to my dismay, he made a few movements with his front end. A judge might view them as a dog simply adjusting his position to make himself more comfortable, but these were almost always the precursors to Flint moving out of position. Had we been in the hall where my dog club trains, I would have immediately repeated the stay command to hold him in position, but in an actual obedience trial that would result in our failing immediately. So instead, I held my tongue and hoped that this really was merely an adjustment.

Flint looked at me in a manner that caused me to hear his voice in my mind saying, *"Hey, there! Aren't you paying attention? Didn't you see me move? Aren't you supposed to say something?"* So, to see whether he could get me to respond, Flint squiggled his body forward another inch or two. I held my breath and glanced at my wristwatch—still more than 2 minutes to go. I looked back across the ring; while my attention had been on reading the time, Flint had moved another few inches toward me and was looking inquiringly at me, waiting for me to do something. Now the pattern was set. Every 10 seconds or so, Flint would make that little swimming movement—never lifting his belly off the ground, but nonetheless inching ever closer to me. He would then pause to look at my face to see my response. Since I said nothing, he assumed that all was well and crept a few more inches toward me. Some of the ringside spectators giggled as they watched my dog swim along the ground.

By the time the judge ordered, "Back to your dogs!" Flint was halfway across the ring. I stopped and stood beside him, effectively right in the middle of the ring, while all of the other handlers continued on to the far side. My little gray dog looked up and wagged his tail, and I could hear him saying, *"Because you have such a clever dog, you don't have to walk all the way across the ring like those other dog owners do!"*

Flint had swum halfway across the ring.

Once we were outside the ring again, Shirley walked over and put her arm around me, "Well, look at it this way: he never actually got up."

In the remaining two trials that weekend, Flint repeated his land-swimming performance during the down-stay exercise. On the last trial a large knot of people had gathered in anticipation of a chuckle as they watched him fail. Perhaps Flint simply felt that his mission in life was to bring some additional laughter into the world.

On a more sober note, Barbara Baker told me, "He's too smart. He has become 'ring-wise' and he knows that in the actual show ring you won't correct him. This may be a problem." Her expression was serious, and she offered no immediate solution at that moment, which worried me a bit more.

❧ ❧ ❧

Solving Flint's tendency to move in the sit and down-stay tests turned out to be an exercise in thinking like a dog. Flint did not hold his position in the ring because I did not correct him when he started to move as I did when we were practicing at home or in the club. So I needed some way to correct him without my direct intervention.

The moment of insight came when I was in a store that sold sporting equipment and saw a spool of "shark line." This is a heavy monofilament fishing line used to catch sharks or other heavy fish. It is transparent but can withstand being pulled by more than 100 pounds of tension. I purchased the shark line and cut a length of about 3 or 4 feet. I then attached a clip to each end. Afterward, before I placed Flint in a sit or a down and told him to stay, I removed his leash, as usual, but now clipped the shark line onto his collar. The other end of the line had already been attached to a stationary object or, when we were outdoors, to a small stake that I drove into the ground. Now when Flint would break his position to move toward me, the tug of the line would correct him. I did not need to respond to every twitch that he made and only had to repeat the sit or down and stay command when he had moved far enough that the fishing line was tugging on his collar.

This worked beautifully. Flint would start to move, get corrected automatically by the tug on the shark line, then look at me in confusion. I would repeat "Down and stay!" and he would settle back into position for the remaining time. Soon he came to expect that corrective tug and simply stopped testing and remained in place. I felt that the problem was solved well enough that we could return to competition.

I had fallen into a very common trap that catches psychologists and other behavioral scientists—the assumption that what works in one situation is apt to work in a completely different situation. So there I was, back in an obedience competition ring with Flint. We were not doing spectacularly well, but our performance up to the group sits and downs was passing. Just two more exercises to go.

I stood and watched from the far side of the ring while Flint held his sit position for the full minute. I was almost giddy when I placed him in the down position and told him to stay. Just 3 more minutes and we would have our first qualifying score. I stood across the ring looking benignly at my dog. Suddenly he looked around, as if noticing that this was a new and different place where the rules might be different. Then, with his belly still on the ground, he made a swimming movement. I could imagine what was going on in his mind. Something like, *"What? No correction? I'm free again!"*

It was déjà vu, complete with the familiar chuckles from the sidelines while my dog swam on his belly out into the middle of the ring to disqualify our otherwise acceptable performance. Another weekend with no ribbons to take home and no legs earned toward his title.

🐾 🐾 🐾

Sometime later I figured out that to solve the problem I had to think more like a dog or at least know what was going on in this dog's mind. The obvious fact was that when he knew that he was tethered he didn't even try to move, but when he felt free, or felt that he was in a different situation, he would test to see if he was still restrained. If the test failed and he was free, he would carefully try to work his way back to me regardless of my command to stay.

"So how do I convince you that you are still tied down when you are not?" I asked him.

"Look at it this way," it was a goofy, patronizing voice that

answered, *"I obviously am not seeing the shark line. That's because us dogs are all dreadfully far-sighted, and since the fish line is close and transparent, it's really hard to see. That means that what tells me that I'm tied to something is the feeling of the tug at my collar. All you have to do is to tug my collar from forty feet away."*

The idea that popped into my mind was simple: Flint must feel the tug *before* he decided to move. That tug had to be felt whether he was physically tethered or not.

Training then became quite simple. Each time I would put the shark line on Flint to hold him in place, after clipping the line on, I would give a sharp downward tug on his collar before I moved away. This served two purposes. First, it confirmed that the clip was securely attached and, second, it signaled to Flint that the line was attached. I mixed this action with some training sessions where I would put him in a down-stay position without tethering him and with no tug. At these times I would come back to face him, then back away a few steps and call him to me. As he walked toward me, his freedom confirmed that he was not tied. What Flint didn't know was that I was building a signal for him. A tug on his collar before I moved meant his movements were restricted. No tug meant that he was not.

Now the real test. Again I found myself in the obedience ring with Flint, and again we were working toward a qualifying score except for the sit and down stays. Now, however, after I removed his leash, I made a show of fumbling with his collar and finished with a sharp tug on it before I stood up. Flint's sit-stay was rock solid.

I returned from the other side of the ring and waited for the judge to say "Exercise finished." At that moment I bent down to fumble with Flint's collar again, and I may even have mumbled something like "Let me check that shark line." Again just before I stood up I gave another sharp tug on the collar. Flint looked at me, and I thought that I heard him give a little sigh. I didn't know whether that was a good or bad sign. At the judge's command I ordered Flint to lie down and to stay, then walked to the far end of the ring. Flint was still lying there. Once he stirred a bit to look behind him. I think that he was looking for the tether, but he seemed to be more clearly trusting that the tugs that I gave him represented reliable information that he was physically anchored in place, rather than relying on the usually less dependable information from his vision.

The judge ordered us back to our dogs, and when the exercise finished I made another big fuss and fumbled with his collar as if removing the shark line. As we left the ring I told him how proud I was of his performance, and he made a little sneezing sound as if to say, *"And what choice did I have, since you left me tied down?"*

When we exited the ring I got congratulatory hugs from both Barbaras, Shirley, and Emma, and Flint got treats from everybody. Barbara Merkley gave a big smile and announced, "Just two more to go!"

🐾 🐾 🐾

We did get two more qualifying scores, not particularly high scores, but nonetheless qualifying. Now Flint had his first obedience title and, since I had taken a dog through to a title, Barbara Baker invited me to teach a beginners' dog obedience class. At our club, the minimum requirement for becoming an instructor for any class is that you have taken a dog through obedience competition to earn a title equivalent or higher than the level that you are teaching. After you serve an apprenticeship as an assistant instructor and demonstrate that you have teaching skills, you are given your own class. This allows these carefully chosen individuals to spend many hours performing unpaid but generally pleasant service to the community.

Having earned his third qualifying scores, Flint was officially now a Companion Dog and therefore entitled to announce that fact by adding the letters CD after his name in all official documents. I was elated and proudly took him home and announced, "Well, Joannie, Flint has now been certified as a CD."

She looked up from her knitting and asked, "And CD stands for 'Crazy Dog'?"

CHAPTER 16

THE GRAY KNIGHT

One day I came home, closed the front door behind me, and immediately heard "Bring that back!" as a flash of gray fur with a carrot-shaped tail and something white dangling from his mouth shot past me and into my office with my wife in hot pursuit. I reached out and circled my arms around Joan.

"It's okay. Whatever he's got this time I'll retrieve it for you," I said and gave her a light kiss on the cheek and walked after Flint.

I stepped into my office and called Flint, who took a few steps forward. On the floor beside him was a small notepad, with a phone number written on the top page in Joan's handwriting, along with a few tooth marks and a splash of dog drool. I gave Flint a pat for coming and picked up the pad. Joan had been on the phone and had written down this number but had accidentally knocked the pad off the end table in such a way that it had skittered across the floor, a clear target for a terrier's chase instincts.

I gave Joannie the pad and another hug. She looked at Flint, who had tagged along behind, and shook her head. There were no harsh words and no later bringing up of the incident.

Over the five years that Flint had lived with us, I had come to understand that my dog was a pretty good barometer for what was going on in Joannie's emotional life. If all was going well, she could tolerate an occasional "event," but if she was stressed, her displeasure with Flint's noisy barking, his high activity level, or his unpredictability could escalate into a major flare-up.

Regardless of her state of mind, Joan never abused Flint. She might yell at him, stamp her foot, or wave her finger in a threatening manner, but when I was away at meetings and conferences for several days at time, she would care for him and feed him, and when I returned, he was never the worse for wear.

Flint seemed to take Joannie's outbursts of displeasure as simply part of her natural behavior that had little lasting consequence for him. Within a quarter hour of any incident, he would be bouncing around the house in his typical manner or comfortably curled up in any of several places where he liked to nap.

Flint always seemed affectionate toward Joan and greeted her at the door with the same enthusiasm that he welcomed me or any friendly visitor. His continuing good cheer and warm nature often broke through to her. When she opened the door on returning home, she would sometimes look at this convivial little terrier and give a bit of a smile. Now and then she would accompany it with a comment like "Hello, silly dog" in the same affectionate tone that we might greet one of our grandchildren today by saying something like, "Hi there, silly child."

🐾 🐾 🐾

Sometimes Flint's behavior would actually amuse Joan. One weekend when I was away at a scientific meeting and called home just to check in and chat for a few minutes, I could tell from Joannie's tone of voice that she was smiling as she said, "You know, Flint really loves you and misses you."

This was a surprising statement from her, so I asked, "What makes you say that?"

"Well, this afternoon I thought that I was having some kind of weird mental experience—maybe telepathy or something. I was in the kitchen baking cookies and kept hearing your voice. I couldn't quite make out what you were saying except that I thought that I heard you say my name and Flint's. This happened several times before I dropped what I was doing and went into the living room."

At that time we had an old phone answering machine that used a large cassette tape. At the front of the machine were two large buttons, one of which played any messages and a second one that rewound the tape. All of the other controls were smaller and placed farther back. I had called home the previous evening and Joan was not home, so I left a message telling her that I was okay and that I loved her. As I usually did when I was away, I left the hopeful instruction, "Give Flint a pat from me."

Joan had not noticed the message until around noon the next day, and after listening, had not bothered to erase it. Flint had heard my voice and his name and must have climbed up on the sofa and leaned over the end table where we kept the phone and answering machine, and, either through happenstance or from watching Joan, he figured out that by pushing one of the big buttons he could hear me speaking and mentioning his name. Once he had learned this, he began to play the message at regular intervals, obviously deriving some pleasure from the sound of my voice and his name.

As she related this story to me, rather than being annoyed at Flint's antics, she gave a little chuckle and said, "It's a good thing that he hasn't figured out how to dial the phone, otherwise he'd be racking up lots of long-distance charges trying to reach you while you are away."

Flint accepted all acknowledgments of his existence as friendly overtures. In his mind, Joan was an integral part of our household pack, and although his primary bond was with me, she was also entitled to his affection, attention, and acts of gallantry—if she chose to accept them.

Perhaps the most dramatic instance of Flint's display of caring for Joan happened one afternoon when she was alone with him. Less than an hour after the event I returned home, and Joan looked at me with a serious expression and told me that there had been an "incident."

Generally confident and independent, Joan grew up in a quiet, law-abiding city in Alberta, and then spent much of her life in small communities and rural settings, in contrast to my big-city, urban upbringing. Having lived in New York, I am always very concerned about household security and safety, always making sure that doors are locked, even when I am inside. I also tend to greet strangers at the door with a dollop of suspicion until I know who they are and what they want. Joan is quite the opposite and often leaves the house to run errands without setting the security alarm. She also greets people who come to the door openly, without any evidence of caution or hesitation.

This time she had heard the doorbell ring, and when she arrived at the door saw a large man standing there who asked if he could use our phone. Because he looked rather scruffy, Joan was more hesitant than usual and didn't want him in our home. Instead, she offered to make the call for him if he supplied her with the phone number. The man scowled at her, and without saying another word, pushed the door open fully and stepped into the house.

She told me, "He made me very uneasy—barging in like that, and I didn't know what to do next. Then, suddenly, Flint was there between us. I have never seen him act like that. He wasn't barking, he was growling. His hair was standing up, his teeth were showing, and he was snapping at the guy as if he wanted to tear a chunk out of him. I never heard him growl like that before—it was really scary."

Flint was not a large dog and weighed perhaps 22 pounds at his heaviest. But confronted by an animal growling, snapping, and displaying its teeth as weapons, the intruder defensively raised his hands and took a couple of steps back, just enough to place him on the other side of the threshold. Joan took the opportunity to rush forward to close and lock the door. A few moments later the man moved away from the door and disappeared down the street.

"I don't know what triggered that kind of response from Flint. He is usually so friendly to anyone who comes to the door. But I was glad that he was there. That guy made me nervous and I certainly didn't want him in our living room."

Joan's admission that she was "nervous" was as close to admitting that she was terrified as I would ever hear. Because the man scared her, she had probably given off pheromones, biological scents that dogs use to determine the emotional state of mind of other individuals, and Flint had responded to her anxiety by rallying to her defense.

"I was glad that he did, but he's just a small dog and the man could have . . ." Her eyes flitted momentarily in Flint's direction.

I put my arm around her and said, "A great general once remarked, 'It's not the size of the dog in the fight, but the size of the fight in the dog that matters.' There's a lot of fight in Flint."

Although she was not particularly expressive about it, Flint had clearly risen in Joan's estimation that day.

To help Joan relax, I offered to open a bottle of wine and I put on some music. I had recently been given a lovely album of Strauss waltzes and Joan loves ballroom dancing. While the music played, I went into the kitchen, I opened the wine, and poured some into two pretty glasses. When I walked back into the room, Joannie was bent over and holding Flint's front paws as he stood on his hind legs. They were waltzing.

I quietly backed out and grabbed a camera that just happened to be on the counter, and took a candid photo of the event, since I might not live to see another performance. I then went back for the wineglasses and by the time I reentered the room, the waltz was ending. I did not tell Joan that I had seen her performance, since I didn't want to chance marring the moment.

Joan and Flint were waltzing.

Joan and I sat, sipping wine and just talking. Later, when Joan got up to leave the room for a moment. I leaned over to pat Flint, who was lying with his head on my foot and said, "You really are a brave and gallant warrior."

"*And a good dancer, too!*" he replied.

Chapter 17

CHANGES

Things were getting a bit tense in my home once again. At first I thought that this was simply a continuation of Flint and Joan's on-again, off-again personality clash. Joan needed order, quiet, and predictability, but neither Flint nor I was orderly and predictable, which was hard on her. But since she loved me, and since everyone expects university professors to be a bit absentminded and inattentive to conditions around them, she pardoned my behavior. Flint's lapses were less excusable.

Flint was once again proving that he had a mind of his own, and his likes and dislikes violated Joan's sense of order and decorum. Joannie would shoo Flint off a chair only to see him immediately jump up on the sofa. She would push him off one side of the bed only to have him jump back up on the other. She would scold him for barking at the door only to have him begin barking at the window.

One day, she had some friends over for afternoon coffee. Flint hung around the group, nosing at the visitors to test the possibility that one of them might scratch his ear or accidentally drop something edible. Concerned that he might be annoying her guests, Joan waved him away.

"Flint, stop bothering these people! Go find something interesting to do."

For once, Flint seemed eager to follow her instruction and dashed out of the room with a great sense of purpose. A few minutes later, he reappeared carrying one of Joan's undergarments, which he dropped in the middle of the floor and played pounce-and-kill games with. Evading capture, he flagrantly snapped it from side to side with great joy, causing great amusement for her company but a great deal of dismay and embarrassment for Joan.

A few minutes later, he reappeared carrying one of Joan's undergarments and dropped it in the middle of the floor.

Flint's favorite toys for playing fetch were all made of hard material. When he wanted to play fetch, he would bring a nylon bone-shaped toy, a hard rubber ball, or a rubber Kong and drop it on the floor in front of me. I would toss it and he would chase after it, sometimes retrieving it and sometimes simply grabbing it and running around for a while. He preferred the hard toys because they clattered loudly when I tossed them on the bare wooden floors in our house.

Often Flint would decide that he wanted me to toss one of his toys when I was sitting on the sofa reading or watching television. He would then scamper around the house until he found an appropriate toy for me to throw and bring it over to me. Since he was neither neat nor particularly organized, however, the toys were sprinkled around in various locations, and he occasionally seemed distressed when he couldn't find one quickly enough.

One day Flint came up with an innovative solution to the problem of having an appropriate hard toy at hand. It involved burying them around the cushions of the sofa. He shoved a number of them into the spaces beside, behind, and occasionally under the cushion at the end of the sofa where Joan habitually sat next to me. His plan appeared to be that, when I was sitting on the sofa and Joan was not, he could unearth a toy, drop it in my lap, and then jump off and wait for me to throw it. I thought that he was very clever to reason that, since I would be sitting on one side of the sofa, the toys must be buried in another place, hence on Joan's side.

Of course, I was thinking as Flint's master rather than as Joan's husband. Within a few hours of his first toy-burying episode, Joan came home, tired from a day in the classroom, and dropped herself heavily onto the sofa. Cruel fate had her landing on a hard rubber ball that Flint had left under the cushion. She fished it out and held it up, "What's this?"

I didn't have time to explain before she went on to also uncover a hard nylon bone and a plastic dumbbell.

"Did you leave these here or was it your dog?" she demanded.

"He was just leaving his toys in a convenient place where he could pull them out to play fetch," I said.

"Convenient for you—uncomfortable for me!" She glared at Flint and then threw the dumbbell-shaped thing at him with the sharp instruction, "Take your dumb toy and find another place for it."

The toy noisily hit the floor and rolled several feet, and Flint happily scampered after it. He snatched it up in his mouth and marched over to Joan and sat in front of her to offer it back to her. I could hear his voice in my head *"Wow! I didn't know that you liked to play fetch with me. Let's do it again!"*

Later that night as we undressed for bed, Joan pointed to a dark blue bruise low on her hip. "Your dog did this to me this afternoon! Burying toys in the sofa . . ." then her eyes filled with tears that she tried to hide by getting into bed and turning her back on me.

Sometimes even well-trained psychologists are slow to recognize the meaning of behavioral changes in their family members or close friends. But at that moment, seeing my wife's annoyance and distress, I finally recognized the importance of the fact that over the past six months or so, Joan had been undergoing some major emotional turmoil. She was worried about her mother, who was growing frail and would soon have to move to an assisted living residence, as well as her daughter, who was considering some major life changes. Also, at this point in her middle age Joan had to deal with her own changing moods and energy level. The end result was bound to be a buildup of psychological stress and depression. Anger requires a focus and obviously, because of their previous history, Flint was the natural target for her.

Flint, of course, was not a completely innocent victim of Joan's irritation. In fact, at the very moment that I had my flash of insight, I was tossing one of my socks into the open clothes hamper in the corner of the bedroom. Thinking that we were returning to our game of fetch, Flint leapt up to catch it, missed, and came down with his front paws on the edge of the straw clothes hamper, which toppled over, spilling soiled clothes on the floor. This was an interesting new situation for my dog, and he began burrowing through the clothes as though searching for some rodent, flinging dirty shirts, socks, and undergarments across the room. Her face buried in her pillow, Joannie fortunately didn't see this.

I called Flint over to me and ordered him to lie down and stay in place while I scooped the clothing back into the hamper as quietly as possible. I then took Flint downstairs with me, poured myself a drink, and sat on the sofa to think this whole situation through. Since Joan was not there with me, Flint jumped up on the sofa as well. He checked the cushion to see if any of his toys were there, but when he didn't find them, he simply lay down with his head facing toward me as though he expected me to tell him something. So I did.

"Well, little gray person, your mom is in a bad sort of psychological state and we need something that will distract her from her current troubles and have her focus on something more positive."

"*Do explain it to me, Dr. Freud,*" came back the answer in a more condescending voice than I usually gave to him. I had no idea where all of this was going but kept on, since conversations with my dogs always seemed more productive than silently ruminating.

"The usual psychological recommendations include finding new interests, engaging in activities that are calming or that fill the mind and keep the person from becoming obsessed with his emotional state. It's even better if those activities also promote a sense of achievement."

"*You could have her start to think about a new house out at the farm, since the old shack is falling down. Tell her that she has to design it and that she will have to be the contractor.*"

"Hmm . . . That is an idea. Anyway, in addition to those kinds of activities, psychologists recommend that women who have a caring personality, like Joannie, but who don't have any of their own children in the house to lavish care and affection on, should find someone to nurture, like a grandchild."

"Well, you don't have grandchildren living nearby. She could nurture me!"

"Sorry, Flint, but you are currently part of the problem."

"Well, then, get her a puppy."

"Yeah, that would be great. Two Flints—that would guarantee a speedy divorce."

"No. Get her a Joannie puppy—something soft and cute and loving. Call it a therapy dog."

At one level this was a ludicrous suggestion. On the other hand, it made a perverse sort of sense. Joannie loves small, helpless things. If I could find a dog that was gentle and needed care and affection, that might help provide my wife with some emotional support. The truth was that I had also been longing for a puppy. I actually believe that the perfect number of dogs in a house is three—an adult dog who keeps you company in the here and now, a puppy for the future, and an old dog for the memories. Although any new dog might be selected to please Joan, I would still end up as its principal caretaker and trainer.

"Hey, little gray person, I know that you understand how much I would like a pup, but I thought that we were discussing what to do for Joan," I protested.

"We are. She'll love a new puppy. Besides, another dog might keep me from getting bored and might keep me out of trouble as well. In addition, I might be able to train him to be my accomplice!"

🐾 🐾 🐾

The following evening Joan seemed to be in a good mood, so I started to present some ideas that I hoped she would like and that might also be therapeutic.

"You know, Joannie, I've just about finished paying off the mortgage on the farm, and since the little shack is falling down, I thought that we might think about building a proper house out there. We could stash the amount of money equivalent to our regular mortgage payments in a bank account and over a few years we could use those funds and my book royalty payments to start work on it. It will be a bit of a shoestring budget, since I don't want to take out loans and be in debt again. That means that you would have to organize the construction and planning to keep us within our resources."

Joan's eyes lit up, and that sweet smile that I had been missing recently returned to her face.

"I could do that," she said. "The adult education program here in the city has all kinds of courses on home design, contracting, and other construction-related stuff. Most are given in the evenings and they're not very expensive. That could be fun."

Since she was in a good mood, I broached the idea of bringing another dog into the house.

"Joannie, I've also been thinking about the problems that you've been having with Flint. I think that one of the reasons that he gets into trouble is that he is bored and is simply looking for something to amuse him. I think that a puppy might help to keep him busy and out of trouble."

Joan was now staring at me with saucer-wide eyes, but I continued.

"Remember that when we got him, I told you that when he was around five years old, I wanted to add another dog to the house, and Flint is—"

I never got to finish that line of thought, since Joan interrupted in a voice that sounded a full octave higher than her usual tone of voice.

"I won't have another terrier in my house!"

"I promise that it won't be another terrier."

"If we get another dog, it has to be the opposite of Flint in every way. It has to be quiet. It has to be loving. It should not be destructive, or chase glints of light or tufts of lint, and it should act like a normal dog. I don't even want a dog that looks like him! No pricked ears, no carrot-shaped tail, no hard coat!"

"I promise that the next dog we get will not be at all like Flint," I said as I grabbed Flint's leash and told Joannie that I had an errand I had to do. I was really dashing out of the house before Joan could think up a set of counterarguments against our acquiring a new puppy. I already knew that I wanted a Cavalier King Charles spaniel, a very affectionate breed, and I had been gathering information with the idea of getting a second dog for over a year. However, I would not mention the new pup again in front of Joan until it was a reality.

As we walked down the front steps, I found myself smiling and said to Flint, "Well, it looks like you're going to get a new brother."

"*Great,*" came the response in a particularly silly voice. "*It might be nice if you got us a cat at the same time so that I could teach him how to chase it.*"

CHAPTER 18

WIZARD

Wiz.

Joannie began to immerse herself in courses and books that would allow her to design and build our farmhouse within the limits of our budget while Flint continued to find ways to unravel her emotionally.

Flint's newest obsession was shoelaces. My guess is that it all started with long shoelaces that flap about when people walk and are commonplace on runners or other soft shoes. These, like fringes, probably triggered Flint's hunting instincts. Instead of chasing and attempting to bite at a shoelace in motion, which could be dangerous because he could get kicked in the process, he adopted a catlike stealth strategy. Flint would wait until people were quietly sitting at a table and then surreptitiously creep forward until he was next to a shoe. Then with the dainty and precise movements that one might expect of a neurosurgeon, he would use his teeth to gently untie the shoelace without attracting the wearer's attention. Once undone, the two strands of laces were stretched out in front of the shoe, and he would move on to the next closest shoe. If, perchance, the laces were tied using a knot that was not easily undone, he did not worry at it, but rather proceeded to look for an easier target. Since Joan usually wore runners around the house, and since she usually tied her laces into a simple bow that could be easily undone by pulling on one or the other loose end, her shoes were often the objective of his sneak attacks.

Neither of us noticed Flint's new pattern of behavior at first, although Joan did complain once or twice that modern shoe-laces must be made of some new material that is more slippery, since her laces were coming undone so frequently. I had found my own laces untied a couple of times and had simply switched to a more secure type of knot even though I had no idea why they were loosening. Of course, there is nothing terrible about untied shoelaces, unless you stand up and one of your feet happens to be standing on the shoelace from the other foot, in which case you can easily stumble and lose your balance. This had happened to Joan a few times, but fortunately each time she was next to a table that she was able to grab and prevent herself from falling.

I discovered that Flint was doing the untying one day when I wandered out to the kitchen to refill our coffee cups and on returning noticed Flint lying on his belly under the table and very gently pulling at Joannie's shoelace. My immediate urge was to stop him with a loud, "Flint, no!" but that would have alerted Joan to his latest example of misbehavior. So instead I simply mentioned to her that her laces were untied and then set myself the task of thinking about some kind of solution to the problem that I could devise without her knowledge of my dog's newest set of misdemeanors.

Later that afternoon, I went to a pet supply house and purchased a bottle of an odorless product that claimed that it could deter pets from chewing or mouthing anything that it was sprayed on. It did warn that the product, although quite safe, tasted quite noxious, so users should avoid getting it on their hands and also be sure that it had fully dried before handling things treated with it.

That night, after Joan had gone to sleep, I rounded up all her shoes that tied with laces and then sprayed the shoelaces until they were thoroughly saturated with this deterrent liquid. I then replaced her footwear in its usual place and went to bed.

The following morning was a Sunday, and I often try to make a special breakfast on Sundays. This morning it was freshly baked biscuits with butter and a variety of cheeses, served with a Louisiana-style coffee with a hint of chicory. I have to be careful preparing food like this because Joannie's sense of taste is much more sensitive than mine, and just a pinch too much chicory could easily have made the coffee too bitter for her. Joan came to the breakfast table dressed in jeans and T-shirt, wearing her favorite pair of running shoes. I smiled because I knew that her laces were quite safe. I wished that I could see Flint's reaction when he first took the noxious-tasting shoelace in his mouth and wondered how many times he would return to try again before giving up.

I poured our coffee and watched Joan break open a biscuit with her fingers. She dabbed on some butter and inserted a piece of cheese. It pleased me to see her enjoying something that I had made especially for her. However, as she bit into it her face took on a look of true disgust.

"Ugh!" she said. "What is wrong with these biscuits? They taste awful!" She spat the half-chewed piece into her paper napkin and then grabbed my napkin and used it to wipe her tongue. She then dashed for the sink, quickly filled a glass with water, swished a mouthful of it, and spat it out. She repeated this process several times, accompanying the performance with sounds like "Ack," "Yuk," and "Blah!" along with several rounds of mopping her tongue with a paper towel until whatever she was tasting faded away.

I quickly sampled a bit of the biscuit on my plate and it was fine. Then it dawned on me. Perhaps her newly treated shoe-laces had not been quite dry when she put them on today. If that were the case, then some of the dog-repellant compound could have transferred onto her fingers when she tied her shoes. Since I knew that she came directly from dressing to the table, it was likely that some of that noxious-tasting compound might still have been on her hands. I like to use a muffin tin to make biscuits since it gives them some shape and they come out a bit more moist. The biscuit was fresh from the oven, hot and steamy. The steam and even some perspiration from her fingers could have been enough to reliquefy the compound and allow it to be transferred to the biscuit, causing it to taste bad enough to ward off even a hungry dog, let alone a woman with very sensi-tive tastebuds.

My problem now was how could I get Joan to clean her hands without revealing what I had done and in the process opening the issue of a new pattern of misconduct by Flint? I quickly improvised—to be more accurate, I quickly devised a string of lies to cover for my dog (and me).

"Oh, I used an old sack of flour, from the back of the cup-board for the biscuits. I thought that it was okay, but maybe somehow it had gone bad or rancid. We have a new unopened sack. I'll make you a new batch of biscuits. Could you wash the muffin tin for me while I mix them up?"

Joan tossed the offending bit of food into the trash can and went to the sink to clean the muffin tin that I used when I made biscuits. "Use lots of soap and water to make sure that there is no residue that might flavor this batch," I added.

I watched her run soapy water over the muffin pan and in the process over her hands, removing any trace of dog-repellant from her fingers. Rather than waste the perfectly good first batch of biscuits, I quietly set them aside to be Flint's dinner. Joan agreed that the second batch of biscuits tasted fine. My secret dog behavior modification scheme remained undetected and Flint avoided having another item added to my wife's growing list of his delinquencies. The noxious-tasting compound did work, because the epidemic of untied shoelaces disappeared from our lives, but I never got to see Flint's reaction to the foul-tasting shoelace. I was quite sure, however, that Joannie had acted out a very creditable version of what his response must have been when she encountered the repellant-tainted biscuit.

🐾 🐾 🐾

The shoelace incident convinced me that I had best get that second dog quickly before Flint invented another form of misbehavior that would get Joan to focus on him again. The dog I felt that Joannie needed had to be a kind of "love sponge," emotionally supportive and loveable in a way that Flint would never be for her. This fit the description of a Cavalier King Charles spaniel, which is a toy breed. Although very popular in the United Kingdom, the breed was then relatively unknown in North America.

Small companion dogs have been around for a long time. The dog I was hoping to get first made its appearance in sixteenth-century England, and is recorded as being a "spaniell gentle, otherwise called *Comforter*." These little dogs were favorites of the British Royal House of Stuart—Charles II in particular.

Tradition has it that Charles kept one or two of his dogs with him at all times. One day, as the king was about to enter the House of Lords, the Sergeant at Arms informed him that the dogs could not accompany him. "Only lords may enter, my liege" he stated. The king promptly issued a decree conveying a hereditary title upon his dogs, making all of their breed members of the peerage. Not only does that entitle them access to the House of Lords, but also to all public and government places. Also, in theory since the decree has never been revoked, if a Cavalier King Charles spaniel were to scratch at the gates of Buckingham Palace, by tradition, it must be granted entry.

These dogs became so popular among the aristocracy and prosperous families that that were casually referred to as "royal spaniels." They appear in numerous paintings spanning the sixteenth through eighteenth centuries, and were the subjects of such well-known artists as Titian, Van Dyck, Gainsborough, and Reynolds, among others. Over time they began to be considered more of a lady's dog. To emphasize that role, they were crossed with pugs and some other toy breeds to produce a smaller dog with a dome-shaped head, low-set ears, a much shorter muzzle, and a pushed-up nose. This is the breed that is currently known as the English toy spaniel in the United States and as the King Charles spaniel elsewhere.

In the early part of the twentieth century Roswell Eldridge went from New York to England looking for toy spaniels that resembled those he had seen in some of the old paintings. He specifically liked the look of the dogs in the 1845 painting by Sir Edwin Landseer, *The Cavalier's Pets,* but all he could find were the newer versions that he referred to as "short-faced Charlies." Rather than give up on his quest, he offered a large prize for the best examples of the old-style dog, which resulted in the "reestablishment" of the breed. It would now be called the Cavalier King Charles spaniel, incorporating the name of the breed's most ardent patron and giving some recognition to Landseer's painting.

🐾 🐾 🐾

Fortunately, a well-respected breeder of cavaliers was less than an hour's drive from my home. After I'd made arrangements, I drove Joannie out to Katie's home to pick up our new dog. I lifted him out of the pen and placed the little white-and-chestnut-colored pup in Joan's arms and watched her melt into a smile and a sigh.

Katie said, "I call him Wizard. His kennel name is Turnworth

Winter Wizard. The Winter part is because he has so much white on him."

"Wizard will do perfectly well as a name," I said, glancing across to Joannie who acknowledged the fact that she was paying attention to our conversation by bending over the puppy and whispering, "Hi, little Wizard," in a soft singsong voice.

I handed her his collar, and she gently slipped it over his head and murmured, "Don't you look handsome now."

It was a good start. Of course, Joan's first encounter with Flint had been all love and warmth as well, but this was a different dog with a different temperament. For the 45-minute drive home Joan sat in the car with Wizard on her lap. She said little but smiled a lot. As we rolled up to the front of our house, she suddenly lost her happy look and, with a voice full of anxiety, asked, "What about Flint?"

"What do you mean?"

"He kills small furry things!"

"It will be okay," I reassured her. "Remember the kittens that he saved. All young mammals have a scent, a pheromone, that clings to them and brings out the protective instincts in other animals."

Although I was convinced that nothing bad would happen, Joan's concerns did make me more vigilant as we entered the house and I placed Wizard on the floor. Joan grabbed at my left hand and squeezed it tightly.

Flint stood about 3 feet away from us and stared at this fuzzy apparition. His tail was high and vibrating, and he approached with a stiff-legged walk. As he drew closer, I could feel Joan's hand clench harder.

Wizard stood watching the approach of the gray dog. A few seconds later he assessed the situation and responded as puppies always do when confronted with a threat—he collapsed to the floor and rolled over on his side. Flint arrived next to him and moved his nose over his inert little body. I could imagine his thoughts.

"*What is this? It looks like something that I should chase, but it smells like a dog.*"

"This is Wizard," I announced. "He is your new brother. Treat him well."

Flint seemed to ignore me, but he lowered himself to the floor next to the pup. A minute later Wizard slowly rolled onto his belly. Our new puppy then tentatively sniffed at Flint's nose, and his tongue came out as if he were licking at the air. Flint stood up, gave a shake as if he had just come out of the water, and turned and started to move toward the kitchen. Without any hesitation, Wizard trotted after him with his tail swinging back and forth. I smiled and dropped his light little leash and let him drag it behind him. Joannie finally let go of my hand and gave an audible sigh of relief.

A few moments later we found the two dogs licking simultaneously from the water bowl on the floor. "I think that they'll be fine now," I said. I looked down at my left hand—the one that Joan had been holding—and noticed that she had been squeezing it with so much pressure that her nails had actually cut into my palm leaving a visible trickle of blood.

🐾 🐾 🐾

A few hours later Joan went off to do some shopping and I was sitting on the sofa reading some research material. I had placed Wizard beside me, and Flint had also jumped up onto the furniture to lie with his head near my leg. Time passed and both dogs fell asleep. Wizard had dozed off while sucking on the tip of one of Flint's pointed ears. I couldn't help smiling. My "great gray hunter" was clearly not going to be a threat to my new puppy.

As if he heard me thinking, Flint opened one eye and a silly voice said, "*This is embarrassing, Hui Shih, the Gray Lion, is now reduced to being a babysitter for a wimpy puppy.*"

"A royal spaniel," I corrected him.

Flint moved his head slightly to look at me and his ear slipped out of Wizard's mouth. The pup did not wake but groped a bit until he found the ear again and continued to mouth it. My terrier sighed, closed his eyes, and returned to sleep without further comment.

CHAPTER 19

TERRIER AND TEACHER

The easiest way to turn a puppy into a civilized dog is to bring it into a home where there is already a dog who knows the routines. This cuts the effort required to housebreak and train by more than half. As a puppy, Wizard watched Flint's every movement and imitated his behavior. When I put Flint out the back door to relieve himself, Wizard galumphed along behind him, watched him, and then emptied himself just a few feet away. When I called the dogs to give them a treat and commanded them to sit, Wizard watched and imitated Flint's responses. I never really had to teach the puppy the meaning of the words "come," "sit," "down," "let's go," and "stay." Wiz understood the basic commands, responded perfectly when Flint was next to him, and more slowly and hesitantly when he was not. A few rewards for giving the correct response to each of these commands when his gray teacher was not around were all it took to for him to add a bit more precision to his performance.

There was, however, an unexpected problem. Whenever I called Flint, Wizard would respond as well. At first I thought that Wiz was simply learning the meaning of the word "come," but I began to worry that he was beginning to respond as though he believed that his name was Flint. I believe that a dog's name is the single most important word that he will ever learn. A dog lives in an ocean of human sounds and, with only the language ability of a human two-year-old, he has to decide which words are directed at him and which are not. Suppose I had said to Joannie, "Why don't you come over and sit down?" when one of my dogs was in the room. How is my dog supposed to know whether or not the words "come," "sit," and "down" in my request to Joan were really meant for him?

Dogs are masters at interpreting body language, so mine can often figure out who I am speaking to based on what I am doing as I speak. Obviously, if am looking directly into a dog's eyes and have his full attention, he knows that I mean for him to respond to "sit" or "down." In the absence of that sort of body language, however, the dog's name becomes the key to his understanding, in effect, a signal that tells him "This next message is for you."

All of my dogs have several names. The least important of them is their official name that is registered with the kennel club and appears on their pedigree certificate, since it is never used in everyday interactions and is usually long and pompous, for instance, Remasia's Our Man Flint. Instead, I use a short, familiar name as the dog's "call name." I don't like to use human names for my dogs because it can be confusing when you call for or give instructions to Fred the dog and one of your visitors or family is also named Fred.

Since there are many times when I want to communicate with both dogs simultaneously, I also need a group name for my dogs. For example, a friend who only has male dogs uses "Gentlemen" when signaling his all-boy collection, while Emma from our club had only female dogs and referred to them as "Ladies." Another friend, a retired army tank corps officer, uses the group name "Troops," while one of Joan's former teacher friends uses "Class" as the group name for her three little lap dogs. I decided to use the word "Puppies" as an alternate name for my dogs, so that when I call, "Puppies, come," all of my dogs should run to me.

Flint was already used to name changes and additions, since I often spoke to him using casual labels as names, like "Scamp," "Gray Warrior," and "Gray Person," when I was talking to him. Ultimately Wizard would respond to "Wizard," "Wizzy," "Wizzer," "Wiz," and "Snarf."

To help Wiz learn his name better, every time that I touched him or petted him I would repeat his name. I also added a little ritual to my life. First thing in the morning, I would get down on the floor and sing a song to my dogs. It was a bad variation of a few lines of the old standard "You Are My Sunshine." Starting with Wizard I would focus my attention solely on him and sing

You are my Wizard, my only Wizard
You make me happy when skies are gray.
You'll never know, Wiz, how much I love you
So please don't take my Wizard away.

I would then turn to Flint and substitute his name, for all of the occurrences of Wizard giving him my full attention. These efforts seemed to do the job. After a while I simply had to say his name and Wizard would look directly at me, and if I told him to stay and then called Flint to me, Wiz would remain in place.

I know that my sitting on the floor singing to my dogs to teach the puppy his name sounds weird, but an online survey (where people could answer anonymously) found that 41 percent of responders admitted that they sometimes sang to their dogs. Of those who did sing to their dogs, 92 percent said that they never mentioned it to anyone in their family nor allowed anyone to hear them. Joan had already overheard me sometimes speaking to, and answering for, Flint, so I doubted that her overhearing me singing to my dogs would further weaken her impression of my sanity. On the other hand, given the nature of my own singing voice and my inability to carry a tune, I felt that it would be a kindness to keep Joan from being subjected to my "musical" performance. Nonetheless, one morning when she had awakened and gone downstairs before me, I was sitting on the bedroom floor singing my little "name song" to the dogs when I was interrupted by Joan's voice coming from the base of the stairs.

"Are you all right?" she asked, with concern in her voice.

"Yes, I'm fine."

"I was worried," she replied. "I thought that I heard you moaning in pain."

When she moved away, Flint's voice added, *"I'll bet that being forced to listen to your singing could be classified as animal abuse."*

🐾 🐾 🐾

Wizard modeled many of his behaviors after Flint. When Flint would scratch at the door to be let back into the house, Wiz soon followed suit. When his water bowl was empty, Flint would noisily push it across the floor to attract my attention so that I would fill it. Wiz didn't quite understand the rationale behind this behavior, but dutifully imitated it, nonetheless. He would push the water bowl over a distance of around 3 feet from its normal place so that it would end up directly in front of the stove or the refrigerator—and then he would carefully push it back to its original spot. Since he was imitating Flint rather than thinking for himself, it made no difference to him whether the bowl was empty or full, and the wet trails of puddles and splashes on the floor were beginning to annoy Joan. So, using my favorite dictum—that technological solutions are often better and faster than behavioral solutions—I simply replaced the metal water bowl with a heavy plastic one with a rubber ring at the bottom that a small puppy could not slide across the floor. Flint seemed to like having the puppy follow him around, and ultimately became quite protective of him. One weekend day, when we were out at the farm, Joan had gone to town to pick up something that would help her plan the new house. I was sitting on the rickety deck that the back door of the "shack" opened out onto. The dogs were wandering around outside, which I allowed since the area was fenced with an orange plastic mesh that was quite adequate to contain two small dogs who never seemed to be that interested in escaping.

The dogs liked to sniff around the outside of the little house, and Flint had shown Wizard where Joanie planted several varieties of mint and some herbs, including lemon thyme, that were quite tasty and that they would gently nibble at. Joannie did not like it when the dogs browsed through her herb garden, but they didn't eat all that much, and the herbs gave their breath a refreshing scent.

I was not paying much attention to the dogs, since I was reading a technical journal and was quite engrossed in some new data. But when I heard Flint give a small growl, I looked up just in time to see a raccoon drop into the yard from a low branch of the willow tree at the far end of the garden. This masked intruder lightly hit the ground, lowered himself slightly, and in a catlike manner appeared to stalk Wizard. The puppy, who had been lying down, simply turned his head and stared at him, apparently frozen. Flint was several feet away and made a mad dash that placed him directly between the raccoon and Wizard. Now Flint's growl had dropped in pitch and become low, sustained, and guttural.

It took several moments for what was happening to register in my brain. Raccoons are omnivorous and eat nuts, berries, insects, and grubs, but nearly one-third of their diet is obtained by hunting birds and mammals. Raccoons regularly kill squirrels, rats, and rabbits. To a raccoon, a 5- or 6-pound puppy could be a target much like a rabbit. This large raccoon, perhaps 20 pounds or more, was clearly equal in weight to Flint and with his fur fluffed out looked larger than my dog. Nonetheless, Flint stood his ground between the predator and the cringing puppy. His growl continued to rumble deeply, broken by bursts of two or three barks, which was his alarm call. "Call the pack! There is trouble here! The barbarians are at the gate!"

When I realized what was happening, I jumped up and grabbed a broom that was leaning against the wall. The word "rabies," popped into my mind, and I was worried that this raccoon was out in the afternoon rather than his usual dawn or twilight because he was crazed due to rabies. The broom no longer seemed like much of weapon against a potentially infected predator, so I looked around for something else. The raccoon made a noise that sounded much like the hiss of a cat, even above Flint's barrage of barks and growls. The rifle in the house was too far away to be of any value, so I grabbed an empty bucket and began to beat it with the handle of the broom. It made a great ringing clamor to which I added by yelling "Back! Back! Back!" in the deepest voice that I could muster.

The noise, my approach, and Flint's threats convinced the raccoon that there must be safer ways to find dinner. He turned and scampered back to the tree, where he crouched on a low branch, staring at us. I continued to approach, beating on the bucket and shouting, while Flint raced forward to stand beside me, adding a cascade of barks to the din. The raccoon looked down from the branch, and with what looked like an attempt at a dignified retreat crossed to the other side of the tree and jumped off well outside the fenced area. He then trotted off at less than a gallop.

I turned to Flint, "Good job, my gray warrior!"

I bent down to pat my heroic dog, and he was quivering. He looked up at me for a moment, and said, in a bad imitation of

Humphrey Bogart, *"Well, the kid seemed to need some help. He really doesn't know the ropes yet. He didn't even bark! I've got to work on that. A dog who doesn't bark can't defend himself or anybody else."* Then he gave a brief wag of his tail and trotted over to Wizard, who was still huddling down and had not moved an inch during the entire episode. Flint licked the puppy's face and moved to his side to give him a poke with his nose. Wiz slowly rose to his feet, and his tongue darted out once or twice to lick the air in front of Flint's face.

Wiz was so young, yet he clearly had to say something. I was surprised to hear how soft, gentle, and composed his voice turned out to be as he first spoke to Flint, *"Thanks. I owe you one—Boss!"* He then turned to look at me and gave a hesitant wag of the tail, *"You too—Sir!"*

Wiz would eventually "talk to me" as much as Flint did, but always in that same soft, composed voice, whereas Flint's voices changed with the mood of the conversation and the nature of the events happening around us. Conversations with Wiz would seldom contain the level of satire, irony, or argumentation that conversations with Flint did. Wizard acted as if he had only one gear in his transmission: he always worked at the same speed, always had a calm disposition, and always talked in my mind with that same gentle and respectful tone that was born the day the raccoon attempted to invade and the heroic Gray Knight, Sir Flint, stood at the battlements to protect his endangered charge.

"Puppies, let's go get a treat," I offered, and we all entered the safety of the little shack. I never did like being outdoors in the country. Give me the comfort of the city and God's good concrete.

🐾 🐾 🐾

Fortunately, for the peacefulness of my house and marriage, Flint never did teach Wizard to bark. Over his entire lifespan, I heard Wiz bark fewer than a dozen times. It is not that he failed

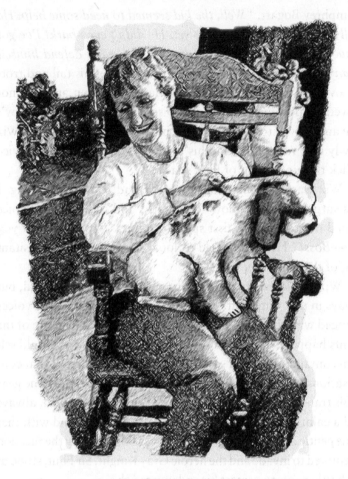

*The surprise was that Joan was sitting on the rocking chair,
with Wizard on her lap.*

to pay attention to situations that Flint felt warranted barking.
When Flint would race to the door to bark at some sound, Wizard would follow along staring in the direction that Flint was looking. If Flint would jump up on the window seat to bark at something he saw through the glass, Wizard would look over his shoulder to check out what had caused his housemate to sound the alarm, but he would never join in.

Occasionally, Flint would look behind to where Wizard was standing. He seemed to be saying, "*Come on, Pup. I'm showing you how it's done and when it needs to be done, so bark already!*"

Apparently, the message just passed over Wizard's head, since when Flint turned to look back, Wizard would also turn to look back to see what Flint was now looking at. The idea of barking never seemed to occur to him.

Wiz, however, did accomplish something without either Flint's or my instruction. One evening I returned home to find Joan lying on the sofa, asleep. Resting on the crook of her arm was Wizard. I smiled and quietly went into the kitchen to begin to cook dinner without waking her.

Later on, when we were sitting and eating, I said to her, "I thought that dogs weren't allowed on the furniture when you were using it."

"They certainly are not," she insisted.

"When I came in tonight, Wiz was sleeping next to you on the sofa."

She looked down somewhat sheepishly and explained it away saying, "He must have sneaked up there after I was already asleep."

A month or so later I came home to find Karen, Joan's daughter, sitting on the sofa petting Flint, who was resting his head in her lap. Joan and Kari were engaged in some kind of mother-daughter conversation that seemed to involve knitting or sewing. The surprise was that Joan was sitting on the rocking chair with Wizard on her lap.

I didn't want to disturb this lovely scene, so I simply greeted them both and offered to open a bottle of wine. Wiz seemed to be having the desired calming effect on the woman I loved.

CHAPTER 20

CAIRN OR CAN'T

ow I had two dogs to train and two dogs to compete with in obedience trials. The early part of Wizard's training was easy, since he had learned most of his basic commands from simply modeling his behavior after Flint's. When he was only about 14 months of age, I put him into his first real obedience competition, and that weekend he earned two qualifying scores. A month later, in another competition, Wiz earned a final qualifying score and his Companion Dog (CD) degree. Working with Flint and my continuing study of dog behavior and training techniques clearly helped speed Wizard's learning.

Meanwhile, I was training Flint for his next degree in *Open Competition*, which leads to a more advanced title, something like a high school degree for dogs. Training at this level is much more exciting because the dog must work completely off leash and he has a variety of interesting tasks to perform, such as retrieving and jumping a high jump and a broad jump. You can teach a dog to jump in a number of ways, but the easiest involves showing him another dog jumping and then encouraging him to join in. In the same way that Wiz was modeling his behavior after Flint, Flint needed someone to model his behavior after. Since Flint focused his attention on me, I had to become the model.

We started with a high jump, which is just a wooden barrier that the dog has to vault over. Initially the jump that I asked him to make wasn't very high, about 4 inches or so. I put Flint on leash, gave a happy "Flint, let's go!" and ran to the jump. As we reached it, I gave the command "Flint, jump!" and I made an exaggerated jump over the low barrier with Flint jumping right beside me. I then raised jump and we repeated our side-by-side jump, now without the leash. This process continued until ultimately Flint and I were simultaneously going over the jump set somewhat higher than Flint's shoulder height.

Flint liked this game and was soon answering my command to jump with a single happy bark, followed by a charge forward toward the jump. Next I had Flint sit facing the jump while I went to the other side. I now called "Flint, jump!" and tapped the barrier with my hand. It did not take a second try. My gray dog answered with that happy bark and leapt over the high jump and then proceeded to circle me several times in excitement.

Another type of jump is the broad jump, which is made up of a series of horizontally arranged boards low in height but covering a wide area—twice the dog's height at the shoulder—that he must leap over. The basic training procedure was the same, with me modeling the behavior and going over the jump with Flint. The big difference was that just after we reached his full jumping length and I went over it with him, I tripped and fell in such a way that the boards scattered noisily on either side of me causing Flint to yelp in surprise and leap back from the site of the accident. He stood there staring at the white boards and grumbling to himself while I painfully picked myself up and rearranged the jump to Flint's jumping length and hobbled back to the starting place.

I was hurting a bit but felt it was important to work through any problems that might arise as the result of my clumsiness, which had clearly startled Flint. "Okay, let's try that again. Flint, jump!" I called to him and painfully vaulted over the broad jump only to see my dog run around it giving the white boards a wide berth. I could hear him in my mind saying, *"Those boards tried to leap up and bite me. I'm not taking a chance on them again! I saw what they did to you!"*

Flint contemplates the broad jump.

Back in the early part of the twentieth century the psychologist John B. Watson showed that if you show a baby a white furry animal and then simultaneously produce a loud, unexpected sound that frightens the baby, the child will learn to be afraid—not only of that animal, but of anything with white fur. In effect, the child has been taught to be afraid of something that he was not afraid of before.

I was now faced with a similar situation. Clearly, Flint had become anxious about jumping over the broad jump. I tried reducing the width of the jump, but he still shied away from it and would not jump with me. He wouldn't even jump over a single board when I called him or tried to lure him with a treat. This meant that I needed some motivation that was stronger than his fear. It dawned on me that his hunting and chasing instincts might work in this instance.

I went to my equipment bag and pulled out a small squeaky toy. It was a fuzzy pillow-shaped object about the size of a tennis ball that made a high squeaking sound when it was squeezed. This was one object that Flint loved to chase and "kill." I then took some long pieces of wood and made a sort of tight corridor with the broad jump in the middle. The pieces of wood, although low, would discourage my dog from going around the jump. Then back to the starting place in front of the jump.

"Hey, Flint! Look at this!" I waved his toy excitedly and made it squeak a few times. "Do you want it? Yeah, you want it!" followed by more squeaking. At this point Flint was dancing around with excitement. I then tossed the toy so that it fell just in front of the jump.

Flint dashed out, grabbed the toy, and brought it back to me, squeaking all the way. I repeated the procedure, only this time I tossed the toy so that it landed over the first board of the jump. Flint again dashed out, hesitated a moment at the board but leapt over, grabbed the toy, leapt back over the board, and returned to me.

This was going well, so I lengthened the throw and the toy went completely over the jump. There was a bit more hesitation this time, but Flint wanted that toy enough that he pushed away his fear and made the jump. With the toy in his mouth squeaking loudly, he jumped back and returned to me. We repeated this a few times with me calling "Jump!" just as he went over. Now I felt that we were ready to try a more formal version of the broad jump again.

Back to the starting point with the leash on him: "Flint, let's go!" and then "Jump!" as I leapt over the boards. I turned to watch my dog only to see that he had stalled in front of the jump and was looking at me with his ears lowered in a fearful manner. I could hear him saying, *"There's no toy for me to hunt and kill out there, and I'm not going to risk my life by going over this monster for nothing."*

I sighed but then had an idea how to continue Flint's "therapy." When he was not looking, I dropped the toy between the boards. This time I let him watch me make the jump while asking him to accompany me—which he did not do. But once on the other side, I picked up the toy and started to make it squeak while I danced around singing, "It's mine. I made the jump, so the toy is mine."

Flint approached hopefully, but I didn't give him the toy. Again when he was not looking I hid the toy—this time near the far end of the jump, just barely out of sight. Again I made the jump alone and snatched up the toy, happily waving and squeaking it. Flint was excited now.

Finally, with the toy again hidden at the far end of the jump, I went back to Flint, attached his leash, and asked "Do you want the toy?" then with a command to go and another to jump, I went over the boards. This time he jumped with me. As a reward I let him find the toy and play with it for a few moments.

Although I had broken through his fear of the jump, another problem presented itself, which was the direct result of the method that I used to solve his fear. This is the bane of psychology: every form of therapy has the potential for not only curing problems but also for triggering others that eventually have to be dealt with as well. Flint was happily going over the jump, beginning with his single bark of joy, but in his mind he had come to suspect that there was always going to be a toy hidden near or in the broad jump. In competition, once the dog completes the broad jump, he is supposed to circle back and sit in front of his handler, who is standing next to the boards. Flint was now making the broad jump, but was then immediately stopping to check around under each of the boards for his squeaky toy.

I had to do a quick fix, so next when he went over the jump, and while he was still in the air, I tossed the squeaky toy in the direction he was going. When he landed, he continued moving forward and grabbed the toy happily. I could then call him back to sit in front of me. Flint had now come to love this exercise because it seemed like play to him and he would indicate how happy he was by making excited up-and-down pitter-patting movements with his front paws while he waited for the command to jump. At that point I knew that his brain was filled with little more than *"Where's my toy? Let me at it!"*

All that remained was to phase out the toy; but here, too, I ended up with a problem that is typical in older dogs and common in virtually all terriers, regardless of age. It is generally easy to teach a dog something new, but once he's learned to do a task in a certain way, it can be difficult for him to learn to do it differently. I'd trained away Flint's fear that the jump boards would leap up and bite him by teaching him that a chance to play with a toy was associated with the jump. In competition there would be no toy, so I had to phase out its use. But when I tried to replace the toy with a treat after he completed the jump, it wasn't as much fun, so there were times when he would suddenly revert back to what he learned first and start searching the area for his toy after taking the jump rather than returning to me.

🐾 🐾 🐾

Eventually, Flint was reliable enough to compete in obedience trials, but occasionally his early experiences with the broad jump would swamp his mind. For example, in one competitive trial Flint had performed splendidly and all that remained was the broad jump. As we stood in front of it, I began to worry when I saw him doing an excited pitter-patting with his paws, which meant that he was in his "chase the toy" mode.

"Just one more exercise, my puppy. Focus! We're almost there," I said hopefully.

At the command to jump, Flint gave his happy bark and then hurdled over the broad jump. When he landed he spun around. He was clearly searching for his squeaky toy. He then looked straight in front of him and dashed out of the ring. Before the ring steward or I could respond, he reappeared carrying a small terrycloth hand towel that one of the other competitors must have used when grooming a dog. With the blue-and-white towel in his mouth, he ran directly to me, snapped the towel back and forth a few times, then sat down. I knew what he was saying: *"Hey, it doesn't squeak, but it's better than nothing."*

Running out of the ring is an automatic failure in an obedience trial. The judge for this trial was known for having a good sense of humor, however, and also understood terriers, since his wife worked with Manchester terriers. He walked over to me, laughed, and then, as if ringing the bell at the close of a boxing match, said, "Ding! Ding! Ding! It appears that your dog has thrown in towel. Sorry, you're out."

🐾 🐾 🐾

Teaching Flint to retrieve was a different problem, since terriers are not natural retrievers. They will chase things, but reliably picking up objects and bringing them back on command is not natural for them. I decided to use what psychologists call shaping or rewarding successive approximations, where you gradually build up the behavior that you want in a step-by-step sequence. The object that Flint would eventually have to retrieve was a wooden dumbbell, so I started by holding a dumbbell in front of Flint as he sat in front of me and telling him, "Flint, take it." Then immediately but gently I rolled it into his mouth and said, "Hold it," while keeping my hand under his chin to keep him from spitting it out. Finally, I told him "Give" and took it from his mouth, then told him "Yes!" and gave him a treat. We repeated this steps many times. After a while I would wait until he spontaneously opened his mouth before giving it to him. Next I held the dumbbell out in front of him, just an inch or two so he had to bend forward to take. Later, I gradually increased the distance so that he was bending down to take the dumbbell from a lower position, until he was picking it up from the floor. Eventually, I would put it down a foot or two in front of him so that he had to take a step, then further out where he had to run to pick it up, until finally I was tossing it 10 or 15 feet for him to go out and get. Each successful completion of part of the exercise ended in a bit of praise and a treat, so Flint liked the training.

Unfortunately, this is a slow process, especially with a terrier. It was not unusual for each step to take a dozen or so repetitions on any given day, and sometimes several days of practice before I could move to the next stage. I rigged my training sessions so that they would be in the evenings when Joan and I usually watched TV. During commercials or when the program had not caught my interest, I would sit on the floor and patiently go through parts of training the initial steps of the retrieving. "Take it" and I placed the dumbbell in his mouth, "Hold it," and finally the release "Give" where he dropped the dumbbell to trade for a treat. This early training took many evenings so it was, perhaps, not surprising when one evening Joan sat down on the sofa and looked at me on the floor getting ready to work with Flint and asked, "Is there anything worth watching on TV tonight—other than 'Take It—Hold it—and Give'?"

🐾 🐾 🐾

Flint eventually learned all of the obedience exercises, and he came to truly love the jumps and the retrieves. He expressed his pleasure the way that terriers express everything—with a bark. When I would send him out to retrieve a dumbbell, he would give an enthusiastic bark as he launched himself toward it, then the moment before he picked it up, he would look at me and give another bark. He would do that for the basic retrieve, where the dumbbell is simply brought back after it is tossed across the room, and also for the retrieve that sent him out and back over the high jump. In addition, he gave a launching announcement bark as he started his run to leap over the broad jump. Those barks, along with the wagging of his carrot-shaped tail, let me know that he was working happily and enjoying the competition and the training. It reassured me that he was not an automation doing my bidding without thinking, but rather a happy member of a team doing what he liked.

Unfortunately, not everyone recognized the joyous nature of my dog's performance. In one trial the judge came up to me as I was getting ready to leave the ring with Flint. I was feeling quite good and confident about his performance this day.

"You know that your dog was barely in control today," the judge said, looking down at my dog with some disdain.

"I'm sorry," I replied, feeling quite confused. "I thought that he was performing reasonably well."

"How can you say that, given all of that barking?" He looked at the sheet on his clipboard, and then continued, "By my count there were five barks. Any more and I probably would have dismissed you from the ring because your dog was not under control."

I was astonished and tried to explain, "He gives those short barks to tell me that he is enjoying himself and that he likes the exercise. He was never out of control."

"Your dog's emotional state is irrelevant. Each time he barks, a judge should deduct one point. That means that if you don't correct that behavior, you will start each competition effectively with five points already lost."

"He barks when he is happy. Should I make the work unpleasant for him in order to earn a few more points in trials?" I asked.

"He is here to do a job—not to have fun! With an attitude like yours, your dog will never amount to much as a competitor."

Looking at the unpleasant scowl on his face, I decided that I would never again enter a trial in which this person was judging. Although I was sure that it would make no difference, I felt that it was necessary to say something. So, as calmly as I could I told him, "Dog obedience is a sport—an entertainment. The day that it stops being fun for me or my dog, I will start looking for a different sport."

Flint and I then turned and walked out of the ring without waiting for a response.

Because God sometimes has a strange sense of humor, it was only a few days after this encounter in the obedience ring that I received a large envelope in the mail. It was a certificate from *Dogs in Canada,* the official publication of the Canadian Kennel Club, that announced that Flint was nationally ranked as the second highest-scoring Cairn terrier in obedience competition that year. I felt a surge of pride and wished I could roll back time to be able to wave this piece of paper in front of that judge, accompanied of course by some witty and cutting remarks about how fine a competitor Flint was turning out to be.

It was then that I looked at the certificate more closely and started to giggle. In the line where it lists Flint's official or kennel name, it should have read "Remasia's Our Man Flint." Instead, this handsome certificate had a misprint which designated him Remasia's Our Man Fling. I was laughing out loud when I held the certificate up to my dog to show him.

Flint was dancing around, as he always did when I laughed, and replied, *"You are always telling me that the elevator to my brain stops one floor short of the penthouse, so why shouldn't the Kennel Club spell my name one letter less than correctly?"*

Although Joan suggested that I return the certificate and have a properly spelled one drawn up so that I could have an accurate document indicating what we had achieved that year, I never did. Flint would never be perfect in competition, and I would never put pressure on him to be perfect, so this certificate was at least as perfect as Flint would ever be. For the next week or so, however, I found myself calling him Fling every now and then.

CHAPTER 21

BEGGING TO DIFFER

aving two dogs as different in their personalities as Flint and Wiz was fascinating to me professionally and personally. Flint was a classic terrier: active, bold, and inquisitive. He was the eternal warrior and hunter and looked at life as a challenge that he would live on his own terms regardless of the consequences.

Wiz was a gentle soul. His idea of a perfect day was to snuggle up to me or Joan when we were sitting on the sofa and to rest quietly. In obedience competition he exerted no more effort than was required. If he had to jump a 13-inch barrier, he would launch himself over it so that he cleared it by at most a quarter of an inch, as opposed to Flint, who would hurl himself far above it as if to inform anybody watching that he also could have jumped 24 inches just as easily.

A great deal of my psychological research involves trying to understand what makes one human different from another in his behavior. For that reason I have often studied groups of people who had different characteristics, such as left-handed people versus right-handers, people who sleep a lot versus those who sleep little, individuals whose births had complications,

and people whose vision or hearing is different from the norm.
These and other apparently minor differences often have significant effects on the way that people behave, their personalities,
learning abilities, and even how long they might live.

Dogs' different temperaments also affect how they learn.
Teaching Wizard to retrieve was no easier than teaching Flint.
While cocker, springer, Brittany or field spaniels all have a hunting and retrieving instinct, toy spaniels like the Cavalier King
Charles do not. The term *spaniel* does not relate to hunting.
The *span* in *spaniel* comes from the word Spain; the dogs were
identified as Spanish dogs even though none of the breeds originated in that country. The term was applied to them because, at
the time, people believed that the most romantic people in the
world came from Spain and so, because most spaniels are so
gentle and kissy, they were equated with Spanish lovers. I often
would hear the soft voice that I had given to Wizard explain to
me why he was resting while Flint was frantically scrambling
around the house on some mission, *"I suppose that someone has
to be on guard; however, I am a lover, not a hunter or a fighter.
It's a tough job being sweet all of the time, but I'm willing to
work at it."*

Flint's true nature was probably best displayed when I
decided to try to teach him to track, with some faint hope that
he might earn a tracking title. As a dog sport, tracking involves
the dog leading his handler over a scent trail that can be a quarter mile long or longer, and can have several turns with several
places where it is crossed by distracting false scents. A highly
recommended tracking instructor named Gary lived about a half
hour's drive south of the city, so I decided to enroll Flint in one
of his classes, held early on Sunday mornings. I took with me a
borrowed harness from Barbara Baker and a new 20-foot long
tracking leash, as well as a plastic bag containing a few hot dogs
thinly sliced into penny-sized disks. Flint had watched me slicing
them and so was hopeful when I took them with us in the car.

To begin the training I had to walk a track across a grassy
field while Flint waited in the car. The trail was marked with
flags so that we nasally weak humans would know where it
was. As I walked, I dropped small slices of wiener every few feet
along the track. The dog was to start by following its owner's
scent, and could pick up these treats if he stayed on course.

Flint caught on quickly. A happy voice announced, "*Ahh . . .
You dropped some hot dog slices. Now all I have to do is to follow your scent and I'll find them all! Watch me sniff. Here's
another bit. Hey, this is fun!*"

"Stan, did you say something?" Gary asked. "After you tell
him to 'Find it!' you should just let him do the tracking. Talking
to him might just distract him."

I was not sure that Gary would understand why I was talking to myself in my dog's voice, so I stopped.

The following Sunday morning the class assembled at
another field. This one was overgrown with very long grass and
weeds. Once again we tramped out a trail, each with two right-
angle turns marked by flags. Again we seeded the path with wiener slices, set a bit more widely apart this time.

I hooked the leash to Flint's harness, and he was giving his
little excitement dance with his front paws. "*It's the hot dog
game. I follow your scent and find all of the treats that you
dropped again!*"

This session started well enough. I gave Flint my scent by
pointing down to a patch of ground that I had tramped down
well, and waiting until he sniffed it. Then, at the command of
"Find it!" he dashed off down my trail, scooping up the wiener
slices that were spaced roughly five or six feet apart down the
track. We couldn't have been on the trail for more than three
or four minutes when a field rat appeared on the track right
in front of Flint, apparently attracted to the bits of hot dog.
Flint's brain went immediately into vermin hunter mode, and he
charged at the gray-brown rodent, which dashed into the high

grass with Flint after him. It was only a short chase. I felt the leash go slack, then jerk a couple of times, and when I finally reached my dog he was standing over a large, fat, and very dead rat. Flint's tail was wagging excitedly. *"All applaud the great hunter!"* announced a silly voice.

This incident really ended any hopes that I might have had of seeing Flint earn a tracking degree. The hunter instinct had been awakened in him, and now his mind was dominated by the idea that the tall grass might contain prey for him to stalk and kill. When I brought him back to the trail that we were supposed to be training on, he completely ignored my scent and was casting back from side to side in an attempt to spring anything else that might be alive in the dense cover. If he happened to cross the track in a place where there was a bit of wiener, he would snatch it off the ground and eat it but he would not return to the trail. Unfortunately, after 10 minutes of frustration while I tried to get him focused on tracking again, he once more plunged into the underbrush and again ran after something. I never knew what it was, since Flint hit the end of the leash before he could catch it, but this second chase confirmed in his mind that his task here was to hunt, not to track, and that ample numbers of vermin were present that could serve as his quarry.

Any chance of progress that day was lost, so I reeled Flint in, explained the situation to Gary, and suggested that it would be best for me to stop training for this session. I hoped that, given a week's time, Flint would return to the promising tracking behavior that he had shown the first day. It was not to be. The following week Flint again completely ignored my scent and all instructions pertaining to tracking. Instead, like a true hunting terrier, he began to cast from side to side through the high grass and suddenly froze in position and pushed his nose toward the ground. He clearly had picked up a scent, but not from my trail. He dashed some 15 feet forward following some kind of scent, and then began to dig frantically. A moment later he raised his head, gave a sideways snap, and showed me he'd caught a mole—now quite dead. This was the end of any hope of controlled tracking behavior for Flint. He was already dashing about looking for something new to hunt when I dragged him back to my side and explained to Gary that I doubted that it was worth our while to continue. Gary suggested that if I wanted to try again I was welcome, but Flint was convinced that any high grass was a hunting range, so I knew that this was a lost cause.

🐾 🐾 🐾

Perhaps one of the most telling differences between Flint and Wiz was their relationship to toys. Flint really did not play with toys except as part of interacting socially or stimulating his hunter instincts. If a toy was tossed to him he would chase it and when he caught it he would try to kill it (especially if it made a noise when it bounced or he bit into it), first by shaking it vigorously then by ripping it apart if he could. Toys that had appendages, like dolls with heads, arms, and legs, he simply dismembered.

This set of behaviors always made me laugh. *"I am the hunter—the king of terriers. Watch me destroy my prey! I am Flint the Ripper!"* he would tell me.

Joannie would hear this and sigh, "Please pick up the bits of stuffing from the toy when the king of terriers tears it apart," she would ask. "You know it's a waste of money buying plush toys for him and then letting him destroy them."

"That's why I only buy used toys," I said. I had found a store run by a local charity that had a big bin of used plush toys that sold for two or four for a dollar (depending upon their size), so that watching Flint destroy them in his game of "serial killer" caused little economic pain.

Wizard, however, was different. He did not play with toys, but rather collected them. If you tossed a toy for him, he would run after it, but when he reached it he would often turn around and return to me without retrieving it, or sometimes he would simply lie down on top of it. Certain toys, however, developed a special meaning for him and he would pick them up and walk off with them. There were around a dozen of these, including a small white wooly sheep, teddy bears of different sizes, a sable-colored rabbit, a green fuzzy dinosaur, and a small moose that was missing one antler (probably due to an earlier encounter with Flint). Wiz stashed these in a small pile in the corner of my office and would sleep on that heap when I was working, occasionally rearranging them or nosing one gently.

Flint and Wiz differed in their relationship to toys.

The importance of those toys for Wiz was clear from the fact that he would defend them from Flint. Wiz never confronted Flint over anything other than those toys. One confrontation was particularly interesting. Flint one day walked over to the pile of toys and lifted up Wizzer's fluffy white sheep. Wiz had just entered the room when he saw this and gave a single bark, startling both me and Flint because Wiz virtually never barked. Flint dropped the toy and Wiz raced to his possessions and stood over them staring directly into Flint's eyes in a direct threat.

I turned from my work and watched, fully expecting to hear a challenging growl from Flint and perhaps a threatening snap. But the two dogs just stood there—eyes locked on each other for many long seconds, until Flint, the "Great Fighter," "King of the Terriers," and "Killer of Toys," turned and with a stiff-legged walk, left the room. As Flint moved away, Wizard, the "Flop-Eared Love Sponge," lay down on the toys and silently watched. *"I don't ask for much,"* said Wizard's quiet voice, *"but these are mine!"*

Whatever passed between the dogs was significant, because although Flint would occasionally look in the direction of Wiz's possessions, he never again tried to walk off with any of them.

🐾 🐾 🐾

It was when I became sick again that I learned another difference between my dogs. Since acquiring the major infection that nearly killed me and contributed to the end of my first marriage, I have been left with an immune system that occasionally goes on strike. When it decides to close down operations, I get sick, often with a systemic infection of some sort. These infections can be quite severe and often worry my doctor again, but fortunately heavy-duty courses of antibiotics have managed to keep me alive until my immune system felt guilty and returned to its normal function. Whenever it is not working at full capacity, however, I can be rendered nonfunctional and can be in prolonged pain and discomfort.

This time the infection mainly affected on my respiratory system, and my breathing was labored. Fluid built up, so I coughed a lot. University classes were not in session, so I did not have to try to be a hero and stagger onto campus to give my lectures. Instead, I took my medication, drank lots of fluids, and tried to get as much sleep as possible to give my immune system a kick start.

Flint and Wiz both noticed my condition because of the disruption of their routine and usual walks. They both also seemed to sense my distress and, in their own ways, responded to it.

I was lying in bed, propped up by pillows, since that seemed to make breathing easier. I was dozing off again when something cold nudged my hand. I looked over the side of the bed, and there was Flint. He banged his nose against my hand several times, and when I finally made eye contact with him, he made a few quick steps toward the bedroom door. When I didn't respond, he repeated the process, this time adding a bark.

"Come on, lazy person. Out of bed! You've got dogs to entertain!" The words stayed in my head since I couldn't even muster enough energy to supply a voice for my dog at that moment. Flint tried once more with more vigorous barking. Finally, he jumped onto the bed and stared directly at me, then looked toward the door of the bedroom. *"Up and at it! Stop being sick!"* the silent voice said.

When I still did not move except to weakly pat his head, Flint slowly curved around my inert body and walked to the foot of the bed. He turned to face me and then lay down with his head on my ankle and gave a loud, dramatic sigh.

While all of this was going on, Wizard simply stood and watched, adding his comment in the form of a longing look toward the door. I wished that I had enough energy to respond to my dogs, but I simply felt too fatigued to do anything. I closed my eyes and must have drifted off to sleep.

Sometime later I was awakened by the sound of Joan coming up the stairs. I opened my eyes to see her come into the room.

"I thought that you were going to rest today," she said in a slightly disapproving voice.

"I am resting," I croaked in response.

"Then what is all of this?" she gestured toward me and the bed.

I looked down. Flint was still lying at my feet. Wiz had come onto the bed as well and was lying in the crook of my arm where he liked to sleep if he could get away with it. However, resting next to me and on top of my chest and stomach was a collection of plush toys. A wooly sheep, several teddy bears, a fuzzy green dinosaur, a moose that was missing one antler . . .

I looked into Wizard's big eyes. *"They make me feel better. Maybe it will work for you too,"* his quiet voice said in my head.

CHAPTER 22

THE INTELLIGENCE OF DOGS

My interest in the differences in the behavior and abilities of the various breeds of dogs has been ongoing for most of my life, although others have shared my fascination. Anyone who owns or loves dogs is bound to go on about the merits and intelligence of some breeds and the limitations of others. I've long collected comments that various people have made about the intelligence of different dog breeds, including TV newsman Peter Jennings's comment on the Malamute: "Their brain [is] like a piece of river rock"; veterinarian Michael Fox's comment on Irish setters: "They're so dumb that they get lost on the end of their leash"; author E. B. White on the dachshund: "Someday, if I ever get a chance, I shall write a book, or warning, on the character and temperament of the dachshund and why he can't be trained and shouldn't be. I would rather train a striped zebra to balance an Indian club than induce a dachshund to heed my slightest command"; or the comment on a TV show by a Los Angeles dog trainer to a woman who wanted to train her West Highland white terrier: "There's not much you can do with a terrier, ma'am."

I had been thinking of systematically ranking dog breeds by their intelligence for a long time, but even starting to define what we mean by intelligence in dogs turned out to be complicated. Eventually, my research showed that there are actually three different types or aspects of dog intelligence.

I labeled the first type of canine intelligence *instinctive intelligence*, which is simply what the dog was bred to do. Thus, retrievers retrieve, herding dogs herd, pointers point, terriers hunt small furry things, and some companion dogs (like Wizard) are bred to love and be empathetic.

The second type of dog intelligence is *adaptive intelligence*. It represents the dog's ability to solve problems and how well he learns, remembers, and benefits from his experiences. This can vary even in a single breed of dogs, so you might find that some Labrador retrievers are brilliant and clever and that some are no brighter than cows. To determine the adaptive intelligence of a dog, you have to test the individual dog. It took me about a year to develop a set of tests for adaptive intelligence in dogs. This is actually a very short time in terms of most research projects, but the work went quickly because I had a shortcut: namely a number of tests that had been designed to measure the intelligence and mental development of young human children, which I adapted and modified for dogs. From these tests it became clear that, in many ways, the average dog's mind is equivalent to that of a human child age two to two-and-a-half years. That one insight explains a lot about dog behavior.

The final form of dog intelligence is *working and obedience intelligence*, which is what the dog can learn to do—the dog's trainability. In humans, this would be the equivalent of how well you do in school.

I had wanted to use the test that I had developed to measure the intelligence of the various dog breeds and combine this with another measure of trainability. Unfortunately, with around 160 breeds registered with the American Kennel Club, the need to test 10 or so of each type would be prohibitively expensive in costs and time.

Fortunately, there were people who already had the information that I needed—namely the people who judge dog obedience competitions. These dog judges are trained to observe and evaluate how dogs perform under controlled conditions. It is not unusual for a judge to spend 10 to 20 hours on any given weekend judging and scoring dogs of various breeds. Because of their extensive experience watching and evaluating dogs, they were bound to have accumulated knowledge about the relative performance of various dog breeds.

To gather data from this group of professionals I first obtained the lists of judges from the American and Canadian kennel clubs and then sent out questionnaires to every dog obedience judge in North America. The questionnaire was fairly long and complicated, and asked the judges to rate each of the dog breeds on several aspects of their intelligence and which specific breeds they would rate as the 10 most intelligent and the 10 least intelligent breeds. To my amazement, 208 experts— approximately half of all the obedience judges listed in North America—responded to my request. Of these, 199 provided complete information in all sections of the questionnaire. In addition, about one-quarter of the judges added letters and notes, many of which contained insights into the way dogs think. Some even added extra statistical data that helped me adjust the placement of particular breeds. Finally, after my preliminary analyses, I telephoned about two dozen of the obedience judges for follow-up interviews that allowed me to clarify some issues and sharpen my interpretation of the data.

All of this work eventually became the basis for my first book about dogs, *The Intelligence of Dogs*, which, in addition to discussing how dogs think, also provided the ranking of the working and obedience intelligence of the 110 dog breeds for whom the obedience judges had provided adequate data. I expected that many people would be interested in the book, but I did not expect all hell to break loose.

🐾 🐾 🐾

The book's publication ignited a massive press response. The whole list that ranks dog breeds by intelligence was printed on the front page of the newspaper *USA Today* and in the lifestyle and science sections of many other papers. The owners of the top-ranked dogs—including the border collie, poodle, German shepherd, golden retriever, Doberman pinscher, Shetland sheepdog, and Labrador retriever—all felt that they had bragging rights. The owners of dogs like the Afghan hound, Basenji, and bulldog, which were judged the least intelligent breeds, were hostile and defensive. I can't tell you how many television and radio reports of my work began with the once popular children's song "My Dog's Smarter Than Your Dog." And I suddenly found myself appearing on virtually all of the television shows that have talk and interview segments such as *Oprah, Larry King Live, Charlie Rose,* and many national morning and evening magazine and news shows.

Joannie became increasingly uncomfortable with my public exposure, feeling that her own privacy was being violated even though the majority of my appearances involved me traveling alone to studios in other cities. She also worried about my decorum during these appearances. One day after I returned home, I found her fuming. In a clipped voice she said, "I just got a phone call from one of my friends, and she said that she saw you on *Oprah* and you were barking! You were demonstrating different dog barks by barking at the camera. I am so embarrassed and humiliated. How can I maintain any sense of dignity if my friends know that my husband was barking on national television?"

I tried to explain: "Joannie, I was talking about the sounds that dogs make. I didn't have any tape clips with those sounds, but those kinds of barks are simple and easy to mimic. I gave some examples of the various barks so that people could understand what I was talking about and so that they could learn how dogs communicate."

"So if you want to talk about how dogs use urine to mark their territory and send messages are you going to pee in front of everybody on national television?" she asked.

Joan came from a family where she had been taught to be quiet and discrete, modest, unobtrusive, no matter what the situation might be. In my family, however, storytelling and clear communication were important. If you had to jump up on a table and pretend to be a monkey doing a ballet in order to make the story more interesting or the make the point that you were trying to get across more understandable, then to not dance on the table would be a violation of proper behavior. Given an irresolvable conflict like this, I chose to retreat, grabbed a pair of leashes, and took my dogs out for an hour-long walk, hoping that Joan's anger would have burned out by the time I got home again.

🐾 🐾 🐾

Eventually, as I feared might happen, the media coverage made its way to my home. The first such was NBC Television's *Dateline*. They sent a crew to film me testing and interacting with dogs. They also wanted to meet my own dogs and asked if they could do some of the filming in my home. Joan would be very uncomfortable having a TV crew there, but she would be teaching and away for most of the day, so I somewhat reluctantly agreed with the idea that part of the segment would be shot in my house, with the proviso that the area must be cleaned up and back to normal before the time Joan normally returned. The

The camera kept slipping so the crew kept adding additional straps and strips of duct tape.

crew descended upon my tiny house and filled my living room with lights, sound equipment, and cameras.

In order to show a dog's-eye view of what it looks like being trained by a human, the crew had a "doggy-cam," a small camera that could be strapped to a dog's head to film what he was seeing. We had made the decision to use Wizard for this segment simply because his head was somewhat broader and flatter, which made strapping on the camera a little bit easier, but even so the camera kept slipping forward to point down toward his nose, and the crew kept adding additional straps and improvised supports ingeniously constructed with strips of duct tape. Wiz showed a remarkable degree of patience and forbearance—more than I had, since I was starting to get edgy about what all of that tugging and taping to properly fix and aim the device was doing to the emotional state of my dog. By the time it was fully anchored and pointing in the correct direction, my poor Wiz looked like a canine refugee from Dr. Frankenstein's laboratory, although true to his breed characteristics, he still wagged his tail and showed few signs of being upset by the proceedings.

Flint was getting excited watching me and everyone else fuss with Wiz, and I thought about putting him in another room until the filming was done, but he was already showing his little front paw prancing movements, which meant that he might be sufficiently wound up that he might start barking if he were separated from me. So I called over one of the crew members and enlisted his help, saying, "Just stand nearby, so he can see me, and hold his leash and he should be okay." He nodded, and I went back to working with Wiz.

As with most things involving filming, the setup took longer than we expected, but finally the lights were on and the doggy-cam was pointed in the right direction and recording. To allow viewers to see and hear what the dogs were experiencing when they received commands, I gave Wiz the signal and command to sit, and he sat. Then I said "Wiz, down," and signaled him to lie down, and he responded. Next I called and signaled him to come. I thought that it went well, but the person doing the directing wanted me to repeat the sequence and to "Make your words a bit more forceful and make your hand signals broader and larger so that they can be more easily seen."

So, as instructed, I repeated the sequence of commands with a louder voice and used much larger hand and arm movements. All went well until, probably because of the pressure of trying to be more vigorous on camera, I did what I often do when I am tired or distracted, which is to use the alternate, generic name that I give to all of my dogs. That means that when I called for Wizard to come, instead of saying "Wiz, come," I made a large gesture and called out "Puppy, come!" Immediately, there was a loud crash, a bright flash, and the smell of ozone. I spun in the direction of the commotion and saw Flint dashing toward me dragging a flimsy tripod that was attached to his leash, and bouncing behind it was a light with a large reflector. Instead of holding Flint as he had been asked to do, the crew member had tied him to the light stand, thinking that he was a small dog and could do little harm. On hearing my command, Flint had charged forward with enough force to completely demolish an expensive TV light.

The room exploded into pandemonium, as I tried to untangle Flint from the lamp he was dragging while trying to avoid entangling Wiz, who was pulling his camera cable behind him. The camera man was standing with his arms clutched around the big TV camera, clearly fearing that the tripod on which it was standing might become the next victim of all of this mayhem. I finally managed to sort out the dogs, and as I sat on the floor unhooking Flint, Wizard sat nearby with the doggy-cam still on his head. "That dog camera didn't catch all of this madness, did it?" I asked.

One of the cameramen shook his head and the interviewer added in a good-natured way, "Apparently not. It might have been an interesting bit. Would you like to have your dog do it again?"

Fortunately, the film from the previous doggy-cam sequence was good enough to use.

We still needed to do the interview segment. Unfortunately the crew had not brought an additional lamp, so we did it outside with me walking the dogs where nature and a bright sky supplied enough light. I thought it best not to inform Joannie about the little catastrophe.

🐾 🐾 🐾

Only a few weeks had passed since the NBC crew had visited the house and once again my living room was filled with lights and cameras. This time a woman was interviewing me and we were sitting on the sofa while the crew set up lights and cameras, when Flint jumped up between us to say hello to this visitor.

The very first dog "trick" that I teach my puppies is to "Give a kiss." I tap my index finger against my own or someone else's cheek, and the dog then moves his head close to the spot that was tapped and gives a little lick with his tongue. It is a cute little bit of behavior that makes children laugh.

To train for this trick, I simply put a little dab of butter on my index finger and then let the dog lick it off. Next I show him another dab of butter on my finger, then touch my cheek, say "Give a kiss," and let the dog come over to lick the butter off my cheek. Next I have him lick a dab of butter off the face of someone else after the person taps a finger to her own cheek. A few rounds of this and most dogs will respond to the word *kiss* and a finger tap by coming over to lick the spot you touch.

Flint knew this trick quite well—perhaps too well. The interviewer laughed at Flint's sudden arrival on the sofa and raised her hands in front of her face in a surprised, amused gesture and said, "He appears to be a kissy dog." As she said this, her index finger landed on the side of her nose, and at the word "kissy" Flint did what he was trained to do—craned his head forward to lick her face. Somewhat startled by his quick movement, she flinched backward, so Flint did what he always did when seeing something move quickly, he tried to grab it. My little gray hunter had had lots of practice and was very quick, and he managed to catch the end of her nose in a nip. The interviewer squealed, swung her arms out to her sides, and toppled the table lamp beside the arm of the sofa. The lamp and its stained glass shade hit the floor with a crash and broke into several large pieces.

Flint had not actually broken the skin on her nose, but there were two little red marks. So while the blonde was in the bathroom putting on makeup, I was cleaning up the broken glass. This time the havoc that Flint had initiated could not be completely hidden from Joan.

While the TV crew continued setting up, I turned to Flint and announced, "I think that this is the last TV interview that we do at home. It's just too hard on the lighting fixtures."

Flint's goofy voice responded, *"It was her fault. She shouldn't lead a guy on like that with promises of a kiss!"*

CHAPTER 23

NOT QUITE A CHAMPION

Flint's escapades with the TV crews brought him back onto Joan's annoyance radar. However, his training was going well and he was now ready for the highest level of obedience competition—the Utility Class. Once Flint earned that title, he would become an OTCH, or Obedience Training Champion. It was a bit more difficult to find time to train him now because of changes at the university.

I often brought both Flint and Wiz into work with me. They stayed in my office during the day, and when I was in the lab or teaching, they slept in a wire pen under my computer table. Often I would take a break from my work in the midmorning or midafternoon to take the dogs out and practice some obedience exercises with them for about 15 minutes. I kept a few training items in a drawer in my desk and improvised high jumps by propping up a piece of cardboard for them to go over. I could also lay down a few boards to act as a broad jump. This bit of training every day made their progress much faster.

Sometimes I would eat lunch quickly in order to leave time to take one or both dogs out, sometimes simply to play. Having the dogs near helped me to deal with the pressures of research

and my administrative duties, which in turn made me more creative and productive. Working with my dogs also provided me
some much needed physical exercise.

Flint would chase things that I threw, but he would seldom
pick them up and bring them back on his own accord unless specifically commanded to do so. It was much more likely that he
would try to "kill" the toy by shaking it to death. A friend had
given me a Frisbee-like throwing disk made of cloth stretched
over a flexible plastic hoop. I thought this had some promise as
a retrieval toy for Flint. Wiz never chased anything of his own
volition, and whenever I would try to entice him, I would say in
his quiet voice, *"I don't do that sort of thing. I am a companion
dog—the 'spaniel' in my breed title is merely honorary."* Then
he would trot off to find someplace to lie down.

This particular day I left Wiz dozing in my office and Flint
and I went off behind the psychology building to a small grassy
area. I waved the flexible throwing disk in front of him and
tried to get him interested in it by chanting "Do you want it?
I know you want it!" in an excited voice. The sun was glinting
off the bright colors of the disk and Flint started to do his little
front paw prancing indicating that he was interested in what
was going on. Next I threw the disk and it flew in a low flat path
over the sunlit lawn while I called out, "Fetch it up, Pup!"

Flint was off like a shot, chasing after it as fast as his short
feet would allow. When it stopped he grabbed it, and, as I had
expected, went into his "kill the vermin" mode, shaking it vigorously back and forth. Because the disk was large and soft,
every shake of his head caused it to curl and hit him in the face.
These slaps made him more excited and motivated him to shake
harder. Suddenly he lost his grip on the disk in the middle of
shaking and it flew through the air on a perfect trajectory—just
as if he had intended to toss it to me. Obviously surprised by
his prey's escape, he stood and stared with his tail quivering
with excitement. I made a quick dash to my side and managed

to catch the disk. Flint barked with what I chose to interpret as approval and trotted toward me.

Since I had the disk in my hand once more, I threw it again, and Flint chased it again. This time, when he grabbed the disk he gave it only a few shakes before releasing it, and it once more flew in my direction—close enough so that by running quickly I could catch it midair. Flint now seemed to be truly amused and barked for me to throw it again. I did, only by this time it appeared that my gray dog had worked out was happening. Now he grabbed the disk, gave it only two shakes, and on the second one released it for me to chase across the lawn.

The game of me tossing the floppy Frisbee to Flint and him tossing it back for me to chase went on for several more rounds. He was clearly enjoying the fact that he could do something to make me run across the lawn. After we had been at the game for around 10 minutes, I had gotten tired of all the running, and since I did have work to do back in my office, I decided to end the game. I hadn't noticed that a small crowd of students had gathered to watch a dog tossing a Frisbee for a university professor to chase. They smiled and two or three of them applauded, so I waved at them.

I had clipped on Flint's leash and started to return to the building when I noticed that one of my colleagues, whose research involved the training of animals (mostly rats and pigeons), was watching with a visitor—someone I identified as an eminent animal behavior researcher who was giving a guest lecture later that afternoon. The visitor looked amused and asked politely, "How did you teach him to do that?"

Feeling rather silly at being caught at play with my dog by such a well-respected scientist, I dodged the question and gave a lighthearted response, "Well, he hasn't fully learned the game yet. He's not very accurate with his throws, and I still have to run a lot to catch it."

As I was talking, Flint snatched the disk that I had been

loosely holding in my hand. He gave a quick snap of his head and released it in my direction. He was only a leash length away from me and instead of arching through the air, the Frisbee hit me right in my crotch. Flint's throw had a lot of force so the impact was hard and it hurt. The breath was knocked out of me and I buckled over in pain. As I tried to strand straight again, I noticed that my colleague and our visitor were trying to suppress outright laughter, and all that I could think to say was to painfully grunt, "Like I said, he is not very accurate with his throws."

🐾 🐾 🐾

Sadly, the era of my bringing my dogs to the university was coming to a close. Peter had resigned as head of the department of psychology and gone on to become the dean of graduate studies. The person who replaced him did not like me personally and used the authority of his office to make life unpleasant for me. He had little leverage to use against me, since my research and writing were internationally acclaimed and respected, my teaching ratings were among the highest in the department, and I carried a heavy administrative load as well. The only thing that he could do (other than making snarky comments) was to take action against my having my dogs at work. In fact, on the very first morning that he took over the office of department head, he sent me a memo denying me the right to continue to bring my dogs into the psychology building. It was a petty action and not really enforceable. Peter was concerned that I would resist this edict and turn the issue into a noisy and unpleasant fight that could harm the image and harmony of the department. He asked me as a personal favor to be a "team player" and not contest this order. My fondness for Peter and my love of the department that I had seen grow to its current mature stature prevailed.

I had always worked longer days than many other faculty members and had been continuously available to provide assistance, guidance, and advice to all faculty and students in the department on issues associated with teaching and research. However, since data analysis and writing could be done anywhere that there was a computer, I really did not have to be on campus to continue to function at a high level. If I could not have my dogs with me in my university office, I decided I would spend less time working on campus and would work at home, where my dogs could keep me company.

My absence was noticed, but since my research productivity continued unabated and I never missed classes, meetings, or required campus activities, our department head was unable to make an issue of this change in my schedule.

🐾 🐾 🐾

The degree of Utility Dog requires dogs to do some fairly complex tasks. In addition to more advanced retrieving and jumping, the dog has to show that he understands hand signals and can identify items by their scent.

For scent discrimination (my favorite exercise), a number of dumbbell-shaped articles made of wood, metal, or leather are scattered around in a sort of loose circle. The dog's owner has touched one of these dumbbells to give it his or her scent, and the dog's task is to find that one and bring it back.

Training Flint to identify and retrieve items by scent was a bit difficult at first. The most common technique for training involves using a pegboard to which two or three unscented articles are tied down with strings and the board is laid flat on the ground. The article with the scent that the dog is supposed to detect is the only one not tied down, although a piece of string is attached to it so that all of the dumbbells look the same.

Flint already knew how to fetch dumbbells on command,

but now he needed to learn that when several articles were present, the scented article was the correct one—or at least the only one that he could be retrieve since the others were anchored in place. Many dog training theories do not take into account the stubbornness and tenacity of terriers, however.

The first time that we practiced the exercise there were three items on the pegboard. One had my scent while the other two were unscented and tied down. I let Flint sniff my hand to remind him of my odor. Then I gave a new command "Find it" but used the same hand signal that I use to send him off to retrieve something. As I expected, he gave the excited *"Here I go!"* bark that he gives when he is retrieving and raced to the closest dumbbell. It happened to be tied down. He grabbed it and when it didn't move, instead of moving off to investigate the others (the way that retrievers, collies, and dogs with nonterrier brains usually do) he began to worry at it, tugging while snapping his head back and forth to give it short, hard jerks. The flimsy piece of kitchen twine I had used to tie it down was not adequate and broke, allowing Flint to march happily back to me with the dumbbell.

After a trip to the store to get heavier string, I tried again. This time on the "Find it" command, Flint again dashed out and grabbed the nearest dumbbell. By chance it was the correct one with my scent. He brought it back happily and was rewarded. He gave me that look and body posture that indicated that he thought that he understood this new game. However, the next time out he grabbed one of the tied-down dumbbells. It didn't move and this time his tugging and worrying actions were not successful in breaking it free. Terriers do not give up easily, though, and he had decided that this was the correct item; the idea of testing the others never entered his head. The piece of pegboard that I had used was a little bit more than 2 feet square, so it turned out that he could keep his jaws locked on the tied-down article and get his hind legs off the board. When he did that, his struggling caused the whole board to move an inch or so. Once he recognized that possibility, the result was predetermined. Using a strange hop-and-bend motion with his hind legs, inch by inch he moved the entire pegboard across the floor until it was in front of me. He then sat beside the dumbbell he had chosen and gave a bark that seemed to say, *"After all that work, I would appreciate a quality treat!"*

The next day I purchased a much larger piece of pegboard and put the tied-down articles closer to the center so that he couldn't stretch enough to get his hind legs off the board and onto the floor. Again, I gave the command to find it and sent him off. He chose one of the wrong, unscented items, tugged and growled at it for a while, but there was no give in it or the board. Obviously frustrated, he came back and barked at me. I could hear him saying, *"I'm smart and tough, but a little guidance would be appreciated."* However, following the process that I was led to understand would work, I simply repeated the "Find it" command.

Flint gave an annoyed growl and dashed back to the same dumbbell that he had been working on trying to lift and tugged at it again. Now he was very exasperated and wound up. He looked back at me and barked and spun around in a circle. In the process he tripped over the scented article and it moved. Although it was obviously a less preferred choice, he grabbed that one and brought it back for his reward. I was hopeful that perhaps we now had the first step toward his solving the problem.

Once again there were three items, two tied down and only the scented one free to move. As before, Flint grabbed at an item that was tied down. Then he stopped and looked at me. Looking back at that article, he gave it a nudge with his nose. It still didn't move. Next he proceeded to the next article and nudged it with his nose. When it moved, he grabbed it and brought it back in exchange for a treat. Perhaps this was a breakthrough?—Not for a terrier—Flint quickly learned that all that he had to do was to push each of the articles and the one that moved could be retrieved. Although it looked like he was using his nose to sniff, it was the physical contact that he was paying attention to. He completely ignored the scent information.

There had to be another way to teach scent discrimination. The obvious technique that occurred to me involved food, one of the few things that really focused Flint's mind. So I put away the pegboard and the strong string and started again. This time I put two dumbbells out on the floor close together. One was unscented and the other I had handled and then rubbed a bit of pepperoni on the shaft. I also carefully balanced a sliver of pepperoni on the shaft.

When I sent Flint out to the two dumbbells, he first approached the unscented article, but as he moved toward it, the other, pepperoni-scented article attracted his sensitive nose. He moved toward it and found the bit of sausage that was balanced on the shaft and quickly swallowed it. At that moment I called "Take it" (his usual command to retrieve) and he grabbed the dumbbell and brought it to me. I exchanged it for another bit of pepperoni.

This was a new game, and after a while Flint was checking out all the dumbbells that I would place on the floor, knowing that one of them had a treat balanced on it and after he ate that morsel, he knew that he would get another by bringing that article back to me. Once that behavior was well established, I put out a few unscented articles and one that had been rubbed with pepperoni, but no actual bit of the sausage was left on it this time. Flint dashed out, checked the articles, and focused on the scented one. He searched the area for his treat and found none. Then the lightbulb lit up in his mind. I could hear him saying *"Well, even if there is no treat here, I can still trade this dumbbell that smells like a treat for an actual piece of food."* He grabbed the scented dumbbell and brought it back to me for the meaty treat that he craved. From then on I did not need to leave a treat on the article. I simply scented the object with the pepperoni and sent him out, and he would carefully check all of the items and bring me back the smelly one.

Eventually, he would have to find my scent, but I chose to get the idea of scent discrimination into his head first. One day I switched to a smelly cheese target treat. I rubbed it on the article, and then let him sniff my cheese-scented hand. When he returned with the scented article he got a piece of cheese. Now came the more difficult part. I moved our training into the kitchen so that I had a sink nearby. First, I scented one dumbbell with meat and then another with cheese. I then washed my hands in the sink and rubbed a bit of cheese on my hand. Next I gave Flint my hand to sniff and sent him out. There were four articles on the floor and two of them were scented, one smelling of cheese and the other of pepperoni. Terrier luck brought Flint to the pepperoni-scented one first and he brought it back to me. I took it but did not give him a treat. Instead, I let him sniff my cheese-scented hand again and sent him off to "Find it." He dashed back, picked up the right object, and returned it for his reward.

Flint quickly learned this new variation of the game. By smelling my hand, he determined which scent I wanted and which reward he would get if he brought back the right item. From there it was easy to go to other scents, like garlic, soap, and of course my own bodily scent. He had learned to sniff the hand that I offered him and then to go to pick up the article with that scent. Now he knew that I was giving him a target scent and there was some sort of reward waiting for him if he retrieved the article that had a matching odor.

🐾 🐾 🐾

Scent discrimination really impresses people when they first see it, partly because our human noses are so weak compared to that of the dog. In fact, unless we deliberately tune ourselves to scent, the idea that we can solve problems using our noses seldom occurs to us. This gave me the opportunity to play some "mind games" with my children, and even with highly educated colleagues and friends.

My kids were still living in Philadelphia with my former wife. Once or twice each year I got to bring them to Vancouver for a visit of a week or two, although Mossy did not make this easy, and sometimes my attorney had to be called on for help. The kids loved to visit and both also loved Joannie. Flint was a major attraction as well, and they always wanted to know what he had learned and what he was doing. Flint also loved all of the extra attention and fondling that he got from them.

Once Flint had learned scent discrimination, I was able to really impress my kids by telling them that I had taught him how to read. I would set a demonstration that ran like this. First, I asked them to draw something, say, a cat. Then I had them print three words on three separate pieces of paper, say, "cat," "dog," and "horse." I then folded each piece of paper into a sort of tent-shaped Λ, with the words facing toward me and Flint. Next, I showed Flint the piece of paper with the picture of the cat, and in serious tones I explained, "Flint, this is a cat. Go find the word that says 'cat.'" I would emphasize the sound of the word dramatically by repeating it and sounding it out something like, "That's the word caaaat." Followed by a quick "Find it."

In response to my instructions, Flint give a little *"Got it, Boss!"* bark and would dash off and always bring the piece of paper with the correct word written on it back to me. We could repeat this several times, with different pictures and different words. I never reused one of the pieces of paper that he had retrieved, explaining that he had left tooth marks and drool that might be clues or distractions. On the basis of this "test" my children became convinced that that Flint was an extremely intelligent dog that could read.

The truth of the matter was that I was cheating, using the same kind of misdirection that stage magicians use. A few minutes before I would let Flint perform his "reading demonstration," I would stop in the bathroom and scrape the nails of my left hand across a bar of scented soap. When the children drew the target picture, I transferred it to my left hand and surreptitiously rubbed a bit of soap on it. I did the same thing with the paper containing the correct word while holding it in my left hand. My right hand, with no soap on it, carried the papers with the wrong words on it. When I was describing the picture to Flint, and saying the word, I held the paper up near his nose, so that he could smell the soap. When he dashed out to "read" the correct word, he was simply seeking another piece of paper that smelled exactly like the one that I placed before him. It was just a variation on the basic scent discrimination exercise, but the illusion that he was reading was very convincing.

Once I also got to show Flint's "reading ability" to a group of psychologists at a party to celebrate Flint's tenth birthday at my home. I had invited some friends and faculty members in the Psychology Department along with their spouses or partners and, given the frivolous nature of the party, had asked everyone to wear something Flint-related. Several came with T-shirts or sweatshirts bearing a dog-related image. One colleague made a necklace of dog biscuits, which she wore. Another eminent psychologist arrived wearing a plastic dog nose, while yet another had a cap with floppy spaniel ears and so forth.

Peter and his wife P.J. were also there, with P.J. defiantly wearing a sweatshirt with a cat on it. Peter, however, was dressed in a tweedy sport jacket, a dress shirt, a Western-style neck scarf, a large silver belt buckle, and a Stetson hat. I was puzzled and asked, "Just how is your costume Flint related?"

Peter smiled and said, "You once told me that Charles Darwin said in *The Origin of Species* something like 'it is scarcely

*Just for fun, I decided to show Flint's "reading ability"
to a set of psychologists.*

possible to doubt that the love of man has become instinctive in the dog.' Well, the man that Flint loves is obviously you. So the most Flint-related thing that I could think of was you—therefore, I dressed the way that you do!"

Peter always knows how to make me laugh, and I did.

Well into the party, somebody asked if I would get Flint to demonstrate some of the things that I had trained him to do. So for fun I tried the "reading" demonstration, using the same technique that I used for my kids. Flint's performance was impressive despite being circled so closely by so many people.

Of course, there was a good deal of skepticism as to whether he was actually reading. Some of my colleagues felt that I must be giving some subtle cues to Flint as to which word to pick out (since no one wanted to suggest that I was deliberately misleading them). To test this, they had me instruct Flint as to which word I wanted and then turn my back so that I couldn't see him sniffing around the cards with the words and thus give him any additional information. Since Flint was operating on the basis of scent, it made no difference, and he always brought the correct card. Then someone suggested that the audience might be giving Flint cues, so I indicated to Flint what the next word was and everybody turned their backs and did not look back until Flint brought me a card—which of course was correct. Now everyone was impressed and puzzled. Their problem was that they were thinking like humans, whose dominant sense is vision and for whom smell is such an unimportant dimension that its part in solving the problem was never even considered.

I thought about explaining Flint's behavior to the group, but then I really considered this performance to be more of a magic trick than a real experiment, and magicians never give away their secrets. So instead I offered to open a bottle of champagne, "To help us all think more clearly and to toast Flint on his tenth birthday." Since this was a party and not a scientific lab, the idea of fine-tasting alcohol seemed more alluring at that moment than the search for truth, and so Flint's ability to read simply entered into the folklore of his life. This was certainly one time when training for obedience competition did have a nearly magic outcome.

🐾 🐾 🐾

In obedience trials Flint had become a reasonable, if not always predictable, working dog, and he was much loved by many of the other competitors who would gather at ringside to see him compete and to see what kind of mischief he might get into. Nonetheless, I was still surprised to receive a certificate from *Dogs in Canada*, indicating that Flint was the highest-scoring Cairn terrier in obedience competition that year—and this time his name was even spelled correctly. Tucked into the envelope with the certificate was a handwritten note, signed with only a single initial. It said, "Congratulations. I was curious and checked our records and your dog has the highest annual point count ever obtained by a Cairn terrier in Canada!"

I proudly showed the two pieces of paper to Joannie, who shook her head and asked, "He may be the number one Cairn ever in obedience competition, but where does he rank when compared to real dogs?"

She had asked a good question, so I checked out the other high-scoring obedience dogs for that year. Flint's record-breaking score was a meager 39 points, while the number one dog in Canada that year was a Border collie with a total of 1,960. I decided not to mention these facts to Joan.

CHAPTER 24

GRAY ON GRAY

On most dogs you can see the signs of age when the hair on their face and muzzle begins to turn gray. Because Flint was a gray dog, I didn't see the age-related gray hair that should have reminded me that he was growing old, and so I treated him as if he were still young and vigorous, with the expectation that he would continue to perform the way that he always had. However, much like an aging human, you can push a dog's body only so far.

Flint's first physical crisis came one evening when we were at the dog club practicing directed jumping, where a dog is sent out across a ring with two high jumps and must leap over the one selected by his handler. Flint liked this exercise and launched himself toward the jump I indicated with his usual happy bark. But as he went over it, he landed awkwardly. When he arrived in front of me he was limping and not putting any weight on one of his hind legs. I thought that he simply had developed a strain or sprain, so I stopped exercising him that night, and assumed that in a day or two the leg would be normal again. I was wrong.

After 2 days, Flint was still not putting any weight on his

hind leg so I took him to our veterinarian, Dr. Moore, who indicated that Flint had damaged his cruciate ligament. "Although this can happen to any dog at any age, it is more likely in older dogs who are still engaged in rigorous activities that involve a lot of running or jumping. He will require an operation if he is going to regain use of that leg again."

The operation was expensive, and after the operation and some time for recuperation, the vet said that Flint's full recovery would require that he start to put his weight on the leg again. Flint was still favoring it and moving around on three legs as if the repaired leg could not bear his weight. I was becoming a bit frustrated trying to figure out ways to get him to exercise the leg properly and to let it carry its normal load again.

The solution came one sunshine-filled afternoon when I decided to take the dogs for a walk along the shore of the bay. The route down to the water's edge took us across a sandy beach and my feet sank into the loose sand on each step. I looked back at Flint and noticed that under these conditions he had no alternative but to put some weight on his hind leg as he plodded through the soft sand that let each leg sink down a bit. This was obviously the therapeutic conditions that we needed.

For the next several weeks, Flint, Wiz, and I had hour-long walks on the soft, sandy shore. Flint's leg gradually strengthened as he was forced to exercise it, while Wizard just seemed to collect sand in the fine hair that made up his coat. When we arrived home after each walk, Flint would flop down as if he were exhausted and watch patiently while I carefully brushed the sand from Wizard's coat.

When we returned to Dr. Moore for a checkup at the end of the month, he was very impressed at how well Flint had healed and how much strength he had recovered in his leg. Flint was now moving normally and the vet announced that if I wanted to have him return to obedience competition, he thought that it would be all right for him to go over the jumps again. I considered this recommendation for a while and decided against it. I had an image in my head of Flint going over a jump and coming up lame again because he had reinjured that ligament, or perhaps damaged another, which was more than likely now that Flint was getting older. A piece of blue-colored ribbon for a qualifying score or even the prospect of him becoming an Obedience Training Champion was not worth the risk.

On our car ride back home, I looked at Flint sitting beside me and told him, "Well, old man, it looks like I'm retiring you from obedience competition. I don't want to risk having you jump anymore."

He answered in a rather philosophical tone, *"As long as I can still jump up onto your bed to sleep, and can still jump up on the window seat to protect the house with my barking, I can survive. And, by the way, I'm not so old. I still have all of my hair—what about you?"*

🐾 🐾 🐾

Other things made me acutely aware that my terrier was showing signs of aging. A slight haze was forming on his eyes, although this didn't seem to affect his vision much at first, and his hearing was clearly going downhill.

The first sign of Flint's fading hearing was that he failed to show up instantaneously at the sound of the refrigerator opening or closing, or in response to the crinkling sound of cellophane as I opened packages of crackers or other food. If Wizard sashayed into the kitchen upon hearing those sound signals that often predicted that some extra food might be available, Flint would sometimes follow him, but more and more often he would not even awaken in response to that activity. Flint had always responded reliably to spoken commands, but now often seemed to ignore my call, especially if he was looking away from me. Outdoors he seemed oblivious of the sound of approaching cars or the noise of kids on skateboards approaching from behind, which before had always caused him to turn and watch them alertly.

I mentioned Flint's diminishing hearing sensitivity to Joannie, who merely said, "Maybe things will be a bit quieter around here since he won't be barking at the sound of every leaf that falls near the house."

Unfortunately for her, that was not to be, since at last Wizard became the accomplice that Flint had always wanted. Flint was sleeping more soundly than he used to, not bolting awake at every noise to sound the alarm with a cascade of barking, but Wizard now seemed bothered that Flint was no longer going to the door or window to bark. Previously, when Flint would bark to alert us to sounds in the street Wiz would always tag along behind him and studiously look over his shoulder in the direction the noises were coming from. Wiz never joined in the barking but wagged his tail merrily as though he recognized that his housemate was doing a good job and one that clearly needed to be done. Now that Flint was not responding to these sounds Wiz began to look uncomfortably in the direction that any noises were coming from and then he would look back at Flint, who was usually napping on the sofa. Rather than take up the job of barking himself, however, Wiz hit upon another strategy. He walked over to where Flint was resting and sounded a single loud high-pitched yip, close enough and loud enough to affect even Flint's diminished hearing. When Wizard's call registered in his consciousness, Flint would open his eyes and raise his head. Wiz would then run to the window or door where he'd heard the sound. This activity stirred Flint into action and he would excitedly race to where Wiz was standing and immediately start barking in response to a sound that he had not actually heard. His own barking apparently sounded lower in intensity to him, and so he seemed to be barking louder and longer now. Wiz stood contentedly but silently beside him, gently wagging his tail in recognition that he had ensured that a needed service for the family was still being provided without requiring a royal spaniel to engage in common canine work such as barking.

❧ ❧ ❧

Dogs with reduced hearing can undergo personality changes. Some may become more fearful or dependent, and some more snappish and apparently aggressive. They startle more easily as things suddenly spring into view or make physical contact without any prior warning. Normally dogs sleep fairly lightly, which means that they are still, at some level, monitoring the sounds around them, which lets them anticipate some events that are about to happen, but a deaf dog may awaken with a growl or a snap if touched while sleeping simply because he did not expect it. In Flint's case this state of affairs resulted in a major crisis.

I was in my home office writing one afternoon when my attention was caught by a huge commotion in the living room. I stood up and was met by Joan who was holding her hand up to show a trickle of blood dripping down.

"Your miserable old dog bit me," she shrieked.

I walked her into the bathroom and washed the blood away from her hand to reveal a small puncture wound on her thumb, which I covered with some antiseptic ointment and a small adhesive bandage. Then I asked her to tell me what had happened.

"He was asleep on the sofa—on my side of the sofa—and I went to wake him up to get him off it and he turned around and bit me!"

"Please, Joannie," I said, "remember that his hearing is going downhill. He probably didn't hear you and was startled awake when you poked at him. He might have awakened in a fright, and of course he would snap at what was touching him."

"He bit me because he never liked me," she insisted.

I tried to explain what she could do to prevent this from

happening again. "If you walked more heavily when you approached him, he would probably feel the vibrations from the wood floor and awaken on his own. Another way is to just hold your hand near his nose and your smell should alert him. He's not totally deaf, so he might even awaken if you clapped you hands a couple of times."

Joan looked at me in disbelief. "You want me to clomp around my own house, stamping my feet, just for the benefit of your dog? You want me to applaud the beast that just bit me so that he can wake up more gracefully? This is my home and I expect to be treated with some respect and not to be bitten by your dog. You are a psychologist. Fix his attitude!"

Although Flint had always been a trial for Joan, this physical assault crossed some critical line in her mind. Joan would not change her behavior to accommodate my dog, Flint was of course too old to change, and his hearing was certainly not going to get better. I feared that there would be more bites, more shouting, and a general escalation of the conflict between my wife and my terrier. The best that I could do was to keep them apart, so whenever I was in the house I kept Flint near me and as far from Joan as possible, sometimes even resorting to the umbilical that I had used when he was a puppy.

🐾 🐾 🐾

The fact that Flint was becoming deaf did not end my ability to communicate with him, because I have always combined voice commands with hand signals. This age-proofs the dog to a degree since, if my aging dog's eyes fail, he can still respond to my voice and if his ears fail he can respond to my hand signals. I could still tell Flint what I wanted him to do, even though he could barely hear me now. I had even made sure that there was a hand signal meaning "Good dog!" so that he would know when I was happy with him.

Because Flint knew his signals, he could still compete in two kinds of obedience competitions where he would not be required to jump. The first was the Veterans Class, which was the same as the first-level Novice exercises, but restricted to dogs who already had their Companion Dog title and were 7 years of age or older. Two or three times that year I entered Flint in Veterans competition and he always earned a qualifying score. Best of all, to my mind, was that people outside of our dog club did not have the least suspicion that he was nearly deaf. It just looked like a normal competition where the handler used a lot of signals instead of his voice.

Of course, Flint did show his age now and then in the ring. In one Veterans competition, for instance, we were doing the long down group exercise. I gave the signal instructing Flint to lie down and he did so. Because he settled down with his head on his paws in a comfortable pose I knew that he was unlikely to break his position. A few moments after I reached the far side of the ring I thought I heard a faint rumbling sound coming from the line of dogs. It was rhythmic, and I couldn't quite identify it or determine where it was coming from. The judge apparently also heard it, and she walked slowly down in front of the line of dogs. When she reached Flint, she stopped and smiled, then returned to her usual position at the edge of the ring.

On her command, "Return to your dogs," I went back to stand beside Flint and all became clear. The rumbling sound was Flint snoring. In the midst of an obedience trial, when he was still in the ring, my old dog had decided to take a nap. It was a strange way to earn a qualifying score in that exercise.

🐾 🐾 🐾

The other class that Flint could still compete in was the Brace competition in which two dogs are linked together with a Y-shaped device that hooks them both to one leash. The objec-

Flint and Wiz win an obedience Brace competition under a Canadian judge.

tive is to do the basic Novice obedience exercises with two dogs together as a team. Most people who participate in Brace competition use two dogs of the same breed, which is mandatory in American Kennel Club trials. When the dogs are closely matched in size and physical characteristics the team can look quite elegant when performing the exercises. However, in Canada there is no requirement that the dogs be the same breed or size, and I rather enjoyed the fact that I could compete with Flint and Wiz as a brace because, except for their heights, there was nothing similar about them. Flint had pricked ears, Wiz had floppy ears. Flint was dark, Wiz was light-colored. Flint had a carrot-shaped tail that he carried upright while Wiz had a fully feathered tail that he carried horizontally. They worked well together, nevertheless, and Wiz had also been trained to hand signals from his puppyhood.

One obedience judge (on loan from the AKC) was quite upset when I arrived at his ring with Flint and Wiz as my brace. He sputtered, "That's not a brace—that's a disgrace. They're not even the same breed. Have you no pride, sir?"

The other three braces competing that day were a pair of well-matched Boston terriers, a pair of golden retrievers, and a pair of Shetland sheepdogs. Those braces did look quite stylish and pleasing to the eye; however, each ran into a problem on at least one exercise, while my mismatched brace of Flint and Wiz was the only one to qualify.

The judge glowered at us as he was forced to give us the high in class. The ring steward who handed the judge the ribbon and the little prize that went with first place was an acquaintance who knew Flint well. I heard him lean over and say to the judge, "You know that the Cairn terrier in that pair is twelve years old and quite deaf."

"Really?" the judge responded, looking down at Flint and smiling at us for the first time. "Good job! I never would have guessed that."

❧ ❧ ❧

I sometimes believe that God has a strange sense of humor. I certainly never expected Flint's deafness to turn out to be a blessing. This situation started with a phone call to my university office.

"Hello, Dr. Coren," said a pleasant female voice. "You

won't remember me, but I took your Introductory Psychology course about seven years ago. There were about three hundred people in my class so you never knew our names. Anyway, my name is Jennifer and I have a bit of a strange request. Do you still have that gray Cairn terrier?"

I was puzzled as to where this conversation was going but acknowledged that I still had Flint.

"I remember that you brought him into class one day to demonstrate animal learning principles. Here is my problem. My grandparents, my mother's parents, were married for 53 years and just around four weeks ago my grandpa died. The two of them had been very close—inseparable. After the funeral Grandma Alice just crawled into her bed and doesn't talk to anyone and hardly seems to recognize anyone. A psychologist looked at her and he said something about posttraumatic stress syndrome, and then told my mom that sometimes when people have been together in a loving relationship for a long time, after one of them dies, the other one just kind of folds up and dies shortly afterward. He suggested that if we could get through to her, interest her in something or remind her of something pleasant in her past, she might 'wake up' again. But Mom is beginning to think that she really can't handle Grandma acting like a zombie, and is worried that we might have to send her to some kind of home.

"When you taught us about clinical psychology, you mentioned therapy dogs and how they sometimes helped troubled people break out of their emotional or mental shells. Before my grandparents moved into their apartment they had a Cairn terrier like yours, even the same color as yours. They loved him a lot. I was wondering if you might be willing to bring your dog over for a visit—sort of a therapy dog visit.

"If it helps at all, Mom is prepared to get her a dog."

I am a sucker for pleas for help, especially when they involve my students or dogs, and this involved both. I did caution her,

"There are no guarantees in this sort of thing. The examples that we talk about when we discuss therapy dogs in class are always the special and remarkable ones, but sometimes therapy dogs are no more successful than the casual visit of a friend or a mental health worker."

Jennifer said that she understood but really wanted me to try. So we set up a time for the next day when I would visit her mother's home.

At the agreed-upon time, Flint and I arrived at a modest, well-kept two-story house. Jennifer, and her mother, Norma, met us at the door. Both bent down to pat Flint, who happily wagged his tail at the attention. They then ushered me upstairs to a small bedroom at the rear of the house where a thin, frail woman, probably well into her seventies, lay partially propped up with pillows.

When we entered the room, Alice's eyes were open, but she didn't respond in any way. Norma spoke to her, "Mom, this is Dr. Coren, a psychologist from the university. He was one of Jennifer's professors and he's brought someone to meet you." Alice did not respond.

I said, in as cheerful a voice as I could, "Hi, Alice."

There were two dining room–style chairs against the wall and I took one and pushed it up against the bed. I patted the seat of the chair and Flint recognized the signal and jumped up to sit on the chair in the place I had indicated. "This is Flint," I continued. "I thought that you might like to meet him. I know that he would like to meet you."

There was no response from Alice, so I tapped the bed's surface to encourage Flint to approach her. He took a step from the chair to the bed, and stood there, tail waving tentatively—expectantly. At that moment Alice's eyes moved to look at him. She stared at him and slowly her head turned toward him. Then a whispery, cracked voice said, "Snuffy?"

Flint took another step toward her, and Alice uncertainly

lifted her hand and swung it in his direction. Flint then stepped
fully onto the bed in an attempt to draw closer to her. All the
while his eyes were only on Alice. Perhaps because of her several weeks of little movement, Alice seemed to lack full coordi-
nation, and the hand that she was moving in Flint's direction
accidentally hit the metal tray on the side table. It crashed to
the floor with a loud enough clang to startle everyone in the
room—except for Alice, who acted as though nothing had happened, and Flint, my hearing-impaired dog.

I did not help the situation any. I made a grab for the tray
when I saw it slipping off the table. In the process I tripped on
the chair, which toppled over with a bang, and then I lurched
into the side table, causing the lamp to topple to the floor adding to the clamor. I really believe that Flint radiated bad karma
for lamps and lighting fixtures all through his life, since so many
seemed to fall over in his proximity.

Flint did not even flinch at all of this commotion, but merely
glanced in my direction and then continued to approach Alice.
She moved her hand again, this time clearly reaching for him,
repeating "Snuffy?"

Flint was now next to Alice, and he gently inched himself
forward until he was actually leaning on her chest. She slowly
raised her hand, touched him, and then began to pet him with
slow, deliberately gentle movements. I had managed to stand
up, and returned the chair to its upright position, glancing at the
tray and lamp that were now on the floor. Neither Jennifer nor
Norma was looking at me. Their eyes were fixed on Flint and
Alice. I repeated quietly, "His name is Flint."

The cracked whispery voice said, "You look just like our
Snuffy dog. You even feel like him. David [her deceased hus-
band] always promised me that he would get me another Snuffy
someday."

Norma stepped to the other side of the bed and asked,
"Would you like me to get you another Snuffy, Mom?"

Flint gently inched himself forward.

There was a pause that seemed to go on for hours, while Alice sat with her eyes on Flint as she patted him with slow hand movements. Finally, she responded in what might have been a wishful tone of voice, "Could you get me another Snuffy?"

Norma's eyes were full of tears, "As soon as I can." I nodded my head and silently mouthed, "Tomorrow."

Norma glanced at me and said tentatively, "Maybe even tomorrow."

Alice momentarily moved her eyes from Flint to her daughter and smiled a wan smile. "That would be wonderful." She then looked back at Flint, who was contentedly resting on her, and said to him, "You could be my Snuffy, you know."

Norma motioned to me and we stepped out of the bedroom, while Jennifer came over and sat on the edge of the bed next to her grandmother.

"This is a miracle," she said wiping tears from her eyes. "She hadn't said more than a dozen words since I brought her here. This is wonderful. But where can I get a Cairn terrier as quickly as tomorrow?"

"On the off chance that Flint's visit might be helpful, I contacted a local Cairn terrier breeder named Glen," I said.

I had originally met Glen when Flint had scored a rare high in class at an obedience trial. Glen had been impressed at seeing a Cairn terrier do well in obedience, but he was quite unimpressed by Flint's looks. "His back is too long, his ears are set too close, and his tail is set too high. Listen, for your next Cairn come to me so that people who love the breed can take pride in a Cairn doing well in obedience who is not quite so badly put together," he told me.

I continued, "Glen told me that he has an 18-month-old gray Cairn that he was keeping as a possible show dog. However, his coat never came in quite the way that he wanted, so he was willing to sell it. That way you'll get a dog that is a young adult and already housebroken, which should make things easier. Anyway, that is one possibility to consider since I don't think you want the hassle of starting with a puppy for your mother."

Norma nodded and we went back into the room. Jennifer was still sitting on the bed next to Alice. Both were petting Flint and they were murmuring something to each other. Alice looked up and nodded at us. Norma smiled and said, "Dr. Coren and Flint have to go now, but tomorrow we'll get you a new Snuffy."

Flint turned to look at me and I signaled for him to come. Jennifer got up and came over to me. She gave me a hug and whispered "Thank you. I think that she is back with us."

As Flint and I sat together in the car on the way home, I started talking to him. Just because he couldn't hear me made no difference, since he always seemed to know that I was speaking to him and he would look at my face attentively.

"You're a good psychotherapist," I said, glancing in his direction. "I was worried when everything started falling over and making all of that noise. I was afraid that you would get upset and ruin the mood. I suppose that it's proved to be a blessing that you are mostly deaf, because it meant you weren't spooked by all of that commotion."

The old familiar voice answered me, *"Yes, just call me Sigmund Cairn, the world's greatest canine therapist. You know being deaf isn't such a bad thing for a psychotherapist. Most of them don't listen to what their patients say anyway."*

A month or so later I received a "thank you" note addressed to Flint and me. Inside was a photograph of Alice sitting on a large rocking chair. On her lap was a handsome gray Cairn terrier and she was smiling warmly at it. The "thank you" note was signed Jennifer, Norma, Alice, and Snuffy.

Chapter 25

SUNSET

My father once said that when you own a dog and observe his life, you learn that it is possible to grow old with grace and dignity. Flint never did anything gracefully or with dignity, however. Although he slept more than he used to, when he was awake he could still career around the house as if he were putting out wildfires, barking when Wizard indicated that there was something to be barked at, and chasing glints of light or flickering shadows that might be rodents or other vermin that needed the attention of the great gray hunter.

Still, Flint now moved a bit more stiffly and was not quite as quick or agile as he used to be. One evening he had difficulty jumping up on the bed. While Wiz slept every night curled tightly against me, Flint only came up on the bed to rest against my legs for the first hour or so of each night. Sometime after I was asleep he would hop off and spend the rest of the night on a floor pillow that I kept in the bedroom for him. If the night were particularly cold, I would sometimes find him on the bed when I awakened, where he had curled up in a nest that he had made of the blankets.

The fact that he could not climb or jump up to the bed bothered me enough that I couldn't go to sleep, so I went down to the basement and constructed a step and covered it with a scrap of carpeting. Then I went back upstairs and put the step near the foot of my side of the bed, called Flint over, and gave the step a little tap. He looked at it for a moment, then stepped up on it and then to the bed. He then proceeded to lie down in his usual place with an audible sigh.

In the morning the alarm clock went off and we got up. Joannie swung off of her side of the bed and as she moved toward the door, of course, she tripped on Flint's new step, nearly falling in the process.

"What's this?" she asked.

"Just a step," I said. "Flint was having trouble making it up to the bed last night."

She gave a little snort and replied, "So if he has trouble biting me, you'll give him some false teeth as well?"

🐾 🐾 🐾

Flint's mind was still sharp and capable of finding novel solutions to problems. Because Flint could no longer hear the scratching and scrabbling sounds made by mice when they found their way into the house, the number of dead mice that we found diminished until we rarely found them.

One evening we were out at our farm, which used to be Flint's prime vermin-hunting area. We were still living in the little shack, since Joannie was taking courses on house building and designing the new house, and we could not quite afford to build it yet. The little shack was a great place to catch mice, since it did not have a proper foundation but simply stood over a crawl space with the wooden floor about a foot or so above the bare ground, and there were gaps in the floor and the baseboards that gave the rodents easy access to the house.

I had just put out food for the dogs' evening meal, which

normally they virtually inhaled in a minute or two. This particular night Flint did something very odd. He finished all of the food in his bowl except for one piece of kibble. He then picked that kibble up in his mouth, moved to a corner of the kitchen, and spat it out on the floor. He then moved across the room and lay down staring at the piece of food.

Wiz noticed this behavior, and opportunistically moved toward the corner to grab this last edible bit, but a low rumbling growl from Flint caused him to change his mind and to put some distance between himself and the dropped morsel. Flint was still staring at the place where he had dropped the kibble when Joan and I went to bed that night.

In the morning we woke up and there was a dead mouse in the kitchen with a broken neck—the clear sign that Flint had dispatched it. Over a number of subsequent nights Flint would continue to leave a bit of kibble in that corner after each evening meal. It was seldom there in the morning. However, now and then we would again find dead mice indicating that Flint was on the hunt again.

Late one night, I was having difficulty sleeping because of a headache and decided to get up and take a couple of aspirin. As I walked out of the bedroom, there was Flint, lying on the floor, staring at the corner where he had dropped the piece of kibble that night. I was about to say something to him when I glimpsed some motion in the corner. Flint shot from his position to the corner, and after two shakes of his head we had another dead mouse. Flint was baiting a trap by placing a bit of kibble in a corner where there was a gap in the baseboard. He had figured out that, if he couldn't hear the mice, he could still see them and catch them if he knew where they would appear and if they stopped for a moment to nibble a bit of kibble. It didn't always work, because sometimes he would fall asleep and miss the rodent's arrival, but it did work well enough to allow him to continue his hunting at least out on the farm.

❂ ❂ ❂

Some aging humans tend to become more religious and spiritual, although to the best of my knowledge no one has ever observed such behavior in dogs. There was one moment, however, when I thought that it might have applied to Flint.

It was a summer night out at the farm, and there was one of those big full moons, such as you find only in paintings. Joannie had been working in the garden all day and had decided to go to sleep early. While she was getting ready for bed, I wandered out on the wooden platform that served as a deck behind the little house. I had a can of beer and had just settled into a chair when I noticed Flint staring at the moon. His back was toward me and he sat unmoving with his head tilted up for a long time. Then he did something that I had never before seen him do. He leaned back his head and gave a long and mournful howl. He was still howling when Joan opened the screen door. She was in her nightgown and she asked, "What's he doing?"

"I think that he has had a religious epiphany and is singing some kind of prayer," I said.

"For which religion would that be?"

"I'm not sure. Maybe the *First Church of the Domestic Canine*? They have a rich and complex dogma, I'm told."

Joannie smiled and disappeared back in the house.

I don't know if Flint's god heard him that night, but the local coyotes certainly did. From a distance I could hear them answering with their familiar yip howls. Within a few moments a veritable chorus of howls was drifting across the field. Sadly, Flint could not hear the musical performance that he had triggered and after a minute or two of further singing he stopped and trotted back to lie down beside me. The wild canine choral continued for several more minutes and drifted away.

"Do you think that your prayer was successful?" I quietly asked him.

His silly voice answered, *"God appreciates a good tenor."*

🐾 🐾 🐾

When we were back in the city again. I was looking forward to a three-day (Friday, Saturday, and Sunday) dog show. Flint was not in competition, but Wizard was, and I was planning to take both dogs out to the show Friday afternoon. Flint loved to socialize at dog shows, and all of my friends from the dog club would be there for me to socialize with as well.

That Thursday night Flint did not try to climb onto the bed but lay on one of the floor pillows, whimpering and shaking. He had eaten his dinner heartily, and had seemed to be all right early in the evening. Concerned, I carefully ran my hands over his body, prodding and pushing gently to see if a specific place was sore. He didn't seem to be in real pain, but to be feeling some kind of general discomfort. I thought that he might just be suffering from some sort of muscle pain from overexerting himself after some vigorous play with our next door neighbor's little girl, Clara, that afternoon. I gave him a half an aspirin and some water and promised to take him to the veterinarian in the morning.

Wizard actually seemed to be more concerned than I was. He stood close to Flint and whined a bit, looking at me and then back to my gray dog. Finally, he walked over to the corner where some clothing was lying on the floor (because the clothes hamper was over full as usual). He rooted around and eventually pulled out one of my sweatshirts. He dragged it over to Flint and, by tugging and pushing with his paws, arranged it like a blanket over him. Flint watched him but otherwise he didn't move or try to shake it off. Then Wiz lay down, with his body touching Flint as if to provide some of his own biological warmth for his friend.

He stayed there for the whole night and never came to bed with me, either.

In the morning Flint appeared to be a lot better, although he was moving a bit slowly. He ate his breakfast—which I considered to be a good sign. Nonetheless, I still wanted to take him to the vet, just to be sure that there was no serious problem.

We went out to my car, and Flint hopped up onto the front passenger seat as he always did when Joan was not with us. He then stretched out on the seat. As we drove I looked out at the bright sunshine that looked like it was coating the world with a yellow butterscotch glow, and I assured him, "You and Wiz will get a really good walk this afternoon in that park near the dog show. We have sunshine predicted for the whole weekend." Flint's only response was a single whimper, which could have meant anything.

I pulled up in front of the veterinarian's office. I noticed that Flint did not pop up in anticipation of leaving the car the way that he always did before. When I went around to his side and opened the door, he seemed to be unconscious and unresponsive. I felt a surge of panic. I quickly lifted him in my arms and raced into the vet's office. His receptionist looked up at me and I barked, "Kay, please get Dr. Moore right away!"

She jumped up, threw open the door to the examining room, and gestured for me to go in. A moment later the vet appeared. He ran his hands over Flint's unmoving body, then he grabbed a stethoscope. A minute or two later he dropped his hands to his sides, looked at me, and said simply, "I'm sorry."

"He was fine this morning," I blubbered.

"He was getting old, and he's gone now," was all that he said.

I looked at that old gray grizzled face and noticed tear tracks running down his muzzle. I had no doubt in my mind at that moment that he had been quietly weeping during our short ride here. I certainly also knew that there were matching tear tracks running down my face.

I stood outside the vet's office. I was in shock. I looked down at the leash and collar in my hand—a leash attached to nothing and an empty collar. I remember that what had been soft sweet sunshine on the way here now cast a hard yellow light that made the world look as if it had suddenly turned to cold unyielding brass.

🐾 🐾 🐾

I have no recollection of the ride home. I just remember opening the door to the house and having Joannie look up at me with distress in her eyes and ask "What's wrong?"

"Flint . . ." I was finding it hard to breathe, hard to talk. "Flint . . . My Flint . . . He won't be back."

Joan rushed over and put her arms around me. Joan might have really wanted to dance in the street at the news that Flint was gone, having lived in such a state of cold war with him for so long. She might have made a cold or cutting comment to express her relief that a being that had stressed her so had died. But she was my Joannie, and she loved me miles above the level of her distress with my dog. So she quietly held me and repeated over and over, "I know how much you loved him."

Eventually, I got control of myself. I was still clutching Flint's leash and collar, and my fingers were stiff as I dropped them on the table. I went into the bathroom and washed my face and tried some deep breathing to get back to normal.

When I returned to the living room I called Wizard over to me. The touch of his soft fur was comforting. I then hooked a leash onto his collar and picked up the small satchel that contained the various bits of equipment and supplies that I used for dog shows.

"Where are you going?" Joan asked with concern.

"I have a dog show to go to," I said, and was surprised at how hoarse my voice was.

"Do you think that that is wise? I mean, being at an obedience competition is just going to remind you so much of him and
it may hurt worse."

I gave Joan a hug and said, "You know I love you, but I need
to be with people who not only knew him but feel the way that
I do about him."

She gave a thin, sad smile and said, "If it does get difficult,
just come home early. I do know how much you loved him." She
leaned her head against mine and whispered softly, "And you
should know how much I love you."

🐾 🐾 🐾

A bit less than an hour later I arrived at the show. Wizard had
sat the whole time on the passenger seat, which he used to share
with Flint. We didn't talk, but I often reached over to stroke his
fine soft fur. When we entered the arena, Shirley and both Barbaras were sitting next to the obedience ring and, as I walked
toward them, Shirley bolted from her chair and came to me.

"What's wrong? You look like a truck ran over you."

I told her that Flint was gone, and was surprised that I could
do it without my voice breaking and without releasing the surge
of emotion that I couldn't hide from Joannie a short time ago.
Both Barbaras got up and crowded close. They asked what had
happened and I told them.

Barbara Merkley then quietly said, "He must have loved you
very much to go that quickly and to not put you in the position
of making that final choice for him," then she gave me a hug.

Someone had pulled up a chair for me and someone else
brought me a cup of coffee. We sat quietly talking. Everyone had
a Flint story to tell and all were funny accounts of his random
and oddly thought-out behavior. As various people came over
to say hello and learned about his passing they added their own
personal observations about him.

Every dog who has shared my life has had its own character with its strengths and foibles. Each had a story and each added its experiences to my way of thinking and my personal psychological make-up. Before Flint, however, the influence of each dog had been confined to the area within the walls of my house and the people living there. Dogs are not suns that radiate their light over vast distances, but rather candles that illuminate the small spaces in which we live—the spaces in which we feel. When they are gone, only those who lived in their limited light recognize that the world has become a bit darker. It was, therefore, a great comfort to me to see that many people had noted Flint's presence, even if just in little observations or amusing scraps of memory. I don't recall if I actually competed with Wiz that day, but I felt somewhat healed and in control by the time that I returned home.

🐾 🐾 🐾

Later that night I had a dream. In it Flint is lying beside the gates of Heaven and an angel comes out to ask him why he didn't come in. In a voice that I don't remember giving to him ever before my gray dog answers, *"Can't I just stay out here awhile? I'll be good and I won't even bark. You see, I'm waiting for someone that I miss very much. If I went in alone it wouldn't be Heaven for me."*

I woke from that dream to find tears on my face, and when I went to wipe them off, Wizard, who had been lying beside me, sat up and began to lick the wetness from my face. In my mind I heard him talking to me in that quiet voice that I had long ago given to him, *"It will be all right. I am here for you. Rest easy— before he went away Flint left me instructions on what to do."*

Over the course of my life I have come to believe that God has created many types of angels—and some of them bark.

AFTERWORD

I have walked out into the field behind our new house on the farm. This is the house that Joan designed and served as the general contractor for. It has been a long time since Flint roamed this field on the hunt. Wizard was my comfort for 7 years after Flint left me, and other dogs joined him, or followed. There was never another terrier, since I had promised Joannie that, but there was my big, elegant, black, flat-coated retriever, Odin—the dog that Joan loved above all others. There was another Cavalier King Charles spaniel, this one named Banshee, who shared my life for a while and who loved plush toys even more than Wiz did.

Right now I am looking at my Nova Scotia duck tolling retriever, Dancer, and my beagle, Darby. Dancer is scanning the field attentively, while Darby has his nose to the ground, the way that beagles always do. Suddenly Darby startles a gray field rat from cover. The rat skitters between the two dogs and heads for the edge of the field where blackberry bushes can provide a safe hiding place. Both of the dogs stand and watch the rat for a moment, then glance up at me, making no effort to give chase.

I am forced to laugh. I tell the dogs, "Flint would have never passed up that opportunity to hunt or at least to chase."

Darby looks at me and in his hound voice says, *"Flint was different, wasn't he, Dad?"*

Darby is the only dog that has ever called me "Dad." He has a typical hound nature, soft, sociable, and as difficult to train as

Flint was—not because he is as independent and innovative as Flint was, but rather because events going on inside his sensitive nose are far more important than the lessons I may try to teach him. Dancer is much more trainable. He loves to work and he calls me "Boss."

"Oh yes," I say. "Flint taught me how to watch dogs, how to begin the process of understanding what goes on inside of a dog's mind, and how to go about trying to train them. But more than that he had a unique and irrepressible personality. If we would have erected a marker over his grave it would have read

Born a dog.
Lived like a lion.
Died a gentleman.

At that moment two of our grandchildren who are visiting the farm appear behind us. Cora is carrying a red plastic bumper on a string, and Matty, a red ball. The dogs start to dance in anticipation. They will chase these toys when the kids throw them, but they won't chase the wildlife. They are not terriers. They are also not royal spaniels who would rather rest beside you than engage in anything as mundane as retrieving.

Each dog is different. Each has two minds, one that belongs to his breed and another that makes him different from every other dog that has ever lived. The sad part is that none of my dogs has stayed around long enough for me to fully understand them, despite all of my psychological training. God gives us dogs to be our companions but demands them back after our short lease on their lives expires.

I watch the kids romping around with the dogs. From the corner of my eye I see Joannie standing at the back door of the house watching the children play with the dogs. She gives that little half smile that I fell in love with so many years ago.

I am missing Flint at that moment, remembering how he used to play with Benn and Rebecca, and wondering how he would respond to Cora and Matty. I feel myself drifting into a blue funk, but as usual I am saved by the tinkling laughter of the children and the excited barking of the dogs. I am also comforted by a remembrance of something that Sir Walter Scott, the author of *Ivanhoe* and other classic novels, once wrote:

> I have sometimes thought of the final cause of dogs having such short lives and I am quite satisfied it is in compassion to the human race: for if we suffer so much in losing a dog after an acquaintance of ten or twelve years, what would it be if they were to live double that time?

ABOUT THE AUTHOR

Stanley Coren, PhD, FRSC, is a professor emeritus in the psychology department at the University of British Columbia and a recognized expert on dog-human interaction. For his contributions to psychological science he was named a Fellow of the Royal Society of Canada. He has appeared on many television shows, including *Oprah, Good Morning America, CBS Morning Show, Dateline,* and *Larry King.* He has hosted the TV show *Good Dog!* which was nationally broadcasted in Canada, and he currently appears on *Pet Central* on the Pet Network. He has also been given the *Dog Writer of the Year* award by the International Positive Dog Training Association. He lives in Vancouver with his wife Joan, and is active in fund-raising efforts for various humane societies.

Born to Bark

STANLEY COREN

A Readers Club Guide

ABOUT THIS GUIDE
The following reading group guide is intended to help you
find interesting and rewarding approaches to your reading
of *Born to Bark*. We hope this enhances your
enjoyment and appreciation of the book.

Book Club Questions for *Born to Bark*

1. Coren's love of many breeds of dog comes through so beautifully in *Born to Bark* as well as in his other books. His fondness for his Cairn terrier, Flint, is particularly strong, however. What is it about the terrier personality that you think he found so appealing?

2. Coren suggests that most people talk to their dogs and that there are different ways that people do this. Do you ever talk to your dog? What do you talk about? Do you actually supply the dog's answers, as Coren does, or do you just think them?

3. Coren's wife, Joan, seems to have had many more problems with Flint than with Wiz. Do you think this had to do with the personalities of the dogs or her personality or both?

4. Flint clearly had a helpful, therapeutic effect on Alice and helped break through her depression. Are there other places in the book, or in your own life or experience, where you have seen dogs providing a psychological boost or improving a person's mood and combating depression?

5. Coren did not want at first to tell the members of his dog obedience club that he was a professor of psychology. Do you think he was right? Do you think this strategy was helpful or harmful?

6. Coren provides an inside look at the world of dog obedience competition. Do you think this is an appealing sport? Do you think you might ever want to train a dog for competition?

7. Do you think the innovative training methods Coren used with Flint as a pup helped them bond with each other?

8. Do some dogs just have a better sense of humor than others? Flint seems so fun-loving and playful—does Coren say this is typical of most dogs or of the smaller dogs or of terriers?

9. Would Coren recommend a terrier—specifically a Cairn—to most families who are looking for a small dog? How would you think he would want to guide people who fall in love with the breed through reading *Born to Bark*?

10. What were some of the main things Coren learned from Flint about canine intelligence? What were the emotional lessons he learned?

11. What type of breed is your favorite, and why? Have you tried any of Stan Coren's training techniques on your dog, and how have they worked? How did you introduce your dog to your children/other pets, and how did they react?

12. Coren writes about Flint's instinctual hunting behavior, but Flint also displayed a different kind of behavior when he saved a litter of kittens from a building about to be demolished. Why do you think Flint saved the kittens? Have you ever seen a dog behave similarly?

13. Flint the Cairn terrier and Wiz the Cavalier King Charles spaniel have distinctly different temperaments and personalities, but Wiz also learned a lot by watching Flint and modeled his own behavior after Flint's. What surprised you about the relationship between these two dogs? How do you think they related to each other and influenced one another?

Stanley Coren is every dog's best friend. His books are treasures for all breeds of dog lover.

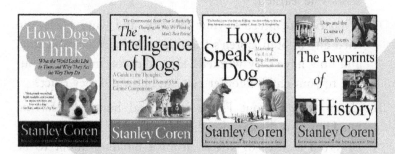

"Well-researched, informative, and fun to read. . . . [W]ill surprise and delight even the most well-read dog enthusiast."

—Deseret Morning News

"Cleverly combines scholarship, opinion, and anecdotes. . . . Read . . . his book[s] with your best friend."

—Dallas Morning News